SENSATIONAL

JOURNEYS

48 Personal Stories of
Sensory Processing Disorder

Hartley Steiner

Sensational Journeys:

48 Personal Stories of Sensory Processing Disorder

All marketing and publishing rights guaranteed to and reserved by:

A proud imprint of   Future Horizons

1010 N. Davis Drive
Arlington, Texas 76012
(877) 775-8968
(682) 558-8941
(682) 558-8945 (fax)
E-mail: *info@sensoryworld.com*
www.sensoryworld.com

©2011 Hartley Steiner

Cover design, John Yacio, III; interior design, Cindy Williams

ISBN: 9781935567318

Dedication

This book is dedicated to the families who have shared their *Sensational Journeys* with all of us. My deepest thanks for your honesty, bravery, and continued advocacy for children like ours. Your stories will provide connection, support, and education for years to come. Thank you.

A special thanks to my husband, Jeff; to my boys, Gabriel, Nicholas, and Matthew; and to my parents, Helen and Stuart and Bob and Dorothy, for giving me the love, support, and guidance needed on my own *Sensational Journey*.

Table of Contents

Foreword

by Lucy Jane Miller, PhD, OTR

Sensory Processing Disorder. Is it real? What is it? How many children are affected? Does it cut across the general population, or is it limited to one social or economic type? Does treatment work? What happens if children don't get treatment? What can I do to help my child and my family?

There are so many questions. So much is unknown. And there is so much individual and family struggle with this disorder.

First, let's get the basic information out of the way, and then we'll talk about the things that really matter to *you,* since you are reading this book.

Sensory Processing Disorder (SPD) is a condition in which sensory information goes into the brain, but the responses that result are inappropriate—sometimes extremely so. To be more technical, it is a disorder of detecting, filtering, modulating, integrating, or interpreting sensory information. The challenge is reflected in behavioral responses, motor skills, and/or self-care areas. Thus, the sensory component is often missed or misdiagnosed, because the behaviors that result are not sensory.

A recent study conducted by researchers at Yale and the University of Massachusetts Boston indicated that 16.5% of children demonstrate significant, atypical sensory processing symptoms by age 8. This was a rigorous prospective epidemiologic study, funded by the National Institutes of Health and implemented by psychologists who were not convinced at first that SPD was real. One of the authors said to me, "I didn't believe in SPD. I thought it was another *disorder du jour.* But I became convinced by my own data."

The Yale study included all children born in the New Haven area between 2003 and 2005. They were tested with a wide battery of tests as infants and toddlers and retested several times thereafter. At age 8, the children with sensory symptoms in early childhood still exhibited sensory issues, but—even more dramatic—they demonstrated *four times* more problems with socialization, *three times* more aggressive behaviors, and *four times* more anxiety than their typically developing peers (A. Carter, A. Ben-Sasson, M. Briggs-Gowan, unpublished data, 2011).

This is not news to any of you parents who are struggling to raise a child with SPD. But for the many, many *nonbelievers* in SPD, these data should make them think twice. Also of great importance is that the impact SPD has on families is *much more substantial* than the impact other psychiatric diagnoses have (A. Carter, A. Ben-Sasson, M. Briggs-Gowan, unpublished data, 2011).

Perhaps this is because when a child has a "real" disorder, and by that I mean one accepted by the medical and psychological community and thus included in the American Psychiatric Association's *Diagnostic and Statistical Manual of Mental Disorders* (called the *DSM),* a family receives support and special treatment services. But because SPD is not included in the DSM, it is perceived by many as "not real," and families are left stranded, alone, afraid, and isolated. Bring your child with SPD in for an evaluation, and you are more likely to hear "just a case of helicopter mother" (eg, hovering inappropriately), or "He'll grow out of it—he's just being a boy," or "Why don't you take a parenting class," than you are to get accurate advice on what to do to treat SPD.

Where should you go for treatment services? If you have insurance or other resources, try to find an occupational therapist with extensive experience in treating children with SPD. If you go to the SPD Foundation Web site *(www.SPDFoundation.net),* you will find a discussion of how to determine if the occupational therapist you are interviewing is qualified. This means much more than being "certified in sensory-integration therapy." (Being certified in this type of therapy is useful, but it relates to whether or not you know how to administer the Sensory Integration and Praxis test, developed by Dr A. Jean Ayres. What you *need to know* is whether your therapist has been well trained and mentored in *treatment for SPD.)* You must find someone with a strong background in building relationships and increasing social engagement, as well as a sensory-integration background. We recommend someone who uses a global approach to treatment; and a must is that you *like* this person and feel that you and your child can trust him or her. Our Web site includes a directory of 10 types of professionals who specialize in SPD. (Those that have been personally mentored by us are designated, and anyone coded in blue is a member of the SPD Foundation. *If you know anyone who you think should be added to this registry, please encourage them to sign up—it's free.)*

SPD is a diverse disorder. There are eight sensory systems— the five you learned in school, the two Dr Ayres brought to our attention (the *vestibular* sense, which is the sense of movement against gravity and through space, and *proprioception,* the sense of the muscles and joints), and the eighth sensory system, *interoception* (which comprises the feelings you receive form your internal organs, such as your stomach and bladder).

Just to make it even more confusing, we believe there are three major patterns of SPD and six subtypes, as depicted in the following Figure:[3]

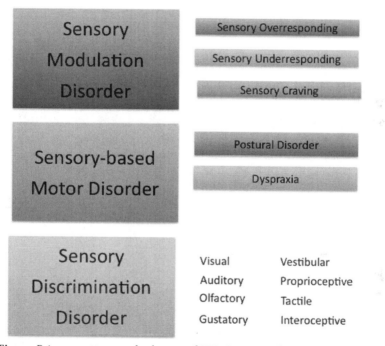

Figure. Primary patterns and subtypes of SPD. *Source: Bialer and Miller, 2011. Reprinted with permission from Future Horizons.*

Since SPD can affect one, two, or more of the senses in any combination, and each child can exhibit one, two, or more of the subtypes, that means there are more than 29,000,000 possible combinations of senses and subtypes that can manifest (8 factorial x 6 factorial [8 senses x 6 subtypes in any combination]). No wonder children with SPD can look so different from each other!

So how do we know that SPD is a "real" diagnosis? To be a valid disorder, the symptoms have to be *universal* and *specific,* meaning that all children with SPD must exhibit the symptoms *(universal)*, and children without the disorder do not exhibit the symptoms (ie, the symptoms are *specific* to SPD.) However, if that definition were to be applied to the diagnoses included in the DSM, we would in fact find that few, if any, of the existing developmental and behavioral conditions meet these very tough criteria.

At the SPD Foundation and the Sensory Therapies And Research (STAR) Center in Colorado, we conduct research to show how close to *universal* and *specific* SPD symptoms are. In 1995, the Wallace Research Foundation began an initiative to study SPD. After funding my research, they were so interested in the findings that they have been funding research to study SPD ever since. In 2002, I founded the SDP Scientific Work Group, which is composed of neuroscientists, neurobiologists, neuroanatomists, and other serious researchers with the kinds of backgrounds we need to figure out this puzzling disorder. The Work Group represents a wide variety of renowned institutions, such as Harvard, Yale, the Massachusetts Institute of Technology, Duke, the University of Wisconsin—Madison, the University of California, San Francisco, and others. (For a complete list of the researchers and the research projects they are involved in, go to *www. SPDFoundation.net* and click on "Research.") This group of scientists has published dozens of papers since 2002. So the next time someone tells you that there *"isn't any research,"* you can say, "That's so eighties!" and send them a copy of one or more of the articles published in peer-reviewed journals by these scientists (which are also available on our Web site).

If you want more information about the sensory systems, the SPD subtypes, or anything else I mentioned previously, refer to either *Sensational Kids: Help and Hope for Children with Sensory Processing Disorder* or *No Longer A SECRET: Common Sense Strategies for Children with Sensory or Motor Challenges* (Sensory World, 2011) to learn more about the SPD subtypes and appropriate treatment options.

Here's the most important thing to know: If your child has SPD, he or she CAN GET BETTER! Not cured, but better. Given the appropriate treatment, most children improve, and improve, and improve. Most will do well with some support mechanisms in place in regular (mainstream) classrooms, and, when they grow up, they will become functioning members of society. With support from their families and therapists, children make remarkable changes. In addition, with intensive education, parents, teachers, and others learn to reframe "bad" behavior into "sensory" needs that can be met. Children with SPD can be super-STARS!

Sensational Journeys represents a unique and wonderful contribution to the SPD literature. Essentially, we are all on a journey through this day-to-day experience we call Life. No one knows what to expect, but as children we do hear a lot of fairy tales that form a template for what we think life might become, if we just wait long enough to grow up. Then, magically, our dreams are supposed to come true, and we will live happily ever after. Right?

Well, that rarely happens. Instead, *Life happens.* So, we have to learn to adapt and grow as we go along.

The journeys that parents of children with SPD embark upon can be difficult, painful, exhausting, and frustrating. Usually, it takes several false starts before a family finds a good match with a clinician. Every family goes through a certain amount of strife. Having a child with SPD exacerbates those difficulties.

Parents and other caretakers are the real heroes and heroines in this journey. Often, they feel alone and without support or even an understanding community. Parents of a child with SPD that has only recently been diagnosed may feel bewildered, confused, and, most of all, terrified about the future. They don't realize that they are not alone, and they have not yet discovered the online parent support villages or the "just right" therapies that will move them quickly forward. If this describes *you,* please know that *you are not alone!* There are millions of children like yours, along with millions of parents who have been through this before.

This book exudes raw courage and honesty. The stories are open and provocative. This book sheds light on what SPD is in a very personal and tangible way. You will read about real people who have experienced real pain and who are brave enough to expose their life's journey in the hope that by doing so, they will help lessen the load that the next person experiences.

Having devoted the past 35 years of my life to SPD research and treatment, I cannot express enough my admiration and gratitude to these 48 families for opening their hearts and lives to us. These in-depth looks at the lives of families who are raising a child with SPD are a kind of qualitative research. This book provides a deep look at human behavior, and by analyzing these stories, we will learn so much about *why* and *how* decisions are made in families with children who have SPD.

My own journey is written elsewhere, but I know that the reason I have devoted 35 years of long days to understanding SPD is because these children and families touch my heart and fill my own need for early and accurate diagnosis…and for believing what patients say!

We have much to celebrate. We know so much more than we did when the Wallace Research Foundation began this initiative in 1995. Ah...if only I knew then what I know now! So many more children could have been helped. And, we are not "there" yet—we have "miles to go before we sleep."*

You will appreciate the honesty expressed by the authors of stories in this book. You will laugh, cry, and stay up late reading the next story. But most of all, what you'll feel is *hope*. *Hope* is the feeling that what you want can happen, and that "things" will turn out okay.

That's the best part about working with kids and families with SPD: There is hope, and there is help! Together, we are building a village—a community—in which people all try to help one another. There is strength in numbers, and, once found, there will be no stopping us! We will change society so that our *sensational* kids and their *sensational* families can truly have *Sensational Journeys*. My hope is that they will be able to participate fully and feel just as much joy and satisfaction as any other person.

Lucy Jane Miller, PhD, OTR

---

* Robert Frost, "Stopping by Woods on a Snowy Evening," stanza 4.

Introduction

I started attending the Parent Connections SPD support group in Washington State in October 2006. I had three kids at home—my oldest, Gabriel, was 5 and had received a diagnosis of Sensory Processing Disorder (SPD) the year before. My middle son was nearly 3, and my youngest son wasn't quite 1. Needless to say, my life was very busy.

When I attended that first meeting, however, and sat down with a group of virtual strangers—it changed me. It changed my perception of my life and ultimately changed my journey. What were these parents doing that I found so profound? Telling their stories. They were retelling the simple stories of their day-to-day life in raising a child with SPD. And their lives were just like mine. The room was filled with, "My child does that too!" and "I had NO idea that was an SPD thing!" It felt like I was home.

Being the overly talkative girl that I am, I quickly jumped in and shared my own personal stories. I talked about my son, his meltdowns, his incessant need to climb, how he licked or chewed or sucked on everything in sight, his love of hot salsa, the way he craved spinning equipment at the playground, and all of his crashing—oh the crashing! I loved it.

That storytelling was therapeutic for me—and not just because I was the one doing the telling. It was healing for those doing the listening, as well. The other parents quickly became my friends, the ones that could relate to my life, and the ones who shared in my joys and stood by me when our family struggled.

Although we did, at times, cry during these meetings, we laughed much more often. We reveled in each other's chaos and at our children's sensory explorations (like flooding the bathroom), and we drank in the knowledge that we weren't alone.

During these good times, it occurred to me that writing these stories down and sharing that kind of connection with other families would be valuable. Then, people could read them and relate to them whenever they wanted to. Boldly, I took to the Internet to write a blog. I was quick to laugh at the chaos of my life—the mess-making and extreme tantrum-throwing that filled my days—and readers loved it.

I had always believed in the power of storytelling. It is one of the most ancient ways we have of passing on information and sharing our history. However, I had no idea how quickly I would find an entire community of special-needs parents raising children with SPD that so effortlessly related to my life. The often daunting and confusing journey of discovery of our children's challenges and working to get diagnoses can leave families feeling alone and isolated—like they are the only ones to have ever walked this path. And it is scary, I know—because I've been there. But, it motivates us to search for others who have walked the same path we are on—to find connection and meaning in what we've been through.

When we find someone willing to share their own story—whether at a support group, on a forum, or through a blog—our path no longer seems so scary. Every time someone tells their story, it moves us closer to achieving awareness, acceptance, and understanding of SPD. And that is what has inspired this book.

Some of these essays were originally featured in the month-long celebration of the SPD Foundation's 30th anniversary on my personal blog—Hartley's Life with 3 Boys. Some essays are new, written by families with a recent diagnosis or those who are just now ready to share their story with the intention of paying forward the support they have received.

I am honored to bring you the stories of more than 40 families who have agreed to share their SPD journey with you. I hope you will see just how powerful storytelling can be.

Warmly,

Hartley Steiner

Chapter 1

Sensory Seekers, Avoiders, and Underresponders

Walk into a room full of parents raising children with type-1 Sensory Processing Disorder (SPD), or *sensory modulation disorder,* and you will hear a chorus of, "Is your child a 'seeker,' an 'avoider,' or an 'underresponder'?" And, just as quickly as they ask, you will find parents happily announcing which camp their child falls into.

Maybe you already know what they are talking about—*sensory seekers* are children who seek or crave sensory input, and *sensory avoiders* are those who generally avoid it. *Underresponders* are those who don't seem to register sensory input at all. Regardless of which subcategory a child belongs to, these are children who don't process sensory information effectively and often respond to it inappropriately.

Many people are surprised to find out that there are children who actually crave or seek input, and perhaps even more are unaware of those who don't register it at all. A common misconception is that *Sensory Processing Disorder* refers only to children who avoid sensory input. That was the false impression I had too, right up to the day I agreed to read *The Out-of-Sync Child,* by Carol Kranowitz. After finishing that book, I quickly understood that my son had SPD—and that he was a "sensory seeker."

It was another year or two after that before I fully understood the third group, sensory underresponders, which is arguably still the most misunderstood of the three subtypes. These children are difficult to arouse, seem to not hear when their name is called, don't feel sensations of hot and cold properly, and may have an unusually high tolerance to pain.

Today, many people are still unaware that children with sensory modulation disorder can be one of these three different subtypes—seekers, avoiders, or underresponders. But, as the families in this section can attest to, they are three distinctly different groups of kids!

The Signs Were Everywhere

by Penny Williams

Isn't it interesting how we worry about all the wrong things? Most of us worry disproportionately about statistical improbabilities—myself included. My unborn child may have a terminal illness. Maybe my family or I will be the victim of a violent crime. We tend not to worry about the occasional little bends and quirks. They're small, so they don't grab our attention.

I worried about having a boy throughout my entire first pregnancy. I was absolutely terrified of having a rough-and-tumble little guy who delighted in revving engines, weapons, and mud. Completely and utterly terrified! I had no idea what to do with a boy, so I felt an unhealthy fear of the unknown. It's a good thing I had a girl.

Right away in my second pregnancy, however, I knew I was having a boy. All that extra testosterone can really wreak havoc on a woman's body! He was definitely a boy—and he was already turning my world upside down.

I began begging my doctor to "get him out of me" on my weekly visits, starting at 37 weeks. I was, by far, the most miserable I'd ever been. Each week, my doctor told me that my son was not ready to come out but that she'd consider it again the following week. She said she sympathized but that it would be a long, miserable, dangerous delivery if he wasn't ready. At 39 weeks, she gave in, and I was admitted to the hospital and induced the next morning.

It took many, many hours before I was finally ready to deliver. By that time I was receiving oxygen, running a fever, and having some heavy-duty shakes. Two labor-and-delivery nurses had spent what seemed like an eternity trying to find my son's heartbeat. It was a rough delivery, to say the least. My doctor was right—my son was not ready! To this day, he still doesn't like to be rushed.

Luke was a high-maintenance infant for the first few months, nursing every 2 hours and only sleeping for short periods. We learned from day one that he had to be swaddled super tightly or there was no hope of him sleeping more than 15 minutes at a time. Within a week or so, I realized that he slept well in his car seat but nowhere else. In desperation, I began letting him sleep in the car seat, even at home, and even at night. That car seat, his vibrating chair, and being held tightly were the only things that could keep him calm. He was a demanding baby.

Luke reached his early milestones a couple of months later than the norm, but I figured it was because he was so roly-poly and fat. The doctors assured me that sometimes boys are slower than girls. If they weren't worried, then neither was I. A couple of months behind wasn't much.

As so many people do with their little ones, we tried hanging Luke upside down to tickle him, or we'd swoosh him from side to side with vigor, like a human swing. He screamed and cried in complete panic every time. So he didn't like to be dangled…who could blame him? He seemed to be afraid he would be dropped.

On the whole, Luke was a very quiet baby and toddler. He was easygoing and spoke more with gentle actions and expressions than with words. One day in his 2nd or 3rd year, however, I noticed that he was suddenly talking incessantly. I had always been grateful that I had gotten a quiet child to balance out his loud and talkative sister—and then I realized I had two very loud children. I reassured myself that he must have reached the age of finally taking cues from his big sister. Being talkative and loud may have been annoying, but it didn't mean there was anything "wrong" with him. I had no idea it was really a sign of something more.

In addition to being talkative, he became very active, too—*hyperactive*. His energy level became much more than we could keep up with. I found myself constantly trying to prevent his rambunctious behavior from causing him physical harm.

Despite his birthday being the cutoff for starting kindergarten that year, I enrolled Luke in school. His intelligence blew us away, and we were sure he was ready, despite being the youngest child in his class. On the second day of kindergarten, his teacher called me in for a conference. "Luke is not in control of his body," she said. "Today, he jumped up unexpectedly and hit me in the nose and broke my glasses. You need to help him learn self-control. He swings scissors around close to his face and the other students, and he's going to hurt someone again. You have to work on these things with him."

Do you see a red flag waving high in the sky? Sure. Absolutely. I totally see it too, *NOW*. But I didn't see it then. I just thought I hadn't prepared him for the classroom setting because he hadn't been to preschool. After all, the teacher seemed to be saying that it was our parenting that needed to be stepped up—to address behaviors we were teaching Luke at home.

Kindergarten grew worse instead of better. I was constantly reminded that he didn't have appropriate classroom behavior. I was told frequently that I needed to be working with him at home. Our conversations with his teacher always seemed to be about our inept parenting. I thought I was a good parent—even great—until that year. His teacher totally had me questioning myself.

I thought that most of Luke's school failures had to do with that particular charter-school environment, so we decided to place Luke and his sister in a mainstream, public elementary school for his first-grade year. I was sure things would be different there.

Just a couple of weeks into the new school year, Luke's teacher lovingly commented on how sweet, kind, and intelligent he was, but that he was too active for the classroom, wasn't finishing his work, and was behind by a grade level. Now, this was a structured environment, with a calm, even-keeled teacher, and I was still hearing that Luke was supersmart but not in control of his behaviors. This time, I saw the red flag right away.

His teacher submitted paperwork with the school administration, describing Luke as an "at-risk" student so that he could be evaluated to receive special-needs help within the school. Meanwhile, I visited his pediatrician and asked for a referral for a behavioral and learning disabilities evaluation. I was going to figure out what was causing this very intelligent child to fail in school.

I read as many books on learning disabilities as I could get my hands on while waiting 3 months for an appointment with a pediatric behavioral specialist. After reading *The Out-of-Sync Child,* I felt certain that Luke had SPD. The specialist diagnosed attention-deficit/hyperactivity disorder (ADHD) after spending just under an hour in the exam room with us. I asked him about SPD, but he told me that Luke's sensory issues were few and secondary to ADHD.

I presumed he knew better than me, since he had 25 years of experience in pediatric behavioral and developmental disorders. I left feeling devastated, but we started treating Luke's ADHD that same week. Part of the treatment program was incorporating occupational therapy. One day, after just a few visits, the therapist asked to speak to me after a session. She sat me down and gave me several handouts on proprioception and "heavy-work" activities. She explained that Luke bounces all around and crashes into things because of a lack of adequate proprioceptive input. His body was having trouble getting a sense for where he was in space, so he had to experience greater force in his physical interactions to feel grounded. That was such an "Aha!" moment for our family! That one piece of information explained so much, and we were finally able to understand many of Luke's behaviors. It was such a gift.

Proprioception not only explained his crashing and hyperactivity, but it also explained his oral fixation, preference for crunchy foods, sleeping with the covers wrapped tightly over his head, and even the need for tight swaddling and only sleeping well in his car seat as an infant. He preferred very tight footie-pajamas as a toddler, too.

Luke struggles with auditory processing, a sensitive gag reflex, supersensitivity to cold foods, a high pain threshold, intolerance for socks and blue jeans, and more, in addition to a lack of proprioceptive input. But proprioception turned out to be the key "missing piece of his puzzle" for us.

Looking back now, I realize the signs were everywhere. From the tight swaddling to the delay in baby milestones, the sudden loud talkativeness, the difficulty controlling his body, the lack of focus in a busy classroom, the bad behavior from a very sweet and kind kid…the signs really were everywhere, but I didn't know enough about SPD to connect the dots. Each instance, by itself, can mean something entirely different. But, when the dots are connected, a clear picture of SPD and ADHD appears. And the picture is very clearly my son.

Penny Williams is the creator and editor of the Web site, A Mom's View of ADHD, at AMomsViewOfADHD.com, where she writes candidly about the everyday experiences of parenting her gifted young son with ADHD, SPD, and learning disabilities. She is a freelance writer and real-estate broker living in the picturesque mountain landscape of Asheville, North Carolina, and has published several essays in ADDitude Magazine, the #1 nationwide publication dedicated to ADHD. Penny is also a contributor in the upcoming book, Easy to Love, Hard to Raise.

Putting It All Together

by Karen Mayes

I'll never forget the first time I thought something was different about my first child, Grant. It began at the changing table when he was 4 months old. While I can't say I looked forward to changing dirty diapers, I did love the one-on-one time it afforded me to sing, play "peek-a-boo," and talk with my blue-eyed baby. Then it happened. His first major diaper rash. I cringed when I saw it. As I laid out the wipes and diaper rash cream, I prepared myself for the screaming and crying that would soon follow. But the cries never came. In fact, he didn't flinch at all. He simply continued playing with the toy I had given him, and, at one point, even laughed as though I was tickling him. I wasn't sure what to think, so I merely pushed away any thoughts I had that this type of reaction was out of place.

Over the next year, I observed more traits about my son that just didn't seem typical. I tried not to compare him with other children, but it was impossible not to notice the growing list of oddities. At times I could rationalize and explain them away (perhaps I was just a first-time mom who was worrying too much), but other times I couldn't shake the nagging feeling that something was wrong.

For example, mealtime for my son has always been an adventure—a very messy adventure. He crams his mouth so full of food that he gags and chokes. Food spills out through his lips and through his fingers, which he uses to try to keep the food in the boundaries of his mouth. However, he has no idea that his face is smeared with food. He could go the whole day without noticing that his face is covered with latest snack or meal.

Then there was Grant's first skinned knee. While we were out for a walk together, he took quite a fall and scraped his knee rather badly. Again, I was prepared to scoop him up in my arms and calm his cries. And again, those cries never came. With blood dripping down his leg, he laughed and continued walking down the sidewalk. He didn't miss a beat. A trend was beginning to emerge. It was a common occurrence for Grant to run into furniture, pinch his fingers, and trip over toys. While that may not be unusual for a toddler who is learning to walk, what was uncommon was that he never seemed to feel pain.

The biggest red flag was when my son touched the hot oven door. We have a rather old oven, and it expels a lot of heat when it's in use. One day while I was baking dinner, Grant walked up and placed his hands on the oven door. He left them there for a long time—too long. I raced over and pulled him away. I placed my hand on the oven door and found that I could keep it there for only a few seconds. That's when my nagging fears fully emerged and could no longer be pushed aside.

Individually, these occurrences could simply be the traits of a busy toddler. Yes, individually, all of Grant's quirks were explainable, but putting the pieces together formed a clear signal to me that something was indeed different. I felt that something was wrong with my son. I began to earnestly seek answers to my growing list of concerns. After an early-intervention evaluation and working closely with a therapist, the pieces of the puzzle came together. A year ago, my son received a diagnosis of SPD. I was both devastated and relieved. It crushed me to learn that Grant was struggling to understand his body, and, yet, I was relieved to find answers and begin the process to help my son.

Grant has come a long way in a year's time. Brushing his arms and legs to "wake-up" the nerves, using mirrors and oral-motor tools at meal time, and implementing various motion and pressure therapies have all helped my son to understand his body and make him aware of his surroundings and sensations. It will be a lifelong journey, but I am glad to know the truth.

Karen Mayes lives in Charlotte, North Carolina, with her husband and two boys. She used to work in the field of finance and data research, but a year ago her life abruptly changed courses. After her oldest son received a diagnosis of SPD, Karen turned to writing as an emotional outlet and to educate others on the disorder through her son's experiences and those of her family. You can follow her at www.akmayes.blogspot.com.

I Need to Tell You...

by Lea Keating

The school psychologist cut right to the chase. "I need to tell you that your son has autism spectrum disorder." It was our second meeting—the one where we would discuss Cole's test results. I was alone this time. Cole had already been observed, and, really, how could I concentrate on anything being said anyway, with his 2½-year-old little body alternating between burrowing into my lap and running headfirst into the walls of this tiny little office? After she told me, I suppose I sat there blank faced and motionless, because after a moment she leaned forward, put her hand on mine and repeated, "I need to tell you..."

It took everything I had to keep from clamping my hands tightly over my ears. The earth seemed to stand completely still—I was acutely aware of the harsh fluorescent lights, the roar of the air conditioner, and the faint smell of onions as she leaned in too close. I didn't want to hear any more—didn't want to feel anymore. This was ironic, because one of the reasons for the evaluation in the first place was that Cole often assumed the very position I now craved, with his hands pressed tightly against his ears, gazing blankly and slightly rocking. A thought flashed briefly through my head—*Aha! Now I understand. What he's doing is self-soothing.*

I wanted to shout, "No. No! You're wrong!" But my heart and my head said, "Yes, I know."

Cole had been working with two wonderful early-intervention therapists for over a year already—a speech therapist and a special educator. They were experts in their fields. I was learning so much from them, but

Cole was making very little progress. The biggest problem was that we only saw each of them twice a week, and even though we tried different times of the day, Cole was never cooperative. He seemed to have two moods—a superhigh energetic state, in which he ran and crashed into everything, and meltdown mode—where he lay on the floor in hysterics. How could he learn how to talk and play if he couldn't calm down enough to interact? The first half of his therapy session was spent chasing him around the house, and the second half was spent receiving a crash course from the therapist on how to constructively play with him during his rare interactive moments.

About a month after receiving Cole's diagnosis, we went to my niece's 3rd birthday party. We had begun to really isolate ourselves at that point. Library programs and music classes had been abandoned long before. What was the point? Cole would just run around the room wildly. I tried chasing him and forcing him into the group circle. I tried letting him run and "modeling" for him how to stay in the circle. But nothing worked, and either one or both of us would leave the class sobbing. It was becoming clearer and clearer that Cole was not like other children. I dreaded going to this birthday party, but my niece is very special to me, and Cole was familiar with her and her house. What he was not familiar with was the noise and the crowd of people we walked into. His hands clamped over his ears as he squeezed his head tightly between my knees. Sensing a meltdown coming on, I took him upstairs where it was quiet. I sat and rocked him, and he started to calm down.

Back downstairs, the party was in full swing, with the other kids yelling and running and playing. I felt so bad for Cole—at some points, he watched as if he wanted to join in. My best friend came over and offered him a toy baby carriage. I held his hand and started to walk with him pushing it. Soon, he was pushing it on his own. He stopped briefly to load it up with wooden blocks. Around and around he went, pushing the carriage. He had a little loop going: through the den into the kitchen, past the hallway, back into the den. Repeat. Repeat. Repeat. For 2 hours. But, he was calm. And—more than that—he was engaged. He smiled and stopped and watched the kids and then did another loop. For the first time in over a year, my husband and I chatted with adults and ate sitting down and didn't have to leave the room with a hysterical child. All was going well, until they were ready to cut the cake. I had the foresight to take Cole outside—we had been through disastrous "Happy Birthday" songs in the past.

I was feeling very pleased with how the whole day went, and Cole was now happily outstretched on his belly on the warm driveway, drawing great big circles with sidewalk chalk. I couldn't remember the last time either of us had had such a great day.

It was then that another mom came outside. She cheerfully, although rather boldly, asked, "Does your son get early intervention?" "He does," I replied defensively, "Cole is on the autism spectrum." *(Go ahead and try to question my parenting skills, I thought—you're not ruining this day for me, lady!)* "I thought so!" she bubbled, "So is my son!" I quickly tried to place her son—he was running around with all the kids inside. He was a bit hyper, maybe slightly quirky, but not at all what I would call "special needs." She continued, "I need to tell you about SPD, occupational therapy, and the sensory diet."

And so, we sat outside and talked for an hour. She called me that same evening, and we talked for two more. I ran out and bought *Sensational Kids*, and then *The Out-of-Sync Child* and *Raising a Sensory Smart Child*. From the first chapter, they all made sense (pardon the pun!). Cole was a classic sensory seeker. He had his moments of sensitivity—especially to noise—but finally, all the running headfirst into furniture, throwing toys, and burrowing under our legs had meaning. It made sense that pushing the baby carriage with wooden blocks in it was both linear and heavy work that calmed and regulated him enough to be able to enjoy the party.

We immediately went for an occupational therapy evaluation and started a sensory diet (a customized regimen of sensory activities created to give Cole the sensory input he craved). The difference in Cole was incredible. He learned how to say his own name on day 2 of the diet. We incorporated multisensory activities into all of his therapies, and he became a little sponge. Every day, we sing, play, and move. Three years later, I am the superproud mom of a very bright, very verbal (and still very active!) 5½-year-old. Shortly after starting occupational therapy, his diagnosis was changed to pervasive developmental disorder—not otherwise specified. This past summer, it changed again to Asperger syndrome.

Cole has become very proficient at managing his own SPD. He knows intuitively when he needs to jump on the trampoline and when he needs to curl up under a heavy blanket. He starts kindergarten this year in a wonderful Montessori school that understands how to promote multisensory learning.

I often think back to that moment when I was first given Cole's diagnosis. I think about how panic and overwhelming fear set in, and how my senses shorted out. I can't imagine feeling that way on a daily—or even hourly—basis. We are *so* fortunate that Cole's condition was diagnosed so early and that he has been able to regulate his SPD. I truly believe that his language and comprehension were locked away because of his overwhelming sensory modulation issues. I need to tell you...that sensory-based therapy and a daily sensory diet have changed my son's life.

I am so very grateful for that wonderful mom who had the courage to share her son's journey with me. Thank you for allowing me to share ours!

Lea Keating is an SPD advocate and blogger and the very proud mom of two high-energy little boys, Cole and Brady. Lea is also founder of the SensorySing! and SensoryPraise! music and movement curriculums utilized in schools, libraries, daycares, and Sunday schools throughout the country.

The Parenting Learning Curve

by Stacy Tudor Mitchell

My four children are spaced very close together: four births in 4 years and 2 weeks. Talk about feeling way behind in the parenting learning curve! As the tired mom of four very young children, I just didn't see at first that anything was unusual. My children are now 9, 8, 6, and 5 years old. Three years ago, my oldest son received a diagnosis of Asperger syndrome, SPD (he's a sensory avoider), and anxiety. However, it is my second-born son that has issues with sensory underresponsiveness. It pains me to think that he is now 8 years old, and it has taken this long for me to come to this realization.

As a baby, it was my second son, Jimmy, who quickly earned the nickname "Snuggle-Bear." Being that he was very cuddly and loving, he seemed to be the opposite of his older brother (who was standoffish and not touchy-feely). Jimmy seemed smaller, sweeter, and gentler in his temperament than his older brother. It wasn't long before I felt the need to protect him from the sometimes-aggressive behavior of his older brother.

When Jimmy was 18 months old, his older brother became much more demanding of my time (he was then 2½ and had not yet received a diagnosis). Yes, the squeaky wheel was getting my attention, and Jimmy would just lie on the couch, content to watch PBS Kids. Back then, I thought, "Wow, what an easy kid!" He wasn't pushy or demanding the way his older brother was. Jimmy certainly didn't throw screaming fits when I needed to run to the grocery store. He didn't seem to notice if I had to go out and wasn't bothered by separation anxiety the way his older brother was. Neither of the boys began talking until they were 3 (again, I didn't recognize this warning sign), but his older brother would often grab my hand and lead me away into the kitchen (or elsewhere) as his way of asking for things. When I got something for his older brother, I'd just give the same thing to Jimmy. Jimmy wouldn't ask…he'd just sit there, wait, and take what he got.

Sadly, I look back now and see that Jimmy was flying under my radar.

Two years ago, when Jimmy started all-day kindergarten, he could barely function. He was exhausted all of the time. Getting him to hold a pencil tight enough to make a legible mark on the page was challenging enough, nevermind getting him to do an entire page of homework. His early writing was feeble, at best. It seemed as though he wasn't even trying. He became very resistant to even getting on the school bus in the mornings. On several occasions, just as the bus arrived at our stop, he bolted and ran away as fast as he could. He was miserable, and getting through each day of kindergarten appeared to be torture for him. I was beside myself with frustration and confusion. At the time, it looked like disobedience, and I scolded him and punished him for this misbehavior. Did punishment correct his behavior? Absolutely not—it only caused him to dissolve in a puddle of tears. Not understanding what the problem was, I chalked this up to another parenting failure on my part (the first being my delay in recognizing the signs of autism in my oldest child).

It was during Jimmy's kindergarten year that I discovered he excelled at preschool video games. It was something he enjoyed, and it kept his attention for a while. Other tactile activities that he enjoyed were painting, building (with real wood and nails), and playing with Legos. I noticed this and thought, "Wow, he really gets excited when he works with his hands." But, I was still puzzled as to why holding a pencil and drawing or coloring was a challenge for him.

There are some challenges that have plagued Jimmy for years, such as making decisions. If he receives money as a gift, he laments over how to spend it. He lingers in toy aisles for long periods, agonizing over what to choose. Often, an hour or so after making a decision, he becomes very upset to the point of crying. He will decide that this toy he bought with his money wasn't something he wanted after all. He will sob and then break the toy or throw it away. There seems to be a correlation between the excitement of having money to spend and the disappointment when that money is gone. His feeling of letdown causes him to be angry at the item he bought.

But, what causes a person to want to break or destroy something they have? This was another behavioral trend that I noticed during Jimmy's early years. If he came home from school with a painting or drawing, I would be so tickled with his artwork. I'd praise him (for it was a rare day that I had such treasures to behold!) for his work. Then, the artwork that he liked suddenly lost its appeal. He would tear it up! The same thing happened if I were to praise his watercolor paintings at home. He'd appear to enjoy the process of painting the picture. Afterward, his mood shifted and he tore up his work. If I yelled at him to stop, he'd dissolve into tears, saying he hates everything. I would be left feeling utterly confused and frustrated with his behavior.

Another ongoing challenge for Jimmy has been his neatness. While his sensory-defensive brother could not cope with the slightest spill on his clothes, Jimmy did not seem to notice that he was wearing half of his lunch on his face and shirt, while the other half sat in crumbles all over the table and the floor. For a long time, I thought he was doing this on purpose, and I scolded him. In retrospect, I am saddened by the negative impact on his self-esteem that my constant scolding must have had. I often feel as though I should stand behind him with a Shop-Vac and a container of wet wipes! Did I mention that my favorite household appliance is my carpet steamer?

Jimmy's challenges with neatness extend to his bathroom habits. Suffice it to say that Jimmy just doesn't see the mess he leaves behind. Again, I've gradually come to realize that he isn't making a mess intentionally—he just can't help it. He needs reminders—frequent reminders—to clean up his mess.

Over the years, Jimmy's attraction to sweets has led me to wonder if he might be hypoglycemic. Sometimes I suspect he recognizes that he doesn't have much "get up and go" and seeks out some sort of stimulant—meaning *candy*. I try to keep protein snacks available, like seeds, nuts, and dairy. I also try to have healthier food ready for him when he comes home from school, rather than wait for him to ask for a snack. I have found that if he gets overly hungry and tired, he is more prone to fight with his siblings or go limp and cry over seemingly simple tasks. For him, the thought of having to tie his shoes is enough of a deterrent to going outside to play. We've compromised, and he wears shoes with Velcro, instead.

Getting ready for the school day has gotten a little easier for us this year. Rather than hollering at him when he fails to rise after the fifth cajoling (which I did every day last year), I have taken a new approach—a kinder, gentler approach. A "no-words" approach. I have found that if I quietly go in and rub his back gently, say 15 minutes before he actually needs to get up, that he is far less combative. Rather than demanding that he do something, I encourage him gently. I tell him that I believe in him. If he says, "I'm *not* going to school today!" I respond by saying, "I know it's hard, but I know you can do it." I rub his back some more, wait a little longer, and allow him to wake up slowly. Most days, I still have to physically dress him, while he lies limp on his bed. But he is fighting less. And that, my friends, feels like a huge victory.

Jimmy is currently on a baseball team and is doing fantastic! It took him a very long time to make the decision to play (and I knew I couldn't force him), but he made that decision on his own, and he's doing a great job during his practices and games.

For any parent, let alone a single parent, getting a handle on SPD is extremely overwhelming. The sensory challenges that Jimmy has are completely different than those of his older brother. I feel that I am running a race—a race to master the sensory challenges of each of my children, so that I can help them learn appropriate coping strategies *before* they become adults. It is a marathon, not a sprint! The rules of this race involve love, patience, compassion, understanding, trust, *and* compromise.

Stacy Tudor Mitchell is a single, work-at-home mom. She lives in Entiat, Washington, with her four children (ages 9, 8, 6, and 5) and her 2-year-old cat, Tiger. Her oldest son has Asperger syndrome, and her two oldest boys have SPD. When she isn't busy managing school, therapy, and sports for her kids, Stacy is usually engaged in her favorite passion—photography.

John

by Domenica Mastromatteo

John was not a calm or peaceful baby. His limbs were always in motion. Even as a newborn, he would arch his back and slip off his car seat if I didn't strap him into it quickly enough. A nurse noticed this at a breastfeeding clinic and suggested I talk to the doctor. My doctor told me it was nothing to worry about.

John lost a great percentage of his body weight after he was born. He became too weak to stay awake for his feedings. Nursing and bottle-feeding tired him, so his dad and I fed him formula with eyedroppers, syringes, cups, spoons—anything that would work. Eventually, we managed to increase John's weight and energy so he could stay awake while feeding from a bottle; however, I would have to press on the bottle's nipple to help him maintain the flow of milk. I tried to continue nursing, but John would yell and arch his back and try to get away from me. He did not want to be held close.

Overall, John was an easy baby and required little attention in his first year. He liked to be alone in his crib or in his swing. He did not want to be held. Yes, it was less work, but it was depressing for me. I felt that I was not connecting and establishing a proper bond with him. I tried to hold him as much as he would let me and began to cherish staying up late at night, so I could hold him while he was asleep. I would always hold him and sing to him while he was sleeping in the middle of the night.

When John turned 1, he was still not crawling or pushing himself up into a standing position. He was content to sit and play with his toys, sometimes staring at one small object with fascination for hours. I had a box of food magazines that I sorted through and ripped out pages to collect recipes, and he loved watching me do this. He was not curious about exploring his environment and never looked into drawers or cupboards. He would "bum-scoot" (shuffle on the floor) to move around. He did smile a lot, had good eye contact, and babbled quite a bit. John was a happy baby and full of smiles, but because he was not crawling or walking, had not developed a pincer grasp, and still gagged on solid foods (aka ate no finger foods), his doctor referred us to a pediatrician, who referred us to an infant development specialist, who eventually referred us somewhere else. No one was able to help. Because no one knew what was wrong.

When John was about 18 months old, he had his first temper tantrum (I think). I had no idea what was happening as he threw himself on the floor, yelling and screaming, arching his back and rolling his eyes. I called an ambulance, thinking he may be having a seizure. When the paramedics arrived, John was fine. They did not think he had had a seizure and suggested it may have been a temper tantrum. I had no idea what he would have been upset about. We had been having a good morning before his "attack." I took him to the emergency room anyway, and the doctor on staff suggested it might have been an atypical seizure. I was still not sure, but the temper tantrums (if that's what they even were?) increased in frequency until he had at least one a day...and then more than one a day. It became very exhausting.

John's smile began to change. He would be frightened by any sound, including the vacuum cleaner or the heaters clicking on. He also developed separation anxiety and needed to be held all the time. I called him my "monkey," as he clung to me constantly and would grab my legs as I walked—at home, as well as in public. He also hated being washed, having his hair brushed and washed, and having his nails clipped. He started getting fussy with clothing, so I dressed him in joggers and t-shirts. He still needed a lot of help getting dressed. He was (and still is) a very picky eater, and he started losing his hair close to his 3rd birthday. The doctor said it was caused by very bad dandruff. I wondered about his diet and whether or not he was malnourished, since he was always so tired and never played on playgrounds or did any of the activities other children his age enjoyed. I paid extra attention to his diet and added extra supplements in everything he ate.

John was finally seen by an infant development specialist about his delay in gross-motor skills when he was about 18 months of age. The specialist suggested ways to help John start walking, and he started walking at 19 months. Then, we put him on a waiting list for speech therapy, as his speech and language development was delayed.

John became vocal (ie, other people could understand him) at 3 years old. Before then, he had a series of sounds that he used to communicate, and I wrote the sounds down so that everyone involved in his care could understand him.

At 2½ years old, John's sister was born. He was very warm and gentle with her, but his tantrums continued and he had trouble sleeping. His sister became mobile very early on, and John joined her on the floor. She is a blessing, as she has introduced him to so many things and so many different ways of moving—including climbing on furniture. Although he attended daycare part-time, he did not imitate other children until after his 4th birthday. His caregiver thought his behavior was not age appropriate, and we had a supported child-development specialist come in and watch him. She helped manage him at daycare but also suggested we have his pediatrician contact Sunny Hill Hospital in Vancouver for an assessment.

After his 4th birthday, John's anxiety became so bad we could barely leave the house. I was tired and burnt out. I pulled John out of daycare and hired a full-time nanny. I finally found a pediatrician that was eager to help us. Our concerns were John's anxiety, his fear of being alone, his fear of sleeping alone, crying in the night upon waking, fears of the dark, loud noises, bright lights, dogs (especially barking), and fear of going out for a walk in the neighborhood.

John loved malls, but he would bolt if I took him into one, so I stopped taking him to the mall or other public places. He was afraid of heights and would not ride a bike, and his tantrums became violent. He began to hit and throw things and said he wanted to kill me. He didn't understand the danger of running into the street. His fine-motor skills were delayed, as were his gross-motor skills. He smiled less and rarely laughed.

Our new doctor suggested he may have developmental coordination disorder, and we found an occupational therapist that diagnosed SPD. The diagnosis of SPD opened a lot of doors, and after learning more about what SPD meant and why he acted the way he did, I finally began to understand my son.

John is now 7 years old. I believe that if we had known about SPD when he was an infant, my little boy could have spent the first years of his life happier and would have been able to catch up to his peers a lot sooner.

He is still struggling, but he does occupational therapy once a week to help him with his fine- and gross-motor skills, as well as his sensory-processing issues. He is learning many new things and feels more confident about himself.

John is smiling a lot these days.

Domenica Mastromatteo is a stay-at-home mom; she dedicates her days to her children. She is very interested in children's mental health. She is also an artist and started painting 20 years ago, mostly with acrylics. She has been a potter (working with clay) for 10 years and continues her art career in many different mediums. She is currently pursuing a career that combines her creativity and problem-solving skills with her interests in infant development, parenting, and personal development.

The First Day of Kindergarten

by Jennifer Kerr Breedlove

As I write this, my daughter is on the bus on her way to the first day of kindergarten. It's a big day for any child, I suppose, and I expect many parents have this combined feeling of pride and dread as the day goes by. I imagine that many of us are staying deliberately close to our cell phones—just in case. But I also suspect that these emotions might have an extra tinge of urgency and immediacy in parents of children with SPD.

My daughter is a beautiful child—bright, warm, and loving. Creative as all get-out, she can play on her own for hours, making up stories and plotting complex epic adventures where Barbie and Luke Skywalker and her stuffed wiener dog go on perilous quests to save one another from the Giant Doll Cradle of Doom. Her preschool paintings have a vibrancy and balance of color that draw the eye and make you look again, because you are sure there's more in there than you see at first glance. Her fashion sense is like her paintings—she puts together these outfits that should be horrific, but somehow…they just work. She loves her brother, whom she alternately plays and argues with. She likes to pretend she is a princess, but she also loves to play in mud puddles and paint her arms brown with it. She befriends neighborhood puppies, caterpillars, and slugs. She is a happy, sweet, curious girl, and there is nothing about her I would change. (Except possibly the fondness for slugs.)

But then, there is the other side. Those beautiful paintings? She spent a year in preschool doing almost nothing else, because painting was something she could do quietly in a corner, away from the noise and chaos of the busy-and-always-moving classroom. She makes up those long stories alone in her room because she has trouble connecting with the other children in her life. She becomes anxious and clingy whenever a new stimulating situation presents itself; if Mom isn't there for her to cling to, the anxiety sometimes escalates into sheer panic. She goes through life with a general attitude of wariness, sure that around every corner, something big and scary might jump out at her—something she can't deal with or process. Being in a room with a constant buzz of sound either revs her up into hyperactivity or causes her to withdraw into herself. The sound of public toilets flushing throws her into a trembling terror.

When someone asks her to stop an activity midstream and change to something else, she comes completely undone and cannot make the switch. She often needs questions repeated, or—once she has heard them—she takes so long to respond that many adults think she is ignoring them or refusing to answer. She desperately wants to please, to fit in, to behave, and to do and say the things she is expected to, but all too often, she misses the target. And, when she thinks people around her are disappointed in her for being afraid or for missing out on some activity or another, she bursts into tears and wails in utter conviction that she is "the worst child in the world."

My daughter has SPD. Last fall, her preschool recommended that we take her for a private evaluation with a neuropsychologist, because of her inability to engage with the larger group and her tendency to regress into toddlerlike behaviors and nonverbal grunting noises when upset or overwhelmed. We went through all the stages most parents do, I suppose—first we wondered what was wrong with the school, causing them to see all these problems we hadn't seen at home. Then we wondered what we'd done wrong as parents to have caused this behavior, to have made this beautiful little girl so unpredictable and difficult to be with. Then we just wanted to shield and protect her from anything that would throw her off-balance or precipitate another meltdown. We started to read, to study, to learn about her sensory uniqueness, trying to figure out what she would need and what would help her. Since SPD does not appear in the *Diagnostic and Statistical Manual of Mental Disorders* and is consequently not on a lot of people's radars, we have felt very alone and disoriented when trying to navigate the world of the different therapies, Individuals with Disabilities Education Act laws, Individualized Education Programs (IEPs), 504s, sensory diets, and so forth to figure out what she is eligible for and what will help her.

Honestly, even after numerous meetings with different teachers, psychologists, special educators, and the like, we still can't say we really know what she needs. We are feeling our way along, seeing what works and what doesn't work and trying to understand our little girl not through the lens of what we expect of her, but rather based on what she sees and hears and feels as she moves through the world. The past summer went well, and she has grown a lot and become more comfortable with her surroundings and with trying new things. We give her the time she needs to think through her answers to questions, we give her the time-awareness she needs to finish an activity and transition to the next, and when she goes in a different direction than we'd wish, rather than assuming defiance or manipulation, we try to figure out what's going on inside her that makes her loathe to choose what we'd originally asked. We've even crossed the public toilet barrier—she is still afraid of them, but she is able to cope with the fear and choose to face it rather than run. (If this sounds like something silly to get so excited about, think about what it must be like to be 5 years old, in a large, cavernous, unfamiliar room, with an ear/brain mechanism that amplifies sounds way beyond an average person's perception. You'd be scared, too!) She is developing some close friendships with neighborhood children. And when I ask her now if she knows what a smart girl she is, she answers, "Yes. Yes, I'm smart. And I'm a good listener."

The next big hurdle: kindergarten. Thinking about it from the nonsensory perspective, it's exciting but nothing particularly perilous: She gets on the bus with her brother, and she gets off the bus at school and walks with the other children to her classroom. She spends the morning in the kindergarten class and then has 20 minutes to eat lunch. Afterward, a teacher from the childcare center across the street comes to walk the dozen or so children from morning kindergarten to their afternoon activities at the center, where they play and learn and snack and rest and play again. A few hours later when school lets out, her brother comes over with some of the bigger kids; then a little while after that, Mom comes to take her home. A full day, a busy day, but just a day, right?

But think of it from her perspective: After eating breakfast and getting dressed in her most favorite comfortable clothes in her familiar and low-key home, she walks to the bus stop...where a giant machine that's an eye-peeling shade of yellow rumbles up and opens its doors, billowing out smelly smoke and worst of all is so loud you can hear it from a block away. Is it any wonder she wants to hide from it? Once she's on, it's not so bad, and the bouncing of the bus is actually soothing and steadying…but then it stops and lets her out at a place with dozens and dozens of children, most of whom are unknown to her. Then she has to walk with the lot of them, surrounded by a distracting buzz of noise, down a long and brightly decorated hallway to her classroom, where there are already so many new and overwhelming sights and sounds and sensations, and it's only 8:20 in the morning.

Now think about the rest of her day: The classroom. The gym. The 19 other children working in the same space. The social cues to learn. The lunchroom, where she tries to remember to eat while processing the perpetual motion all around her and the rising buzz of voices. And, most of all, knowing that if things get scary or overwhelming, Mom and Dad aren't there to run to and hold. How scary must this all be for her?

For that matter, how scary is it for Mom? Because now, as I write this, she is probably off that bus and in her classroom. She is on her own. We are lucky to live in a school district where we have a lot of support from a wonderful staff who will spend a lot of their time during the first weeks of school in the kindergarten classrooms, observing the children to make sure they are making the adjustments they need to, and, if not, to help get them what they need to succeed. After a few weeks of class, we'll develop a 504 plan for her, once we see how she adjusts to her new environment and determine where the pitfalls and stumbling blocks are. I will do my best to let go of the tendrilly little weed of false hope twisting sneakily through my brain, the one saying, "maybe all her issues will just go away once she's in a positive schooling environment or the right classroom or has the right schedule or reaches the right age," because it's a familiar little thought that's presented itself through numerous other transitional moments during the past year.

The fact is that my daughter is who she is, and "who she is" is a wonderful, bright, and sweet child whose brain processes sensory input differently from that of other children. She will learn to make her brain work for her, and she will learn to work in the way that's best for her brain. And she will thrive.

And today, she got onto a school bus and started kindergarten.

Jennifer Kerr Breedlove is a musician, author, composer, and "green" blogger. She lives in Chicago's west suburbs with her husband and two children, is pursuing a doctoral degree in choral conducting, and blogs regularly at www.greenmomintheburbs.wordpress.com.

One Step Behind

by Heidi Andress

You would never guess Joshua is a "sensational" kid. He does an amazing job of flying under the radar so that all anyone ever sees is the imaginative, funny, clever kid he is. And maybe that's why we didn't get help until he was almost 2½. He'd always passed the developmental milestones, being as broad as they are. But the nitty-gritty is in the details of those milestones, and that's where I'd always known something was "off." Since birth, I'd been compiling a list of "quirks"—behaviors and preferences that didn't seem typical but didn't fit together in any sort of sense. As with many kids with SPD, there was some seeking behavior and some avoiding behavior, but there was no label to describe him fully. Until the term "underresponsive" popped up. And that fit perfectly.

Joshua bailed from the womb 5 weeks early—without warning or explanation—and I think we used that for a long time to explain why he often seemed…inert. Skimming the journal I've kept since the day he was born, I see I also used phrases such as "unmotivated," "not self-directed," and "lacking curiosity." These are terrible ways to describe any baby, especially your own! I don't mean to sound like he just *laid there*, like a log—he engaged, he made eye contact, and he occasionally smiled and cooed. He didn't seem listless or dull-eyed. He "appeared" normal. But he also spent a huge amount of time just *watching*. Watching everything. Pensively. He had the perfect poker face, which was completely unreadable. Sometimes, I wondered if "anything was going on 'upstairs." Now I know he was just using all of his little baby brainpower to process his great big world.

Basically, Joshua's problem is that his brain is so busy processing everything around him, and doing it so thoroughly, that it takes a bit longer to send a message back to his body as to what it should be doing or feeling, and much of the time, the message sent back seems to be messed up. He's constantly one step behind. By the time he's caught up, everyone and everything else has moved on to the next step. Joshua's other, related problem is that he's way behind in motor skills, both gross and fine. His Peabody Developmental Motor Scales assessment came back littered with scores of "below average" and "poor." He was about a year behind, which shocked everyone. It explained why he asked to be carried after walking a mere 10 steps. And why he screamed when another kid approached the stairs he was trying to climb down. And why he stood around at the playground, exploring nothing but the sandbox. Maybe even why he insisted on wearing rain boots every day—for 18 months straight.

So how do we help our son navigate this sensory, physical world? We had, by chance, developed many "tools" before we even knew what the problem was, just based on what seemed to get Joshua engaged. I now talk with a fair amount of animation in my gestures and exaggeration in my face and speech. Maybe it works because he doesn't have to process the subtleties of normal communication—I don't know. I've taken on a calm, relaxed manner about everything with him, because if I get amped up and anxious, so does he, and from there it's a downward spiral.

Because Joshua needs lots of time to process, we often venture out to the same few places and do the same few things. We've been attending Gymboree twice a week since he was 10 months old. He knows the teachers, the equipment, and the songs and games. It's that much less "processing time" he needs before he can get comfortable and engage. We also don't overschedule him, because even though toddlers take a long time to transition in general, Joshua takes twice as long as that. So one outing or activity a day is plenty, unless we're feeling especially daring. And when we are out and he says he needs something, like lying down on the floor in a quiet place, we listen to him and find him a spot on the floor. Finally, we try to break everything down into microsteps. There is so much we, as humans, do with our bodies automatically and take for granted, but Joshua needs help with these things, along with extra time to break it all down. Fortunately, he's a quick study.

Along with that great poker face he was born with (which I'm hoping to somehow bankroll into retirement money), he's also gifted with responding well to all sorts of treatments and therapies, for which he's undergone more than his share in his short little life. Jaundice. Torticollis. Food concerns. And now weekly occupational therapy for sensory and motor-skill issues. We call it "playing at Miss Sherri's," and that's exactly what it is for him. She gets him to work hard without him even knowing it. For me, though, it's a lot of work. A session with Miss Sherri is a subtle dance. She leads, and I follow. She'll engage with Joshua while talking to me at the same time about what she's seeing from him, and what she's hoping to see. I play along with whatever game they're attempting and quickly work to come up with a way to get him to "buy in" to the activity. Joshua won't expend his energy unless it's made interesting and relevant to his interests. Trucks usually do the trick. It's exhausting work for both of us, and, afterward, we go home and chill for a very long time.

I'm an optimist, but when the chips are down, what keeps me pushing through? Guilt! Though I'll tell you what I don't feel guilty about (that maybe I should). When Joshua was 12 months old, he ate frozen meals for lunch. For months on end. Trader Joe's Chicken Tikka Masala. And that Indian fare can get spicy! I don't care—it was all he would eat, and he was finally eating. He also watches probably a bit more TV than recommended. This started as a suggestion from our food therapist—let him watch a video and just spoon food into his mouth until he gets used to it. And it worked. But he also really took to watching videos. The thing about that, though, is that he doesn't "zone out" when he watches them. I think he uses them as a way to understand and engage with the world without all of the extra sensory stimuli the real world offers. And, when it comes to TV, he's great at self-regulating—after two videos, he turns the TV off by choice.

There are other things I don't feel too guilty about. He's still attached to getting a bottle of milk before nap and bedtime. And around 2 AM each night, he half-wakes and calls for me to come sleep with him—and I do. He's always needed someone to touch while he sleeps. And, finally, we haven't even started potty-training yet, and he'll be 3 soon. These are what I call "battle issues," and for now, I'd just like to spend my energy on winning the war. So I don't feel guilty about much, but the one thing that keeps me going when I'm super tired and just want to be done for the day is that, well, I believe I'm the reason Joshua is this way. I feel that he got SPD from me, passed through the genes. It's hard for me to see myself in him, like a mirror. Obviously, I didn't mean to give him this condition, and I'm really sorry about it and I hate to see him deal with it every day. The silver lining is that I'm well positioned to give him so much help. I know what he's going through, and what it feels like, and how to help him make his way through.

And, just so we don't end on a sad note, there's been great progress in the 4 months Joshua has been in therapy. We're not going down playground slides quite yet, and he still has scrawny biceps. He still stands while eating. And, he still doesn't seem to notice when he's been hurt, as evidenced by the huge, bloody, torn toenail he didn't know about the other day. He will still sit in too-hot or ice-cold bath water forever, without saying anything. But now he's so comfortable with occupational therapy, he just struts in and instantly turns into what Miss Sherri calls "his bold self," owning the place and exploring in comfort. He's stopped spitting out food and no longer needs toy trucks held firmly in his grasp to sleep. And, finally, for the first time ever, he told us yesterday that he was actually hungry.

And that, my friends, is progress.

Heidi Andress *lives in Seattle and enjoys being a stay-at-home mom more than she thought she would—although she really looks forward to going back to work someday.*

Ponytails

by Renee Knoblauch

I am a stay-at-home mom of two amazing kids. I have been married for more than 20 years, and I was told that we would never have any biological children of our own. I wear several hats—not only am I a stay-at-home, homeschool mom, but I also provide "daycare" to two sisters, one of whom has periventricular leukomalacia and cerebral palsy. My days are spent trying to keep up with them all, the house, and everything else.

We adopted my 8-year-old daughter, Ann, from within our family. She came into our lives when she was 9 months old. We also have a biological 5-year-old son, who is all boy and doesn't lack in energy. We found out I was pregnant 3 days before our adoption was finalized. Our son is also a superhero little brother, as he acts like a "big brother" much of the time. He swoops in to help his big sister avoid meltdowns and gives her lots of love and compassion.

Ann's medical issues include stroke, blood clotting disorder, SPD, obsessive-compulsive disorder, and mental retardation. Three years ago, it was discovered that she has a microdeletion in one of her chromosomes. At this time, the geneticists are not aware of another person who has the same deletion. We are still discovering new issues all the time.

The day that I saw Ann for the first time at the airport, I knew that something wasn't right. Even though everyone told me she was a perfectly healthy 9-month-old girl, my "mommy instinct" was ringing loudly. She looked like a rag doll, with her head all floppy and tucked into her chest, as if her head was too heavy for her body to support. Shortly after she came into our home, she was diagnosed as having had a stroke. The doctor estimated that it happened at around 10½ weeks old. We were told not to worry about her delays and that she would catch up in time. She was far behind most kids her age and wasn't meeting her developmental milestones, yet I was still told that she was okay. But things didn't add up—it was like we had a puzzle that was missing some pieces.

Ann hated to be held for long periods of time. I just wanted to cuddle with her, but she would push you away if it went on too long. She loves to hug and is a very loving child who will hug anybody—as long as it isn't for too long.

Ann was always hungry and thirsty. Her body didn't seem to know when to stop. Gaining weight was never an issue—she looked like a toothpick. Eating was a challenge and still continues to be a significant challenge to this day, because she gags on just about everything. Smell and texture are big issues for her. She will not eat meat. She lives on peanut butter. I can name the foods that she will eat on both hands. Additionally, I have to monitor what she eats or she will just keep on eating. Like clockwork, 15 minutes after any meal, she asks me for more food. She only drinks water, and wherever Ann is, there is a cup somewhere nearby.

I always dreamed of a little girl with long hair that I could braid and put in ponytails. Ann has short hair. She yanks it out in chunks. Every morning, I pick up wads of her beautiful curls. She has little bald spots from pulling it out. Her hair is uneven in the back, with patches of long and short hair. I know when it gets to a certain length that it is time to cut it. My little girl then gets mistaken for a little boy who wears pink. No ponytails around here.

She continually bites her hands. She bites herself when she is frustrated or mad or sometimes for no apparent reason at all. She has permanent scars on her hands. It doesn't seem to faze her that it should hurt. Trust me—I know how hard she bites, as I have felt it numerous times!

It seems unimaginable to me that someone cannot feel hot versus cold. Pain doesn't seem to register in her brain the same way it would others. When she wants to get your attention by tapping your arm, it feels more like hitting. Ann and her brother love to tickle each other. It starts out funny, but then it ends with her brother screaming, "Ouch! You're hitting me!" Yet, her face tells you that she was only trying to tickle her brother and not trying to hit. Her "tickling" becomes a very hard, painful hitting. It's like she can't feel the difference between a soft touch and a hard one.

When she plays with Barbie dolls, it sounds like they are at war with one another. In reality, she is trying to make Barbie "babysit" a baby. All you can hear is "thud," "thump," and her dollhouse furniture falling down. It isn't her intent to make the dollhouse and its contents go all over the place.

Ann doesn't know when to go to the bathroom most of the time. She is my 8-year-old in diapers. I will ask her if she is wet, and she will say, "No, Mom, I'm dry." I will check her and find she is walking around with a loaded diaper. After meals, she looks like a 1-year-old child who is just learning to eat. It doesn't even register that she has it on her face—and she could care less. She walks to her own beat. The world is passing her by at the speed of light, while she is slowly inserting herself into it. Everything takes so long to accomplish—school, getting dressed, getting out the front door—and that is just the tip of the iceberg. Getting her attention and getting her motivated is a daily ordeal. I tell others that I could record myself and hit play. I have to tell her to do things several times. During conversations, her attention wanders and she has to be told the same thing several times.

I was so frustrated with the doctors who told me nothing was wrong with her. I was with her 24/7. I wanted to take one of the specialists home to follow us around for a day. I felt like no one listened, much less believed me. I first learned about SPD from her physical therapist. I had never even heard of SPD before! I went home and researched it on the Internet and read just about every book out there. I was going to be armed with as much information as possible when I met with her pediatrician. I was convinced that she had SPD. All those pieces of the puzzle fell into place. Ann received a diagnosis of SPD several months later.

She was already involved in speech, occupational, and physical therapy, and she was given a sensory diet. Ann thrives on heavy work and play. She pushes herself when it comes to therapy.

Every morning, I find her cuddled up with her head covered in her weighted blanket, and I start her sensory diet with a good rubdown before she even gets out of bed. The rest of the day is filled with many different activities. My home is littered with mini-trampolines, exercise balls, and all kinds of weight-bearing therapy tools. When we don't administer the sensory diet, we see a stark difference in her, like night and day.

Our life is filled with adventures with our daughter. It certainly is not dull. We have been given a gift by the name of Ann, and I am grateful for her therapist in helping us navigate this world of SPD. Life is not as dramatic now. Yes, we still have lots of drama, but knowing what I am dealing with sure does makes it easier.

Prior to staying at home with her two children, **Renee Knoblauch** *worked full time, served as a foster parent, and cared for her aging mother. She loves blogging about her adventures at* reneek-littlehomeschoolonthe-prairie.blogspot.com/.

Chapter 2

Stand-Alone SPD

I have found that there are still many misconceptions about SPD running rampant on the Internet. People claim one thing or another about what it is (or is not), but the most common myth I hear is that SPD is always a symptom of another disorder—like autism. According to research conducted at the SPD Foundation in Greenwood Village, Colorado, this isn't true. Their research shows that 75% of children with sensory issues have SPD as their primary diagnosis.

Children with a stand-alone diagnosis of SPD are at a distinct disadvantage when it comes to receiving therapy and school-based interventions. Families of these children are on the front lines of dealing with the effects of SPD not being recognized by the medical community, and they are supporting the SPD Foundation to get SPD included in the next edition of the *Diagnostic and Statistical Manual of Mental Disorders*. This would be a key step in getting these children the help they need.

The stories that follow relate the journeys of families who have SPD as a stand-alone condition—from knowing something was amiss, through the often-challenging maze of finding the right help for their child, to arriving at the diagnosis of SPD.

We're Not There Yet, but We're on Our Way!

by Kristen Jordan

My second son, Nash, joined our family on October 11. I was 28 when he was born, my husband James was 27, and his older brother Wyatt was 21 months old. Nash had physical problems from birth, such as torticollis, where one muscle in his neck was shorter than the other. Within a few months of birth he was undergoing physical therapy, and around that time I received a diagnosis of thyroid cancer and spent the first 9 months of Nash's life in and out of surgery, treatment, and recovery, having to take care of myself instead of doing the normal, day-to-day things I would have preferred to do with my infant son. James and my mom took on full-time care of the boys and the house. James, who managed to continue working full time, came home from work or changed his schedule to make sure Nash made his physical-therapy appointments, on top of having to take me to and from the hospital in Seattle for my own treatments.

My mom became "SuperGrandma" and reprised her role as a full-time parent and a help to James. Sometimes she was at our home night and day, making sure daily things were done and everyone was happy and fed. I was here physically, of course, and a part of everyone's lives, but anyone who has been through any type of cancer or has known or cared for someone with cancer knows that it really is one of the few times when you have to put yourself first. So, needless to say, I was "checked out" of their lives mentally, emotionally, and physically more than I wanted to be.

I was just starting to feel better and become a daily participant in family life again when Nash turned 1 and Wyatt was about to turn 3. When I started to become the main person in the boys' lives again and assume my role as stay-at-home mom, we started to focus on some of Nash's milestones that he was a little behind on. Nash had just been released from physical therapy, and the delays in hitting his milestones were only minor at the time. Being only 1, he wasn't doing much except for starting to walk and babble. I felt bad, as if we weren't able to focus on his needs like we did with our first son. I secretly thought it was our lack of work and attention to his milestones that was causing him to lag behind, minor though they may have been.

We spent the next year working with and focusing on the boys, and by Nash's 2nd birthday, we realized he still wasn't progressing as much as he should. We started to worry about his speech, as he could say very few words (and later would altogether stop using some words he used previously), and he seemed frustrated that he couldn't communicate. Nash became agitated easily and started hitting his head against the wall. He became inconsolable in certain situations because of the lack of communication, like at the grocery store or in a restaurant. He was also very antisocial at playdates or in any situation involving other children (other than his brother).

I remember leaving a family lunch one afternoon with Nash screaming and crying, and nothing we did helped. I thought I was the worst mom, not knowing what was wrong with my son and not being able to help him. It didn't help that well-meaning family and friends kept telling me it was normal and only the "terrible twos" coming on. My "mommy instinct" told me it was more than that, and that we needed to get help. We spoke with our family doctor about it, and she referred us to a children's therapy center for an evaluation. We were also sent to a neurologist. It was agreed that Nash would benefit from speech therapy right away, which he started right after his 2nd birthday.

Nash took a few weeks to warm up to his speech teacher, but after he did, he started benefiting right away. He spent 1 hour a week with her, and she gave us endless insights and information to work with at home. He thrived with the tools she gave us. After Nash was settled with the speech teacher, we met with an occupational therapist, who went over his evaluation and information from the speech sessions. She and I focused on his other problem areas, like social skills and gross- and fine-motor skills. I remember her mentioning something to me about his sensory-processing abilities. She gave me some activities to work on with him at home and said we would meet up again in a few weeks to evaluate his progress. She went over a sensory diet she wanted to try with him, as well as "heavy work." She explained how giving him physical activities to do helped with his sensory input, and she advised that we have him do these activities before going to a store or on an outing or doing something where I needed him to focus. I remember telling my husband about it, and we both thought, "She wants us to have him push around a laundry basket with heavy things in it before we go to the store? Umm…OK." The store was one of the harder places to visit with Nash, as he became so upset. Usually, we just wouldn't take him, or James would be on standby to go sit in the car with him or walk with him outside so I could shop.

When we finally tried administering "heavy work" before an outing or errand, we saw immediate results. I thought it was a fluke—that Nash must be tired, or—just the opposite—that he must be having a good day. So we tried again, having him do "heavy work" before a family dinner out at a restaurant. It always yielded a positive experience afterward, with no acting out and no tantrums. We couldn't believe it!

The occupational therapist came back, and we explained how each and every activity worked for him and how he responded. She spent the next few weeks after that trying more things and giving us more tools. I remember the day she brought us the paperwork about SPD. I remember thinking, *It has a name—a label.* Knowing that SPD had a name was at least *something.* We went back to see our neurologist, and he said he wanted to continue seeing Nash through his 3rd birthday and that we would reevaluate after that. Nash's 3rd birthday is coming up in October, and we are working on transitioning Nash out of the birth-to-three early-intervention program and possibly into a program with our local school district. Having the right tools and knowing more about SPD has allowed us to help not only Nash, but our older son Wyatt, as well, who is believed be dealing with a lot of sensory issues himself. He will be seeing an occupational therapist later this summer for an evaluation. The good news is that the tools we already have allow us work with him right now and start early intervention to help him cope with his day-to-day sensory issues.

The saying "It takes a village to raise a child" has never been more true for our family. While this is just the start of Nash's (and our family's) journey with SPD, we are lucky to be a part of an amazing, supportive, and very informative SPD community.

Kristen Jordan is a 32-year-old stay-at-home mom who lives in Kent, Washington, with her husband and two amazing little boys. She spends her free time blogging about her family's personal journeys with SPD and her life after having thyroid cancer. She also enjoys photography and sharing her family's journey through pictures.

How We Came to See SPD!

by Joyce Herrmann

Hello! We live in Texas and have two kids with sensory issues. However, we didn't even know about SPD until almost a year ago. Our kids Emma and John are 8 and 6 years old, respectively. We always knew that things were a little different with our children, but we thought they were just personality quirks.

John started going to preschool at age 2. Usually, kids bring home art projects and pages they have colored, but John never did. He always drew very lightly on paper and never enjoyed coloring very much. He also had trouble holding and using eating utensils. When he was able to hold a pencil or a fork, he often switched hands. John would say, "My hands are sticky—I can't touch anything!" Some of the other "quirky" behaviors were drooling past the teething stage, being excessively ticklish, being unable to ride a bike, and refusing to attend the musical, "The Wizard of Oz." (John sat with Daddy in the theater lobby while I watched the show. The tickets weren't cheap!)

All of the teachers at John's daycare center just loved him. He was pretty quiet and not much trouble. He didn't seem to excel, though, and never wanted to learn his letters, draw, or color. We were told that he may need to stay in prekindergarten for another year. I consulted with a psychologist and tutor in our area, and she said not to hold John back (as did John's dad). Against my better judgment, I sent John to kindergarten at our local public elementary school. I was worried. About a month into the school year, we received a letter from John's teacher, stating that he was having trouble using the scissors. I was afraid that John was going to get kicked out of kindergarten! We scheduled a conference, and John's teacher asked if I had heard of "sensory-integration disorder." I said I had not, but I would look into it. I went home and Googled it, and found out that the name had been changed to SPD. I found a Web site about it and then a checklist. I went through the checklist and was amazed. All of John's "quirks" were listed as symptoms! Here was my "Aha!" moment. I finally figured out what John had.

Upon reading more, I found out that occupational therapy was imperative. I scheduled John for an appointment with our pediatrician, and she assigned the SPD diagnosis on the basis of the checklist that I carried with me to the appointment. John started therapy 2 weeks later. What an amazing chain of events—and what a wonderful kindergarten teacher! More often than not, John still persists in playing rather than doing his schoolwork, but he's surprisingly clear when he focuses.

Emma also shows some possible signs of SPD. Her symptoms are mainly related to clothing and food. She will not wear stiff clothing, like jeans, and her pants cannot have buttons, zippers, or snaps. She likes for her clothes to be tight and wears leggings and t-shirts or skorts. She is a picky eater, as many kids with SPD are. She talks loudly and has trouble focusing in class. Emma started relaxation therapy about a year ago, and she takes medication for attention-deficit disorder (ADD). It was hard for us to come to the realization that, yes, ADD medication is probably necessary for Emma. She took isdexamfetamine dimesylate for the last month of school this year, and she was able to concentrate and write neatly. However, when she started taking the medication, she had daily meltdowns and trouble sleeping. We are getting ready to try atomoxetine hydrochloride. Emma's other symptoms include not being able to sit still, messy written work, and variable and quickly changing moods.

This summer, we have had the kids in music camp, drama camp, tutoring, picky eaters' class, and swimming lessons. All of these things have helped them to grow and hopefully have helped them with their sensory issues. We are giving John another year in kindergarten this year, and, in retrospect, are very happy that he was enrolled in kindergarten last year. Since he underwent occupational and physical therapy almost the whole school year, he came a long way. We believe him to be smart, but we cannot tell if he knows things or not because he usually does not share with us what he knows. Now I can ask him about the letters of the alphabet, and he doesn't hesitate to answer. He is learning to read—but once again, I don't know how well. He learned to swim this summer and is able to swim on his own now. He started the summer by insisting on holding onto a "pool noodle" and now jumps off the diving board by himself. Lately, he even swims underwater and is not scared to do so. He talks more confidently now than he did in the past. I think he will excel this year in kindergarten!

In learning about SPD, I have figured out that I too have had sensory issues all of my life. I was painfully shy as a child and would cling to my mother. I did not like the noise that other children made and clearly remember one time when my mom went to work out and there was an area for children to play. I cried because the children were too noisy and rough, and I sat outside of the play area by myself and read a book. It is so cool that I've been able to learn about my children *and* myself at the same time! I've since learned that kids are supposed to be somewhat more boisterous and that I was an exceptionally quiet child. I remain very particular about my surroundings and environment (especially temperature).

My husband is still "on the fence" about our children's problems, and although he feels that they will simply outgrow them at some point, he believes that the therapy is, in a lot of ways, "tutoring" them and will directly help them in school, in any event. He is opposed to Emma's ADD medication in principle, and we have had a lot of conflicting discussions about it. As a practical matter, he now accepts the low dosage as being helpful to Emma's concentration. John has made rapid advances since his treatment began, but he still insists that many things be done for him that he should do himself, like buckling his seatbelt and turning certain lights on and off.

I think getting SPD into the *Diagnostic and Statistical Manual of Mental Disorders* would help not only with insurance coverage and addressing John's problems at school, but it would help get SPD "out there." How lucky were we that John's teacher's son had a friend with SPD? If she hadn't spoken up, we would have never known what was wrong. What if I hadn't listened to John's tutor and his dad and had held him back in prekindergarten? We never would have gotten help and would still be struggling. Let's get SPD "out there" so that more people, parents, doctors, therapists, and teachers know about it!

Joyce Herrmann is the mother of two children with sensory issues. She worked for 14+ years as a financial analyst and still takes contract jobs from time to time. She decided to stay at home to be able to devote more time to her children and their school functions. Her daughter is 9, and her son is 7. Her children's sensory issues are very different from each other—her daughter experiences texture issues with clothing and food and tends to talk VERY LOUD. Her son is the more extreme case and has received a diagnosis of SPD. Now Joyce likes to blog about SPD in the hopes of helping others.

A Day in the Life of Kodi

by Mary Hamblin

We became the proud parents of Dakota, or "Kodi," on August 1. From the very first day, he was a wonderful and happy boy. He cried normally and did everything a baby should. By the time Kodi turned 1, he was ahead of the doctors' charts for growth; in fact, he was in the 95th percentile for height and weight. At first, we started him exclusively on breast milk. As he began to grow, we started to introduce new foods.

Around the time he turned 1, we began to see things that just didn't fit a typical 1-year-old. We tried to give him baby food, but he would rather nurse or have whatever we were eating. We had those wonderful mesh bags you can put food into for babies to gnaw on, so we gave him food in those. I had been noticing that he was a very headstrong little boy already, and he liked to have things his way.

Around 15 months, he was really not saying much to us at all and just babbling, if you want to call it that. Maybe I didn't think about him not talking as much as I should have. Both my husband and I were late talkers, so I just figured he was going to be one, as well. Kodi knew some very basic sign language and was using that to communicate with us, when he was not yelling or screaming at us.

He was starting to throw some big fits about changing his diaper. I had been a good mom and tried to read all the books I could on parenting. I was doing what they said—to give him a special toy that he only got to use while changing his diaper. But neither distraction nor rewards helped. My husband and I both became very good at changing his diaper while he stood up—even the poopy ones.

By the time he turned 2, Kodi was still not talking as much as he probably should have been, and his fits about changing his clothes and diaper were becoming extremely bad. He was so very hard to calm down, and both my husband and I were at our breaking point. I don't know if giving him time-outs was more of a time-out for us than for him! We tried several things. If we sat him in the corner, we wound up having to hold him while he fought us. If we put him in his room and shut the door, toys ended up broken, and we were both afraid he would hurt himself. We couldn't seem to find a solution.

At Kodi's 3-year-old checkup, I talked to his pediatrician about his lack of verbal communication. She recommended a wonderful service to get him evaluated through the school district. What we found out was a shock, but a blessing. Kodi had a speech problem and was not able to articulate his needs, which was why he was having all the behavioral problems. At least that was what I thought. We got Kodi into speech therapy right away. We started to see a big difference, but then at the same time, I noticed some other problems.

I decided to ask his therapist about Kodi licking everything and wanting to put everything he could into his mouth. She said that she would talk to one of the occupational therapists about it. She also gave me a sensory profile to fill out. As I read over it and marked the different boxes with things Kodi had trouble with, I was starting to get a sense that something more was going on with our son. After two or three sessions of Kodi being observed by an occupational therapist, a plan was devised to help our son.

Our first at-home assignment was the Wilbarger brushing protocol. Every 2 hours, the kitchen buzzer went off and we brushed Kodi. Not only was his licking and sucking on items becoming less and less, but he was sleeping better at night. Sleeping has been and still is a problem for him, but when we first started the brushing, the difference in his ability to fall asleep was like night and day.

We started to notice a changed, happier little boy. Because Kodi was happy, he became motivated to do other things. He was still very headstrong, but as therapy progressed, so did he.

We went through a phase where he became upset each and every time we went to therapy. I realized that the waiting room was becoming too much for him to handle, and I suggested to his therapist that maybe we could meet her in the back and see if that helped. That little change in his routine worked. He was able to go to a room that was in a calm place, so he didn't have to worry. He no longer fought going to therapy.

During that year, his occupational therapist wanted us to start a therapeutic listening program. I could not believe how much those headphones cost. It seemed unbelievable to me that I was going to buy $150 headphones for a 3-year-old! But, I thought that it might really help him. There were seven different music CDs, which—in the beginning—truly seemed to help. He did great with it. He didn't care where he listened to his music—at times it would be at home during breakfast or even out at the store. We made sure he listened twice a day, and he was again a totally different little boy. His sleeping habits became even better, and he even figured out how to use the potty.

By the time Kodi was 4, our lives changed quite a bit. We added a new baby boy to our family, and Kodi's dad lost his job and decided to join the navy. We moved in with Grandma and Grandpa while Dad went to basic training. This change threw Kodi into total defensive mode. He refused any brushing and had fits that you could not imagine. He was just not taking the stress in our lives well at all. He refused to change his clothes and only wanted to do things that allowed him to barely function.

I consulted with his occupational therapist, and we decided that he needed more therapy time to give his little body a jump-start. We increased the therapy sessions to twice a week for a month. It was working great, and Kodi was happier and coping with things better. He was even letting me brush him. We had been with Grandma and Grandpa for about a year, when we moved again.

This move turned his little world upside down again. Since we moved out of state, he has been without therapy services for 3 months. He's on a waiting list, and we are still trying to deal with his "issues" daily. We were able to put up two swings in our home, and he can swing whenever he wants. We have also made our home a home of sensory freedoms, which means he can jump and crush into almost everything.

I did let him know that we were going to be brushing again, and he actually allowed me to brush him. He is still having a hard time with changing his clothes, and he doesn't like to change into pajamas at night. Instead, he wants to stay in his clothes, which is fine, as long as he gets dressed in the morning.

We finally saw a neurologist about getting an official diagnosis of SPD. The doctor did agree with us and wants Kodi to continue to receive both occupational therapy and speech services. Our newest trial with Kodi is trying to find a preschool for him. We live in Virginia, and when children turn 5 here, they are placed in kindergarten. Kodi, however, is not ready for kindergarten, and he turned 5 in August. The school district does not seem to care whether or not he is ready. They will not allow him to be enrolled in a preschool program where he can receive the attention and help he needs to get ready for school.

We visited the school principal with Kodi. At that visit, Kodi was jumping around and we were asked if he had attention-deficit/hyperactivity disorder. I said, "No, that is all sensory behavior for him—he is seeking input, and when he is in a new place he jumps around." She looked at me like I was making it up, but it's the truth. It seems like an uphill battle to find the help that my son needs. We want what is best for him. As parents, we will fight for our son, we know our rights, and we will help him get what he needs.

Mary Hamblin is the mother of three handsome, active little boys. She currently lives in Virginia, where her husband Aaron is stationed in the navy. Mary loves being a stay-at-home mom and certainly has more than enough to keep her busy. Her days are never dull. Dakota, her oldest, received a diagnosis of SPD when he was 3 years old. He's almost 6 now and has been receiving services since his diagnosis. Mary is active in her church and is close to her family. When she has free time, she enjoys running and just finished her first 7K.

Our Long, Strange Trip to Diagnosis

by Brandi Bernatow

When my first child was born, I was overjoyed. I did not quite know what I was in for. Luckily, in this case, ignorance truly was bliss. I think it is a blessing that Andy was my firstborn. Since I was a first-time mom, I did not realize what a difficult baby he was. Well, I take that back. I realized he was a difficult baby, I just didn't realize that all babies were not that way.

I should have noticed right away that he was not a "typical" child. He was born at 2:33 AM, and they brought him back to my room at 8 AM. Everyone kept commenting on how bright eyed he was and how curious he seemed to be about his environment. He was awake that whole first day. Every single minute! He never even closed his eyes. I finally called the nursery at 5 PM and asked the nurse why he would not sleep. I mean, I thought babies were supposed to sleep a lot—especially newborns. Apparently he didn't. The nurse whisked him away to the quiet nursery, and eventually he fell asleep.

Looking back, that should have been my first clue that something with my precious baby was not quite right. Andy did not like to sleep. He was overstimulated so easily that his brain just would not shut down and allow him to drift off. If I put him in his swing, he would stare at the legs of the swing as he went back and forth, back and forth, but never fell asleep. The only way to get him to sleep was to swaddle him tightly, put him in a dark space, and play a white-noise machine in the background. He had to go to bed at the same exact time every day, with his bedtime routine done in the same exact order. I did not realize that this was abnormal—I just thought he was quirky.

I learned very early on that Andy had to be on a schedule. If his bedtime was 7 PM, he had better be in bed by 7 PM or he would not sleep. I could not miss bedtime by even 5 minutes, or forget about it. We did not go out in the evenings. I had to run errands in between naps and whenever I could steal a couple of minutes here and there. People thought we were ridiculous for being a slave to Andy's schedule. Everyone always said, "If he's tired enough, he will sleep!" It may not have been ideal, but it was our life, and it was not worth the aftermath to push the schedule even a few minutes either way.

As Andy grew, we eventually overcame the sleep problems. That's when the tactile issues started. He suddenly hated to have his hands dirty, his hair washed, anything on his face, and his fingernails clipped. I thought he was just being a toddler. "Toddlers are not supposed to like to sit still," I told myself. "He is just asserting his independence," I said. If only it were that simple. Next, almost overnight, the food issues began. It was just before his 2nd birthday, and he started refusing everything I put on his plate. Andy went from eating Mexican food, guacamole, fruits, veggies, meats, and cheese to only eating a few select foods. He would no longer even touch foods he had eaten a few short weeks before. Worse than that, he would not even allow them on his plate!

I mentioned some of Andy's quirks to his pediatrician at his 2-year checkup. She was unconcerned and told me the food issues were just a phase that he would grow out of. She was the expert, so I believed her.

By his 3-year checkup, things were worse. It had progressed to him only wanting to eat certain brands of things. All chicken nuggets were not created equal. He loved macaroni and cheese but only if the noodles were shaped like characters. If they were regular noodles, he would not eat them. He would eat yogurt only if there were no fruit chunks in it.

Dinnertime was a battle every night. It was horrible and involved lots of pleading, begging, crying, and frustration. Forget trying to make him eat something he did not want to try. That would result in him instantly vomiting on his plate (and no one wants to finish eating after someone vomits at the table). We tried making him sit at the table until he tried a bite, but that did not work, either. He would rather sit at the table for hours than eat a single bite of roast beef.

The pediatrician told me not to make a big deal out of his food issues. She said if he would not eat what I prepared, he could have a peanut butter sandwich instead. We tried that, and he ate peanut butter every single night and was happy as a clam. It didn't feel like a good solution.

By his 4th birthday, there was no improvement. It got to the point that Andy did not want to sit at the table if we were eating something he did not like. If his brother was eating something messy, Andy would gag at the sight of his brother's messy face. Vomiting at the table was practically a daily occurrence.

The pediatrician was not very helpful. She insisted that he would eventually grow out of his "pickiness." She said it was a power struggle and a phase and advised us to just keep letting him eat the peanut butter sandwiches.

I was so frustrated! I was tired of people who did not "get it" giving me advice on how to get him to eat things. I was tired of hearing that he would "eat when he was hungry" or that he "would not allow himself to starve." I was tired of being judged as a bad mom, like I was somehow responsible for the way he was acting. I was tired of people saying I should be harder on him, or that I should just force him to eat it. I knew there was something more to it than pickiness. I knew it was not just about the food, but I didn't know what it was. I could not get anyone to really listen to what I was saying.

When Andy was about 4½, he became very wiggly. He was constantly wiggling his legs, he could not sit still in a chair, and he was jumping on the furniture nonstop. He would remove all of the couch cushions, put them in a big pile, and dive on top of them over and over and over again. It was as if he was not comfortable in his own skin.

When I took him back to the pediatrician for his 5-year checkup, I refused to leave her office until she addressed his eating issues. I was sick and tired of being unheard. I was tired of battling my child every day. I was tired of the nagging feeling that something about my son was different, but I could not put my finger on what it was. I wanted answers, and this momma bear was not going to leave until someone helped me.

The pediatrician was caught off guard a bit but gave me the name of an occupational therapist that dealt with feeding issues. She suggested we start there. I called and made an appointment for an evaluation the same day.

When we arrived for the appointment with the occupational therapist, I was given a sensory checklist to fill out. I was shocked, and a little confused, because I thought my son just had a feeding issue. However, as I worked my way through the checklist, it became very apparent that it was much more than that.

The occupational therapist we saw was amazing. She went through the checklist with me and explained that my son had SPD. Right then and there, I felt like a weight had been lifted off of my shoulders. I was not crazy. I was not a bad mom. The feelings I had that something was just not right with Andy were correct. He was different, but not broken. There was a way to help him.

It was then that I decided to make it my mission to educate the world about SPD. I was angry that I had never heard of it before and that my pediatrician had never seen the red flags or mentioned SPD to me. I was upset that my son had struggled for years with this disorder without me being able to help him. Most of all, I was sad that there weren't any other people I knew in the same position for me to talk to and gain support from.

Looking back, I feel like that day was a turning point in our lives. Nothing has changed—he is still the same little boy with the same issues as before. Yet, we finally had a name for what were living with. Things finally made sense. My feelings of concern as a mom were finally validated. And, for the first time in years, I felt like I understood my sweet little boy.

Brandi Bernatow is a nurse living in the Midwest with her husband, two boys, and newborn daughter. Her oldest son received a diagnosis of SPD and attention-deficit/hyperactivity disorder at age 5, after years of her insisting that something was different about him. Her younger son recently received a diagnosis of a milder form of SPD. Her days are spent trying to mediate between her auditory-hypersensitive older son and her auditory-hyposensitive younger son, while also caring for her newborn baby. In the rare event that she has any free time, she enjoys scrapbooking, reading, and spending time outdoors with her family.

Trust Your "Momma Instinct"

by Laura Pittman

Joshua is our firstborn. I grew up not knowing much about kids, or babies, even though I got my bachelor's degree in psychology from the University of Colorado at Boulder, with my focus being child and adolescent development. Maybe that has been a blessing! It has been 4 years since Josh was born, and it is still emotionally draining to recount his first 18 months of life. It is one of those "if *only* I knew then what I know now, how different would Josh be?" things. Then I remember that everything happens for a reason, and so now my hope is that his story—our story—can help someone else navigate through theirs and see that they are far from alone and that there is hope—and a lot of it, too!

Josh was born via planned cesarean at 39 weeks 5 days. He was small at 5 lbs 12 oz. He couldn't keep his body temperature up, and they kept putting him under the heater, not on me for warmth. Josh had the hardest time nursing and didn't seem to have a strong sucking reflex. Does this sound familiar to anyone else?! Again, if only I knew what I know now…I thought I had read the right books and "how-to's" for raising a baby and nursing, but, as it turns out, I felt pretty unprepared. Breastfeeding is not as natural as some might think, so from hour one, Josh had strikes against him and was well on his way to showing even more developmental concerns. However, what I did hear from nurses and doctors was, "Don't worry, it'll get better—give him time!" Jump ahead to week 10, and nursing stops altogether. Like I said earlier, I never did the babysitting thing or spent time around babies growing up, but what is amazing is how automatic your "momma instinct" is and how quickly it kicks in. I was always petrified that this maternal sense would be lost on me, and of course it wasn't.

Joshua's first 10 months of life were bliss. After I successfully buried the birthing and nursing troubles in the recesses of my mind, I thoroughly enjoyed Josh and his laugh, smile, and sense of humor. He's always had one! Of course, looking back onto even that time, I see the signs of sensory-processing issues. He would take forever to fall asleep for naps. It was as if he couldn't calm down or get his system to be quiet. He would kick his legs against his crib mattress—you could hear a "bang! bang!" coming from his room. He was definitely a late crawler. In fact, he had his own way of moving around. He would literally get into a backbend, flail his arms back and forth, and scoot around on his head.

Little did I know how important it is for the developing brain to be successful at crawling. This developmental milestone activates the brain's corpus callosum, where the nerve endings form pathways to each other across the two hemispheres of the brain. Crawling is a cross-lateral skill, and it sets the child up for success in the development of gross-motor skills. Joshua's crawling stage was very short, and every time I saw him "move" around, a voice in the back of my head started to "hum."

People around me told me not to worry, he just does things his way, he'll "get it." Which was true, but it didn't quiet that "hum" in my mind.

We moved from Ohio to Illinois when Joshua was 11 months old. He started drinking cow's milk the next month, had his 1-year well-baby appointment, and truly hasn't been the same kid since. Josh began walking around 13 months old, he only said two to three words, and he still had not said "momma." Then the tantrums began. Again, I'd hear, "Oh, all kids do that. It's his age." At this point, you can insert any type of parenting advice that may apply—I think I've heard it all. However, his tantrums were just so intense and frequent. If you looked into his eyes, you could see that he was "not there" anymore. We would get into the car—meltdown. We would come home—meltdown. I would leave him anywhere—meltdown. I'd go to pick him up—meltdown. You get the picture.

Once he started walking, it didn't last long. He then began running—and when I say "running," I mean that he ran everywhere! At times I'd have to literally pick him up and hold him so he could catch his breath. I was scared he didn't realize how tired he was getting and would pass out.

Josh also never could follow directions. You'd ask him a simple two-step request, such as, "Go get the book and come sit in my lap." He wouldn't even look at me, he would go somewhere else, or—you guessed it—he would have a meltdown. This part of the story really breaks my heart, because if parents are not aware of SPD or what to look for, many think this is simply a behavioral issue and that assertive parenting can fix it. This is not true! SPD is a neurodevelopmental issue. Josh did not know how to motor plan and therefore didn't know how to get started on things.

Time-outs would have no affect on Josh, as he liked being by himself. Spanking did no good, either. The deep pressure and sensation of spanking actually felt good to him. It was something he could actually feel at that point.

And so, that "hum" in the back of my mind had become a loud voice in the front of my mind. My "momma instinct" was going off like crazy. We went to the doctor's office for Josh's 15-month checkup, and he hadn't grown. Some tests were run, my concerns were communicated and, yes, I received the "let's wait and see" line. Since he was a boy, and the firstborn, and since my husband and I aren't the loudest or most talkative people anyway, we decided to give him a couple of months to "catch up," since he was late in the other developmental areas, too. Hopefully you can see how wrong this was. This is why I cringe as I write, because if he was late in achieving some developmental milestones or simply skipped them altogether, then this was the *reason why* he needed to start early intervention as soon as possible and not "wait to see" if he wound up doing it all on his own.

Then the tipping point happened. One Sunday morning when my husband and I went to pick Josh up from his Sunday school room at church, he had his usual meltdown, but this time he added hitting his head against the wall. It took everything in me to not completely fall apart and start crying right then and there. My son was hurting, and he was in pain, somewhere...he couldn't tell me, he couldn't even call me "momma," but that is when I started educating myself. The first book I read was Jenny McCarthy's book, *Louder Than Words*. I remember calling my mom late one night, crying after I finished it, because it described Joshua perfectly and that scared me more than anything. One big piece that the book talked about that had eluded me until then was his gastrointestinal issues. Josh was always constipated, walking on his toes, and flailing his arms. This pushed me to finally listen to the now-screaming voice in my head to take action. I started him on a gluten-free/casein-free diet and called the early-intervention program in Illinois. This program is wonderful and was a true lifesaver. We had Josh evaluated, and he qualified for speech therapy, occupational therapy, and sessions with a nutritionist. We were incredibly blessed because our occupational therapists were trained in sensory processing, and it was a match made in heaven!

Not even a month into his therapy and his new diet, Josh said "momma!" He was 2 years old and finally said the word I had waited so long to hear. His therapists introduced my husband and me to the term "SPD." We had never heard of it. My research and time went toward learning more, and, finally, it seemed like we had a plan. Not only did we now have a "sensory diet" and knew the difference between the vestibular and proprioceptive systems, but everything seemed to be helping! Josh was becoming Josh again! We knew to add some weight to his backpack or put ankle weights on him, and his running subsided so that he was able to actually sit down, play, and hold his attention on one task (even if it was for only 2 minutes).

Obviously, it's hard to write down everything that happened in those first 2 years, but what I can definitely say is to listen to that "momma voice" that could be going off within you. Trust it, and run with it. Joshua just turned 4. If someone was to meet him and spend some time with him today, they would probably think he is a typical fun, loving, and very active little boy. Early intervention is truly the key, so if there are any concerns— get an evaluation. Look up your state's early-intervention program. Ask your doctor for that information if you don't know where to start. In our experience, all of it was free in the beginning. Once we started therapy, we paid a monthly fee on the basis of our family income. It was nothing in respect to what we got in return: our son being happy, able to communicate, and finally starting to thrive.

What I have learned, besides the importance of listening to my "momma gut" and trying to act as early as possible, is that this is a journey. We take steps backward with regard to progress, and then there will be big jumps forward. My hope is that people will see that there is help, that they don't feel isolated or alone, and that they are able to better understand what they are experiencing: In other words, to speak up and be an advocate for their child. Joshua is unique because there is no one else exactly like him, but his story, unfortunately, is not so different from thousands of kids out there, whether they are aware of it or not. Please, don't be afraid of joining the journey we are all on.

We have moved again. This time the Air Force moved us from Illinois to Colorado. We were ecstatic. If you don't know what the STAR Center and the SPD Foundation are, check these Web sites for more information: *www.spdfoundation.net* and *www.starcenter.us*. They are located in Denver. Joshua started therapy at the STAR Center last week. We are so excited and even more hopeful to start this next part of Joshua's journey.

***Laura Pittman** is a military wife with two kids. Her family's first blessing was a 4-year-old boy with a diagnosis of SPD at age 2 and then pervasive developmental disorder—not otherwise specified at age 3. He would likely not be identified as being on the autism spectrum anymore! They now focus on his SPD, diet, and supplements, and on helping him learn self-coping skills. Their 2-year-old daughter is a blessed handful and tries her hardest to keep up with her older brother. Laura has her BA in psychology from the University of Colorado at Boulder and blogs about her experiences at* www.followinggodalongthespectrum.com. *She and her husband both try to find joy and have a grateful heart in all circumstances, because they believe all things work out for good reasons (no matter how difficult that can be to remember some days).*

Throwing the Plans out the Window

by Lindsay Bartholomew

I admit, I am an obsessive planner. I plan every detail far in advance. When I found out I was pregnant, I had a girl's name and a boy's name picked out within a month, and I knew every detail of the nursery I would prepare for either a boy or a girl. When I found out I was having a girl, I was beside myself with excitement. Having a little princess was something I had dreamed about (and planned for!).

My pregnancy was full of things *not* in the plan…I know, I know, there is only so much control I can have over the situation. I was sick the entire time, and the last month I was on bed rest. My daughter was due after the new year, but I had to be induced on Christmas night. At 7:23 PM on December 26, perfection was born—and it was complete and overwhelming love at first sight.

That night, I knew something was amiss. My daughter would not stop crying and only slept for a few minutes here and there. Two days later we were sent home, and I was exhausted and in a fog.

I have complicated emotions about Emma's first year. It was an extremely joyful, stressful, and sleep-deprived time. Emma had severe reflux at 1 month old (which continues even now), and from 3 to 7 months old, she remained the same weight. She was nursing but struggling to eat enough. We introduced solids at 6 months, but she gagged, sputtered, and got sick, so we had to stop. At 8 months, she had a nasal-gastric tube placed so that we could feed her that way. However, the nurse that performed the procedure inadvertently caused complications, and Emma ended up in the hospital with aspirated pneumonia. Toward the end of that year, Emma's dad decided that this whole marriage/parenting thing was not what he thought it would be, and the decision was made to get a divorce.

During her first year, I started noticing that Emma was supersensitive to temperature, touch, noises, and being outside her comfort zone. She only wanted me and constantly needed to be skin-to-skin (usually nursing), wrapped tightly in blankets or being carried in a sling. I thought she was just a "high-needs" baby and would grow out of it. I kick myself now for not paying attention to all of these things—I was so wrapped up in her health issues that I missed it. At 11 months, a gastronomy tube was placed, and we were referred to an occupational therapist for feeding therapy. Not once did this therapist mention sensory issues.

Being a mother was a lot harder than I had ever imagined it would be. I was so jealous of friends and their babies or babies I saw in the store or in a restaurant, snoozing away in their car seats. Emma cried and fussed the entire time. I stopped going to restaurants and avoided social functions because they were so stressful.

Although there were a lot of struggles, there were also a lot of wonderful and amazing things that happened that year! I always worry that when I explain Emma, people will think, "Wow, what a grouch," but I promise you that the good memories are just as etched in my brain. That first smile, first laugh, rolling over, standing, and walking—you name it, those memories and 1,000 more are all there and just as clear. I learned so much about myself through my experiences with Emma and have become a better and more patient person that I ever thought I could be.

Through Emma's 2nd year, we continued to struggle in achieving weight gain and finding answers for her stomach issues. In my head, I knew there was something more, but I just couldn't put my finger on it. Emma started acting out with what seemed to be stress-induced behaviors. She pulled out her hair and eyelashes, threw herself into walls and furniture, bit her nails to nubs, and scratched herself. On top of that, she was still not sleeping well and took hours to fall asleep, only to wake up an hour later. We did a sleep study with her, which showed that she had severe restless leg syndrome. She was given medication for that, along with melatonin. To this day, these meds don't seem to make a difference in her sleep pattern.

Developmentally, we started noticing delays in speech, social skills, and motor skills. We seemed to get into a decent groove with her health toward the end of last year, and it was in that time that I was really able to focus on her other struggles. I contacted our local early-intervention program, and they put her in the Early Head Start program and set us up with an occupational therapist for feeding therapy. The therapist, Joel, came for his first visit in October, and within 15 minutes told me that she had some severe sensory issues that were causing some of her eating problems and odd behaviors. Sensory issues are what he decided to address before anything else. Emma struggled through preschool and became easily stressed with all the noise and kids, but I knew it was important to continue to expose her to new experiences.

Now we are approaching the end of Emma's 3rd year. We are still working with Joel one to two times per month, and Emma is also receiving weekly occupational therapy through the local children's hospital. Her therapist there has been amazing and totally gets the sensory thing! We work with a child psychologist, as well, to help get a handle on her anxiety and sleeping problems. I know how blessed I am to have a primary care physician, gastroenterologist, psychologist, occupational therapist, and even a pharmacist all working together as a team, helping Emma deal with everything from her stomach and weight-gain issues to her sensory struggles. Everyone on Emma's medical team agrees that Emma has SPD, and we all work together to make sure she is getting everything she needs.

I am still learning every day with Emma, and I have learned that planning 1 year ahead is just not something we can do. I worry about how she will do in school, and how she will keep up with her classmates. Will she make friends? Will she grow into this? Every day is a guessing game, so I have learned that I just need to take it one day at a time. Sometimes I am exhausted—physically and emotionally just "done for." Between going to appointments, sticking to routines, making sure Emma's sensory needs are met each day, struggling through some serious behaviors, and working with her to get her to go to sleep and stay asleep, I am so tired! Just thinking about starting all over the next day is enough to make me want to cry sometimes. But, the day starts whether I am ready or not, and I wake up to a slobbery kiss and a "wuv you, mama." I love Emma with every piece of me and only want her to be happy and well adjusted. I will do everything in my power and more to make sure she has every opportunity available to her!

Emma never ceases to amaze me, despite all that she has struggled through in her short little life. She is a teeny-tiny firecracker, full of spunk, smiles, and endless energy! Every day for us is a slow but promising and wonderful step in the direction of understanding and adapting to a life that just didn't go as planned.

Lindsay Bartholomew is a single mom who has dedicated her life to understanding her daughter's special needs and making her as comfortable, happy, and regulated as she can be!

He's Not a Bad Kid— He Just Has SPD

by Teri Frost-Tibben

When my partner and I were talking about whether or not to have children, we thought our biggest concern was that our child would be teased for having two moms. We moved back to the city from the suburbs to be in the most diverse environment possible for child-raising. At our 20-week ultrasound, we were told that our son would likely have a cleft lip and palate. We again thought—okay—we can deal with this very correctable condition through a series of surgeries. Nothing prepared us for a much harder issue, however—SPD.

We chalked Nathan's sleeping problems up to his surgeries at 3, 6, and 12 months. He had to wear "no-nos" on his arms for 10 days after each surgery to keep him from touching his mouth, and this obviously interfered with his sleep. Eventually, however, the only way to get him to sleep was to hold him and rock him, put him down in his crib without waking him, and sneak out of the bedroom while trying to remember where those creaky spots were in the floor. We couldn't stand to let him "cry it out," so we did the best we could. No one got much sleep.

Nathan started daycare at 6 months old, and I quickly cursed my fate as the parent on pickup duty at the end of each day. The daycare provider complained that Nathan wouldn't nap. Who gets bad reports about their *infant*?

We had to change to another in-home daycare provider for unrelated reasons, and by that time Nathan was able to get around. In her frustration, the daycare provider said she was going to have to tie him into a high chair upstairs with her during naptime because he wouldn't sleep and was bothering the other children. I felt ashamed and completely helpless. My father-in-law volunteered to come every day at naptime to prevent this from happening. Fortunately, it never came to that, and we eventually enrolled Nathan in preschool.

To our chagrin, the napping issues continued, and added to them were new behavioral issues. Nathan was hitting and biting other children, and the school's color-coded behavioral chart had no effect on him whatsoever. It was awful to go there every day to pick him up, dreading the day's report.

Once Nathan started kindergarten, things went from bad to worse. On the second day of school, the phone rang and it was the school's social worker, telling me that another child had bitten Nathan. I was so relieved that he wasn't the biter, I momentarily forgot to ask if he was all right! Many calls from the school followed, and, unfortunately, he was the one in trouble. He was sent home from kindergarten for hitting another child on the head with an apple in the lunchroom. His teacher said he was constantly running into other kids and sometimes knocking them over in his attempts to get from point A to point B.

I started to recognize the school's phone prefix on the caller ID and dreaded answering the calls. The school's only answer was to send him to the office or send him home for the day. Again, whose kindergartner is sent home from school? By the end of the school day, Nathan looked exhausted, and his shirts were soaked from him chewing on the sleeves and collar.

At home there were increasingly awful meltdowns, and we walked on eggshells around Nathan. We did whatever we could to avoid setting him off. The day we realized we needed help, Nathan ate his behavioral chart from school to prevent us from seeing it. He then hit and kicked my partner and chased her around the house when she tried to get away. The most worrisome aspect was wondering what would happen in 5 or 10 years when he would be physically stronger than we were.

Desperate for help, we turned to Nathan's pediatrician. She suggested that Nathan had attention-deficit disorder or attention-deficit/hyperactivity disorder, but she really had no idea. Through contact with several friends and doing some research on the Internet, we started honing in on SPD as a possible explanation. We took Nathan to an occupational therapy center, where he was evaluated and received a diagnosis of sensory modulation disorder. "Eureka!" we thought. We finally have a name for what's going on and a plan to treat Nathan. To our great surprise, our health insurance approved 12 months of twice-weekly occupational therapy.

I provided a copy of the evaluation for his teacher and school social worker, anticipating their cooperation. The reality was much different, however. The teacher complained about his oral aids because "saliva is flying everywhere." Calls and e-mails to the social worker were answered only about half of the time, and while the principal was kind and reassuring during a meeting, nothing happened to get any help at school. The social worker told us verbally that our son didn't qualify for an Individualized Education Program (IEP).

A chance conversation with another district employee led me to contact our district's parent advocate. She immediately got the ball rolling, and the same day, I received an e-mail from an employee in the district's Office of the General Counsel, who worked to ensure compliance with the federal laws governing special education. I now knew the big guns had been called in. We finally got a 504 plan written for Nathan on the last day of his kindergarten school year. The proposed accommodations were minimal, but it was a start.

Nathan worked hard at occupational therapy, and we saw some wonderful changes. He loved to swing, crash into things, and jump into piles of pillows. The therapy center and his therapist made things fun for him but kept working at the goals they had set up. Things at home improved, and Nathan's aggression toward us and other children decreased dramatically.

Feeling hopeful for the school year ahead, we walked into the first-grade room for open house night, and my heart sank. If someone had asked me to describe the worst possible physical environment for Nathan, it would have been this large, open room, divided into four classrooms by short "walls" of bookcases and cubbies. There were no doors. The noise and visual stimulation would drive many adults without sensory issues to distraction, and I couldn't fathom how my child would ever be able to learn in that environment.

We are now halfway through the first-grade year, and it's not going well, although Nathan has made amazing progress in every other area of his life. After the parent-teacher conference where his teacher opened the meeting by stating, "Nathan gets here in the morning and just decides what kind of day he's going to have," we decided it was time to request a formal special-education evaluation. Having educated ourselves, we knew that by law, the school had to perform this evaluation within a specified time frame.

We showed up for the meeting wondering if this was going to be one more fight with the school. As each staff member gave their report about the tests they had conducted with Nathan, we were relieved to find that his academics were in the average range. It was heartbreaking to hear from the school psychologist that although he's obviously a bright child, he seemed very discouraged. This was no surprise to us, based on how much he has struggled in school.

Fortunately, they found that he did meet the criteria for an IEP on the basis of "emotional/behavioral disorder" criteria, since SPD is not recognized and he's far too social to meet the autism criteria. They will soon begin a small amount of one-on-one and small-group time that we hope will help.

Facing a crisis like this has been terribly hard on our family. It's isolating and depressing. We live the roller coaster of feelings every day, and Nathan's "bad days" are bad for all of us. There have been many times we have felt like failures as parents when we miss the cues that a meltdown is on the horizon or are too busy to do a needed therapy activity. We have had to restrict our own activities and his, but we are much more aware of how to structure things so he can have a good experience—either by doing a therapy activity before and afterward, or just watching for signs of sensory overload so we can step in quickly with a remedy. We have to help Nathan regulate his moods and energy level, as he can't do it for himself yet.

Being "doers" and "fixers" it is so hard for us, because this isn't something we can fix easily or quickly for our beloved son. I have cried at work more times than I can count and stopped wearing mascara on my bottom lashes because I was crying it off more often than not. But, when I feel like I can't go on, I think of what Nathan has to deal with and how he wakes up every day, ready to try again. It's humbling.

Several things have preserved our sanity over the past couple of years. First is our occupational therapist, who has been wonderful. She really "gets" Nathan and treats him firmly but kindly. She laughs at his wisecracks and actually seems to enjoy spending time with him. The other parents in the waiting room have also been lifesavers. We celebrate the accomplishments of our kids and commiserate in the challenges like no one else can. Online support has become increasingly important to me. More than once, I have read a blog entry or something on an SPD Web site that has been just the thing I needed that day to keep plugging away.

While we are far from the finish line, there is so much good news that keeps us going. Seeing Nathan doing so much better at sports, having friends, and starting to understand that he's not a "bad" kid are the things that make it all worthwhile.

Teri Frost-Tibben lives in the Minneapolis area with her partner and marvelous 7-year-old son, who received a diagnosis of SPD at age 5. She works for the federal government and devotes her free time to reading about SPD, connecting with other special-needs parents online, and thinking of new and creative ways to get her son to do his occupational-therapy activities, vision-therapy homework, and schoolwork.

I Wouldn't Change It If I Could

by Chris Jurecko

How can the countless things you have been through during the process of raising a child with special needs be put into words? How can anyone other than you find the joy in hearing your son who has SPD finally say, "The tag itches me," instead of ripping all his clothes off and screaming at the top of his lungs if I were to try and put them back on? My personal opinion is that no one can fathom the individual situations that every parent of a special-needs child goes through on a daily basis. Everyone's experience is so unique that a single victory is enough to bring tears to your eyes, but it would take hours to explain its significance to someone else. I always knew I would love my children, no matter what, and I think everyone has fantasies about what their child could be. But, very rarely do you find someone who has expectations of raising a child with special needs. I am a father of three beautiful children, a daughter and two sons. My two sons, Riley and Carter, both received a diagnosis of SPD.

Our family's deep dive into the world of SPD began long before our first trip to an occupational therapist. In the first year of Riley's life, we thought we had the toughest, most advanced little guy on the planet. We were already talking football and calling him our little "Urlacher." He felt no pain, and his physical development was on the fast track. He was so ready to get moving around that he never actually crawled. At 4 months of age, he began bear-crawling, with his knees off the ground, and he began taking his first steps at 7 months. By 8 months he was full-out running alongside his big sister. He developed a noticeable six-pack before his first birthday because he would use his abdominal muscles to pull himself up onto chairs and tables, which he promptly jumped off of, over and over again. Our doctor was under the impression that he was a Superbaby and that his development was well beyond "on track." All of these traits seemed wonderful at the time, but as we look back, they paint a very different picture today than what we were seeing at the time. In reality, if we had known that he had SPD, we would have realized that even though he was getting hurt on many occasions, he did not know how to process that sensation and therefore didn't react. In addition, his desire to crawl and walk so early derived more from a desire for deep physical input that he could not get from lying on the floor, which drove him to start crawling and walking at such a young age.

As time progressed into his 2nd and almost 3rd years, Riley began developing more fears and taking fewer risks. He had acquired the nickname "Smiley Riley" from his grandpa, but that trait began to fade away, as well. We watched him slip into his own world, not knowing exactly what we were seeing or how to handle it. We heard an opinion from everyone… the doctor said his development was still on track and there was nothing to worry about. We heard that boys develop more slowly than girls, to give him time, it's just a phase, and on and on. The truth was that my wife and I were seeing something far different than any doctor or family member could see during their limited time with him. We were watching him turn inward, shutting the outside world out. He started turning cars and carts on their sides to spin the wheels. He spun himself endlessly without getting dizzy. He acted out in preschool when he could not articulate what he wanted with words. He lined up blocks in perfectly straight lines, even color-coding them. He refused to try to write anything because his hands could not make what his mind wanted them to, which caused him immense frustration.

It was actually part of an old episode of the TV show "Scrubs" that came to my mind when I saw Riley lining up his blocks over and over again. That was the first time my wife and I discussed the possibility of Riley having autism, and we decided to take him to a group of specialists to be tested. Through the tests, we discovered that Riley was not on the autism spectrum, but rather that he had SPD and would need lots of different weekly therapies to help him cope with the symptoms.

That diagnosis was one of the hardest experiences we would go through as a family, but it was also one of the greatest experiences. Once we got a result from the specialists that explained Riley's behaviors and made sense to us, we were able to move forward with getting him the help he needed. I really have to give my wife, Kelly, a huge amount of credit. She took this diagnosis and plowed into the unknown wall of SPD head-on. She spent hour upon hour researching SPD and finding out how to treat it, including food, clothes, therapies…you name it, she did research on it. She gave me things to read when I got home from work, explained everything she could to me, and filled me in on the progress Riley was making or what therapy sessions Riley was taking part in that day. It was awe-inspiring to see that level of dedication from my wife, and it really made me proud to be her husband. It was a lot of hard work, and there were plenty of obstacles and rough patches along the way, but Riley has made enormous improvements since we began working with him, and I cannot bring myself to imagine where we would be today if we had not gotten him help or if we had let him try and "grow out of it."

Riley continues to go to therapies and a special-needs school today. Through the process of securing an SPD diagnosis and participating in treatments for Riley, we were able to spot the defining characteristics of SPD in our youngest son, Carter. Owing to the fact that we knew what we were looking for and we were able to get Carter into physical and occupational therapy as early as possible, he was able to "graduate" from SPD therapies, and he no longer shows any symptoms.

SPD is still not something that is well known in society, or even in the medical community in some cases. It is always a challenge to be out in public when Riley is having a tough time because he looks like a normal little boy, so it could seem like he is just misbehaving to onlookers. That doesn't concern me so much—after all, I am not responsible for what other people think. My concern lies with the effects those people may be having on Riley because they do not understand what is really going on. My wife took an oath to herself that if we were able to help Riley, she would dedicate herself to raising awareness about SPD and put all the information she spent hours researching into one place, so other parents could access the information quickly and get answers as fast as possible. Out of that desire came *www.spdparentzone.org,* and it has been a huge help to me.

The last piece of the puzzle that has made such an amazing difference in our lives has been all three of our kids playing together. Addison, our daughter and our oldest, helped Riley in his darkest times by playing with him the way he wanted to play. Our kids are all great friends today and spend much of their time together, playing and using their imaginations. It is such a wonderful thing to see them in action and watch them help each other. Life is not perfect, and nothing is wonderful 100% of the time, but I am so grateful this is the hand I was dealt in life.

Chris Jurecko lives in the northern suburbs of Chicago with his wife and their three children, two of whom have SPD. He currently writes at Dad-ComesLast.com, his personal blog about his life as a husband and a father. He is also a board member of the nonprofit organization, SPD Parent Zone.

Chapter 3

SPD with a Diagnosis of Autism

About 25% of children who receive a diagnosis of SPD are also assigned a diagnosis of something else. Most commonly, it's an autism spectrum disorder, such as autism, pervasive developmental disorder—not otherwise specified (PDD-NOS), or Asperger syndrome.

According to the SPD Foundation's research, more than 75% of children with autism have sensory issues. But, keep in mind that the reverse is not true.

Many children who have high-functioning autism, PDD-NOS, or Asperger syndrome are first identified as having sensory symptoms, and that is what is addressed first. It is later, as these children grow up, mature, enter school, and are faced with larger social challenges that the other indicators of an autism spectrum disorder come to light.

Here are the stories of families who have experienced a similar path to mine—a diagnosis of both SPD and an autism spectrum disorder.

Connor's Story

by Emma Benefiel

It wasn't long after Connor was born that I knew something just wasn't right. There were little signs right from the start. He was unable to self-regulate his body temperature at birth. After many tests, all of which yielded normal results, it was an unknown issue that was probably caused by my fast delivery. Five days later, we ended up in the emergency room because Connor wasn't waking up to eat. After 3 days of continuous testing and finding nothing wrong, he was discharged as just needing time to adjust. At the time, none of this was really sending red flags up for me. The doctors were running every test they could think of and the results kept coming back fine, so everything must have been fine.

After the trip to the hospital, I was just happy to be home and to have a healthy little baby. Things did go well after that. He was such an easy baby—I used to think, "How did I get so lucky to have a baby this easy?" Connor did not like to be held as an infant and preferred to be on the floor staring at the wall. We just thought he was a hot baby, and that is why he didn't want to be held. How little we knew then. Part of me thought this was really cool—I could get so much done because he didn't want my attention. The other part of me was bothered by this, as it didn't seem right. Babies want to be held. At our checkups, I would bring this up with our pediatrician, and he told me not to worry and that Connor was fine. I believed him.

Around 4 months old, I really started getting the feeling that something was just not right. When I would voice my concerns to people, they would tell me not to worry—he was fine. As we started to approach the months where babies start to have their milestones, Connor wasn't having them. No rolling over, no sitting up, and no trying to grab things. Once again, I voiced my concerns and was told that he was fine and that he would catch up. This continued until he was 13 months old, and we went in for his checkup. At this age, Connor could not sit up on his own or pull himself up to stand. Walking wasn't even an option. At this age, all Connor could do was roll over and do some commando crawling. Once again, I was told by his doctor that Connor would catch up.

We ended up seeing a doctor at the children's hospital for another issue, and it was at that appointment that she voiced her concerns about Connor's development and said I should have him evaluated. I can't explain to you the feeling you get when you finally have someone validate your concerns. I left that appointment so relieved that someone had finally listened to me, yet so sad that, yes, there really could be something wrong with my son.

It wasn't long before Connor underwent evaluation, and it was clear that he was very delayed in several areas and would need therapy. At 15 months old, Connor started occupational therapy, and at 19 months he started speech therapy. I really thought that in 6 months, he would be discharged and we would be able to move on with our lives. Connor is 5½ years old now, and he still receives both occupational and speech therapy.

When Connor started therapy, I still really wasn't thinking that he had any disorders or anything of that sort. I just thought he needed help catching up. As we continued with therapy, I really wanted to know why we were in therapy—what was causing this? Around the same time, my sister-in-law brought up SPD. I had no idea what that was—I had never even heard of it before. I asked Connor's occupational therapist about it, and she really wasn't able to explain it to me and didn't seem to think Connor was really affected by it. As we continued therapy, I wanted to know why we were facing these issues. We found a new doctor for Connor, and after one visit with him, we were off to the children's hospital. At the age of 2, Connor got his first diagnosis of autism: pervasive developmental disorder—not otherwise specified. I cried all the way home. My first order of business was to get on the Internet and read as much as I could. I was still confused as to why Connor had all these other issues with his fine-motor skills, gross-motor skills, balance, and the like. In all of my reading on autism, these things were not discussed, so I still didn't know the whole picture. The professionals were unable to answer my questions. I spent many hours on the computer, and I think between the information I got from my sister-in-law and the Internet, I really wanted to know more about SPD. My biggest break was finding the SPD Foundation Web site, and from there I was able to find our current occupational therapist, who specializes in SPD. That changed our lives.

Finally, someone explained to me why Connor couldn't walk until he was 2, why he couldn't pull himself up to a standing position, and why he didn't like to swing. It was all starting to make sense to me. Even though it really wasn't, and I felt so lost.

Living with SPD changes your whole world. It affects every aspect of your life. Every day—every event—is planned carefully. Just going to a birthday party can be exhausting. Will there be too many people? What will the noise level be? We have to make sure Connor isn't overstimulated; usually, it's just easier not to go. I would never have thought SPD could affect such things as Connor being able to climb the jungle gym, but it does.

Connor is severely impacted by SPD in most areas: vestibular and proprioceptive systems, hearing, and self-regulation. We live a life of highs and lows. Just when we think we are safe and doing well, a small thing like the weather changing can throw us into chaos. It is an extreme balancing act just to have calm in our house. Finding the right therapist and support group has been our lifesaver; without these I do not know how we would have made it.

We have come a long way in the past 2 years, but we still have such a long way to go. We still struggle with knowing how to give Connor the sensory input he needs and how to explain to other people what SPD is. I look forward to the future and what it will bring us. Both Connor and I can only grow from our experiences and all the new things we learn.

Emma Benefiel was born and raised in the Greater Seattle area. She is married to her high-school sweetheart and is the mother of two wonderful kids, a 15-year-old daughter and a 6-year-old son who has autism and SPD. Emma works in the medical field and enjoys hiking, white-water rafting, and spending time with her family.

From Birth

by Alysia Krasnow Butler

That's my answer when people ask me when I first noticed something was a little "different" about my son. From birth. Well, really from day 2. I could hear his cry as the nurses brought him to me from the nursery. At 2 AM. 4 AM. 6 AM. Those poor nurses tried to keep him there so I could get some sleep, but he just wouldn't settle down. He had a completely distinct cry from the rest of the babies at the hospital, and I'd be awake and ready for him by the time they arrived at my room. On day 4, one nurse had to walk him around the hospital floor while another one discharged me because he was so unhappy. It may be hindsight, but I think even then I knew he was going to be more challenging than my older son.

There were more signs along the way. He would nurse until he spit up, and then cry to nurse again. He refused to take a bottle or a pacifier and always wanted to be held when he slept. My older son had a milk/soy protein intolerance, so we thought that might be it. We removed so many things from his diet—and mine—including all corn products. While that helped with the spitting up, he was still so unsettled. My neighbor at the time said he looked "uncomfortable in his own skin." Her words were so prophetic, since that's exactly what he was and is now.

One major sign of something "different" was his erratic sleep pattern. He would only sleep next to me or on me for naps and at night, and he seemed to wake every 45 minutes. I told the pediatrician that I thought he was waking up every time he peed. She said that seemed impossible but referred us to a sleep study clinic at the children's hospital when my son was 2 and still not sleeping through the night. One overnight electro-encephalogram and one 24-hour electroencephalogram later, the results showed "brain blips" but nothing "abnormal." We were told to put him in his crib, to let him scream—even if he threw up—and to clean it up and let him scream some more. Looking back now, we realize that not only would this never have worked with our son, but it was actually going to make things worse. I spent many nights crying through his screaming and finally gave up on the crib. Pregnant with my third son, I was sleeping on the floor next to his toddler bed in his room. It was the only way to get him out of our bed.

Eating was a whole other issue. At 9 months old, he refused all the stage-three foods after gagging on the chunks. At 18 months, he was still living on stage-two baby food because so many things he tried to eat came right back up again. He went 4 months without gaining any weight, and we were in the pediatrician's office monthly for weight checks. Nothing we tried worked. He wouldn't eat anything cold, hot, or chunky or foods that he had gagged on previously. The food repertoire was getting smaller and smaller. Multiple visits to the gastroenterologist showed nothing physiologically wrong with him. We were rapidly approaching the end of our rope.

Our glimmer of hope came after he turned 2 and was evaluated by our local early-intervention team. While all of his reports came back in the "normal" range, there were definite differences regarding his sensory-processing abilities. His sensory profile came back showing issues with sensory-seeking (his need for constant touch) and sensory avoidance (textures/temperatures of foods). The occupational therapist enrolled him for services under "clinical judgment." This meant that even though his results didn't officially qualify him for early-intervention special services, she thought he still needed help. She was right. We all needed help.

The team introduced me to the term "SPD." At its most basic level, they told me that my son just couldn't interpret the world around him properly. Everyday noises, smells, textures—things that wouldn't normally bother someone—bother him a great deal. They explained that we all have sensory issues, but most of us develop coping strategies to deal with them appropriately. People, and especially kids, with SPD have no idea how to cope.

The occupational therapist came every 2 weeks for 6 months. She had my son carrying heavy workout balls around the house and knocking down stacks of blocks. She would set up pegs and have him stack them or pull out her "goo" and hide little animals in there for him to find. I'll admit, at first I thought the things she was doing were a little hokey, and I wasn't quite sure what the purpose of it was. But I saw results quickly. His body was much more settled when she left. He didn't fling himself at his brother or crash into the furniture. As the sessions progressed, he could sit and attend to a task or a story. He would actually ask for the heavy ball or the pegs when she came, as he started to learn what his body needed.

She introduced us to the "therapeutic body sock" and the weighted blanket for the first time—two things that have become permanent fixtures in our house.

The feeding issue was trickier, but she tried to work with him on that, as well. We scheduled our sessions around lunch, and she'd sit at the table and eat with us. With her help, we got him to try soup and macaroni and cheese. To the outside world with kids, it must have seemed ridiculous to celebrate the fact that our kid was eating such kiddie food staples. But for us, it was a major victory. The occupational therapist showed him how to hold a spoon properly, and by the end of our 6 months, he was able to eat yogurt by himself. This was a far cry from where we started—with me spoon-feeding him at 2½ years old.

I'm not sure where we'd be now without her intervention. I am now familiar with words like "proprioceptive," "vestibular," "joint compressions," and "sensory diet." When the school district took over his case at age 3, I knew what he needed during his preschool day and how to ask for it. We're lucky that we have an amazing team at our son's preschool who understands sensory issues. Because SPD isn't a recognized diagnosis under law, our son couldn't get services specifically for his sensory issues. The school's occupational therapist secured special services for fine-motor–skill problems, and because of that she's been able to get a sensory diet in place for him during his school day. His aides and teachers understand him well enough now to know when he needs a "sensory break"—a walk outside or in the hallway, 100 jumps on the trampoline, or just a quiet space to chill out away from the noise of the classroom.

In December, our son also received a diagnosis of autism spectrum disorder. His official diagnosis is pervasive developmental disorder—not otherwise specified. I believe that much of his autism spectrum disorder is driven by his sensory issues. His lack of understanding of social space, his inability to regulate his volume, the stimming (repetitive body movements), his impulsivity—all seem to stem from his SPD. However, the autism diagnosis helped us understand all this much better and allowed us to get our son more help, which he needed at school.

After people ask me when I first knew something was different about my son, the next question is always what the hardest part about it is. There are many things that are difficult for me personally: the lack of sleep, the schedule, the 24/7 hands-on parenting, the worry. But the hardest part is clearly watching my son struggle with controlling and understanding his body and watching my other boys struggle to understand why their brother is so different. There have been so many people who have said that SPD isn't real—that it's just overindulgent parenting of kids who are just badly behaved. To those people I say, "spend a few days in my house." Watch my son run laps through our downstairs or spin in circles because he can't calm himself down. Watch him gag on a strawberry or refuse to eat ice cream because it's too cold. Listen as my older son stomps away in frustration because his brother is screaming so loudly after his yogurt wasn't opened correctly. Help me as I pull my son off his baby brother because he's trying to get a "squishy hug." Spend the night and see the way my son needs to fall asleep with his hands in the crook of my neck to calm him under four blankets, and be there when he wakes up at 2 AM to crawl up against me in bed, jamming his feet under my legs.

You may call me accommodating, but this is not overindulgent. This is me, after 4 long years, finally understanding my son. And this is my family living with SPD.

Alysia Krasnow Butler is a stay-at-home mom to three boys, ages 8, 4, and almost 2. Her 4-year-old received a diagnosis of autism spectrum disorder, and since then she has become his tireless advocate. She writes about her boys and their journey at trydefyinggravity.wordpress.com. *Her work has been published in* The Boston Globe *and* Bay State Parenting *magazine, as well as online, including* Mamapedia *and* Autism Speaks "In Your Own Words."

Alex's Story

by Michelle Bookman

I first learned about SPD during an in-service workshop presented by a local child psychologist through my employer. I was working as a family therapist and, at the time, saw a lot of children for therapy. During the workshop, a new book was referenced, called *The Out-of-Sync Child,* by Carol Stock Kranowitz. As I read the book, I couldn't help but feel that much of the information seemed too familiar. One of my sons, Alex, who had recently started school, bore a resemblance to many of the characteristics found in the book. Upon completing this workshop, I learned that Ms Kranowitz would be presenting a half-day seminar at a facility in my community. The seminar was free and open to the public for teachers, therapists, and parents dealing with children with sensory issues.

I registered to attend and reread parts of the book in preparation. As the date grew closer, I found myself feeling anxious—not only because I feared what I might learn, but also because I desperately wanted answers as to why my child was different. Even in preschool, Alex's teachers had warned me about his odd behaviors and how he didn't respond the way the other children did. Alex was labeled "hyperactive," but there was more to it than that: He was fussy about clothes, food, temperature, and light. He had frequent temper tantrums. He was clingy, yet not comforted by touch. I hoped Ms Kranowitz's seminar would give me some answers.

I was impressed with her presentation skills and knowledge. I left the seminar knowing what I had to do: have Alex evaluated by an occupational therapist. I felt, beyond a shadow of a doubt, that this new information would allow me to help Alex.

He was already struggling in school, with the demands of being in a classroom all day, needing to focus, and having to stay still. His kindergarten teacher had told me she was "sure he has oppositional defiant disorder," as well as attention-deficit/hyperactivity disorder (ADHD), and that he "stuck out like a sore thumb" because of being different. Alex was quickly growing to dislike school. We scheduled an appointment to have him evaluated.

After completing multiple checklists and rating scales, Alex was evaluated by an occupational therapist. The results of the evaluation were clear: Alex had multiple issues with sensory processing. He was overresponsive to light and sound, underresponsive to pain and touch, and sensitive to fabrics and food temperature and texture. He craved movement and deep muscle pressure. He started outpatient occupational therapy once a week. This continued for 1 year, followed by less frequent occupational therapy for several more years (he was finally discharged at age 13). He also eventually received occupational therapy services at school through an educational services agency for a period of about 4 years to focus specifically on his handwriting, which was problematic owing to his immature pencil grasp. I wish I could say that occupational therapy was a "cure" for Alex. It wasn't. It certainly helped, as he was able to get the "input" he needed in a safe environment. We were able to learn what helped him organize and what was frustrating to him. With the support of the educational services agency, we were able to help the school to understand these things, as well.

Alex is now 14 and about to start high school. He has unfortunately received diagnoses of some other issues that have complicated things, such as ADHD, anxiety, and Asperger syndrome. His sensory issues are not as noticeable in some ways, but they are still there. He has never been able to go see fireworks because of the loud noise, but he can now tolerate a movie theater. He doesn't need to swing or jump excessively anymore, but he craves deep muscle pressure, which he gets from wrestling with his brother. His diet is more varied, but he doesn't let his foods touch each other and eats most things lukewarm. He won't eat anything with gravy or cheese. His body temperature runs hot, so he wears shorts all year round and hates coats. He will not wear any clothing with buttons or zippers and won't wear denim or certain other fabrics. Probably the most difficult thing for me is that Alex does not like to be touched. I literally have to pay him if I want to hug him. He just does not like that kind of touching.

Being the parent of a child with sensory issues can certainly be a challenge. If I didn't have the information I have about SPD, though, I would be even more frustrated. I would recommend any parent who has the chance to meet Carol Stock Kranowitz to take advantage of the opportunity. I do not know how many years may have passed without getting the proper care for Alex if I hadn't first heard the words "sensory dysfunction." Alex may always be a little quirky, but at least I understand why he is that way, and I can appreciate the special gifts he possesses. He is, after all, my first-born son.

Michelle Bookman has a bachelor's degree in social work from Juniata College and a master's degree in social work from Widener University. She has 20 years of experience primarily in hospice social work and outpatient mental health. Michelle has been married for 18 years and has two sons— Alex, who is 15, and Ryan, who is 8.

A Gentle Boy with a Giant Fear

by Lou Tecpanecatl

Raising our oldest son up to this point has been an amazing and reward-ing experience, but it has also presented us with a unique challenge. Diego entered the world just before 10:30 PM on a Monday in early March. Right from the beginning, he made everyone around him acutely aware of his presence. We noticed rather quickly that he cried a lot and for an extended period of time. I would leave the hospital for maybe 30 minutes to get some food, and when I came back, I could hear one baby crying louder than the rest. It was Diego. This would become a common occurrence, as we spent the first 9 months of his life without much sleep. He was unable to "self-soothe," making it nearly impossible to put him down for a nap or to rock him to sleep at night. He was always so determined to stay awake and fight sleep, even if he was exhausted, making him more and more agi-tated by the minute. We finally realized that we would have to put him in the stroller and rock him to sleep. We did this whenever he was supposed to nap and again at night before moving him to his crib. This may not seem like a big deal, but we used the stroller method to put him to sleep until he was 3 years old! While he napped during the day, everyone had to be really quiet because they did not want to be the one to wake Diego up. If that happened, we would be dealt an unforgettable display of screaming and crying. Any time he was awakened before he was actually ready to get up, he would be in a horrible mood for at least an hour afterwards. We spent most of our time walking on eggshells, since we did not want to make any sudden sound or movement that would startle him.

In addition to having sleeping problems, Diego would vomit all the time. To fully explain his throat and stomach sensitivity, I will try and put this into perspective. During the first 12 to 15 months of his life, I cannot remember a day he did not throw up. Not one single day. The worst were the days he threw up three times or more because he got so upset, and it would take a long time to calm him down again. He had a problem with acid reflux, which caused projectile vomiting, and that usually meant that his baby formula ended up all over us and the furniture. By the time he was 3 months old, we took him to a gastroenterologist, and he was given a prescription for a medicated powder to help control the vomiting. After finding a formula that he was able to hold down (at least most of the time), we faced a similar problem when he started eating solid food. My wife and I were so stressed about his feedings, because half the time he could not keep the food down.

We watched him hit all of his physical milestones early, and we were amazed at how quickly he learned to walk. By the time he was 10 months old, he was practically running circles around my wife and me. He had powerful legs, made stronger by the fact that he preferred to squat down while playing. He appeared unable—or simply found it too uncomfortable—to sit on the floor with his legs in front of him. In hindsight, I can see all the early signs of sensory-related issues. The major problems have always been his sensitivity to loud sounds and being touched against his will. The food blender was his worst enemy. It could only be used to prepare his food if the kitchen door was closed and he was either upstairs or being consoled by his mommy in the other room. He was not able to tolerate the vacuum cleaner or other loud, sudden noises. As time passed, it also became obvious that any physical contact would have to be done on his terms. If he felt like hugging your legs or wanted to be picked up, then that was allowed; but if he did not request the contact, he refused to be touched at all.

By the time he was 2 years old, we had quite a few concerns about our son's behavior, and we decided to consult with a neurologist. At that time, usually when he got overly excited, his body shook and his face turned bright red. We were unsure about the severity of the issue, so we decided to have him examined. The neurologist ordered magnetic resonance (MR) imaging of his brain and an ambulatory electroencephalogram to examine his brain activity for 72 consecutive hours. The electrodes were to be attached to his scalp on one end and to a battery-operated pack that recorded his brain activity on the other. Diego had to be sedated for the MR imaging and to have the electrodes put in place. Since the wires were 3 feet long, for the next 3 days, someone had to be that close to him at all times to carry the backpack. We went back to get the results and were very relieved when we found out the test showed he did not experience any seizures. However, it was at this same follow-up appointment that we received news that would ultimately change the course of our lives. The doctor, after both observing our son and having a lengthy discussion with us, diagnosed our son's condition as autism spectrum disorder.

Diego is now 4 years old and is currently attending a preschool for children on the autism spectrum. He is a sweet and caring little boy who loves to watch DVDs and play with his toy trains. He is remarkably intelligent and has an impressive visual memory. He does, however, struggle with a speech delay and behavioral problems. He has not received an official diagnosis of SPD, but his extreme sensitivity is a major part of his life and presents itself as the core of his developmental delay. For example, when he is sick and has to visit the doctor, both my wife and I, along with one of the nurses, have to physically restrain him just so the doctor can examine his ears, nose, or throat. The fear he has of the examination and the thought of being touched by the doctor are so intense that he fights to get up and run away. We have also abandoned any notion of taking him somewhere outside of our home to get a haircut. We are forced to trim his hair ourselves because he thrashes violently and screams throughout the entire process. Since he is big for his age, I hold him in my lap while my wife cuts his hair. By the time we are finished, his voice is hoarse from the yelling. Because he can only tolerate certain food textures, he is a very picky eater. The issue he has with vomiting has stayed with him throughout the years, but thankfully to a lesser extent. If he gags while eating, even only slightly, he will force himself to throw up everything he has just eaten. Just recently, we have come across a problem with clothing. He has become nearly impossible to dress in the morning because he does not want to remove his pajamas. The pants and long sleeves he sleeps in are very comforting to him, and he throws a fit when he is forced to change. He has even carried a pair of pajamas with him to school and kept them by his side as a soothing presence in his hectic day.

As his father, I am amazed at the way he is able to hold it all together and how he has adjusted to attending school on a daily basis. The improvement he has made with his spontaneous speech is impressive, and I am in awe of all he has accomplished. Yet, it is very hard for me to see him get really upset and start having bad tantrums. If I am alone and I start to cry, it is not because my son has autism, but because of my inability to take away his fear. At night, after he has fallen asleep and before I go to bed, I peek into his room to catch a glimpse of him sleeping. He always looks so peaceful. I like to think that his mind is able to relax and that he can escape for a short time from the confusing and overstimulating world around him.

*As a parent to a boy with autism, **Lou Tecpanecatl** has dedicated himself to learning all he can about developmental disabilities and the best ways to help his son learn and communicate more effectively. Originally from the Midwest, Lou graduated from Ohio University and has since moved to New York. His blog, Our Life with Diego, is where he writes about his views on autism and his son's journey.*

Full Circle

by Melanie Chance

Day 1. "Your son tried to strangle a child today." This matter-of-fact message is written with the swift precision of a teacher's handwriting. I stare at it in disbelief as I review Caleb's agenda book—a daily ritual. "What?" I exclaim out loud. "That is NOT possible!"

"Caleb, did you squeeze someone's neck today???" I ask. My little 6-year-old boy, blue eyes sparkling behind raggedy blond hair, says, "No, Mama. I just gave him a hug."

I write a reply to the teacher's message: "Please call me to discuss. Caleb feels he was only hugging."

Day 3. The phone rings, and I answer. "Hello, is this Caleb's mom? This is his teacher. I'm calling to find out if Caleb is always like this." "Always like what?" I ask. "Well, he seems to be just a bratty little kid who never wants to do what he's told," she says flatly. "No," I reply, "Certainly he is *not* always like that. What on earth do you mean?" I can hardly believe the conversation I am having. "He won't do what he's told and refuses to listen. I was just wondering if he's like that all the time."

Day 30. The phone rings. So many calls have transpired over the first months of school, and I've heard so many defeating and demoralizing comments made about my beautiful child, that I am now conditioned to physically cringe at the piercing sound of a ringtone, stress hormones coursing through every vein. "Hello, is this Caleb's mom?" I try to maintain my pride in this most cherished label. "Yes," I say firmly. "This is Caleb's gym teacher. I'm calling about Caleb's behavior. He is all over the place and can't seem to calm down. He's pushing other kids and falling down all the time, slamming up against the walls. I'm having to pull him aside throughout class." "I know," I say, "I've been getting a lot of these calls, and I just don't understand what's going on with him. He has always been the sweetest little boy and has always used his words and not his body to express himself. He's such a great kid." "Really?" says the gym teacher, "That doesn't sound like the Caleb in *my* class."

Day 65. I arrive with Caleb at his homeroom and sit down in a chair the size of my purse, bracing for the meeting we are about to have with one of his teachers. I am feeling smaller than the smallest child, more vulnerable than the class pet in his corner cage, more terrified than the student who suddenly realizes the test is *today*. I coach myself in the third person: "Melanie is a strong woman. Melanie has gone through a lot in her life and has fought to succeed. She is intelligent, kind hearted, and worthy of having her own legitimate opinion in matters of her son's education. She is entitled to her own voice, and she will use it here today." "Really?" the voice of my inferiority complex intrudes, "That doesn't sound like the Melanie in *this* class."

What *is* it about sitting in a teacher's classroom as a parent that can send you right back to your worst experiences as a child? The teacher begins by explaining that Caleb's *behavior* must change. It is *unacceptable*. To do her part to help Caleb change his *behavior*, she describes the class meeting she held that day. In what feels like a surreal moment stripped from a melting Salvador Dali painting, she tells me she had all the children sit around Caleb while he listened. She instructed them each in turn to tell Caleb what they didn't like about him. "You hug too tight," "You talk too loud," "You push too hard," "You act too crazy." And all my little Caleb hears is, "I don't like you," "I don't like you," "I don't like you," "I don't like you."

With the genuine smile of Mother Theresa, she acts as though I should be thanking her for modifying my son's behavior (when obviously what I have been doing isn't working). I am at once stupefied, enraged, confused, sickened, and…silent. I cannot speak. My insecurities, my unpreparedness, my complete shock, my own confusion with Caleb's behavior—they have all frozen my tongue. I nod. I say things I don't remember. We leave.

Day 66. The next day, the full trauma of what transpired hits us both. I feel wracked with guilt and shame that I did not speak up in the meeting, that I did not condemn the teacher's actions or call out her lack of understanding. Caleb…is broken. My sweet, naïve, eternally optimistic 6-year-old was spirited away in the night, and in his place is left a brooding boy who calls himself "stupid" and "bad" and hits himself in the head as a matter of habit. He refuses to return to school.

Day 71. I have hatched a plan to find my lost son. It is a secret, crazy plan. It means sending a letter to the school, advising them to gather Caleb's belongings for us to pick up. It means homeschooling, not returning to my career after my recent maternity leave, and changing the entire course of the life we had planned for our young family. At the time, I believed it would mean reinventing myself. Now I know that it was always about finding *myself* in the journey to find *my son.*

Day 283. Seven months of homeschooling (with an infant in tow) later, and we are who we were always meant to be: happy, confident, self-loving, and not self-loathing people.

We have so many things we didn't have before: diagnoses and labels (Asperger syndrome, SPD, giftedness), therapists for occupational therapy and speech therapy, a fun social skills group, a sensory diet, a sense of who we really are as a family and as individuals, a total acceptance of our differences and our inner beauty, our voice. Challenges and uphill battles are never far off on the horizon for families like us, and the next will surely be Caleb's longing to return to a classroom that doesn't understand him. But in the meantime, we have found ourselves, as well as a virtual community that understands every messy bit of the journey.

Day 365. I'm having coffee at a favorite café with a good, good friend. She wraps her thin fingers around a hot mug and says, "Ben's been behaving differently…he's crashing into everything all the time and hitting people. He shrieks randomly for no reason, yet he can't seem to tolerate loud noises. He can't look at me when I'm talking to him and seems to shut me out. Do you have any idea what might be going on? He's such a great kid."

"Yes. *Yes he is,*" I reply, "And yes, I think I do have an idea…"

Melanie Chance is a pen name for the mother who wrote this story. She homeschools, blogs, and advocates for increased understanding and acceptance of those with autism and significant sensory-processing differences. She hopes that one day all children will find the acceptance and accommodations they need to feel safe at school.

Her Name Is Grumbled- All-the-Way

by Emma Apple

Our sensory journey really started long before I realized. My daughter was born via cesarean section, after a relatively difficult labor, and after a year of trying to conceive and being told we would need help to do so because I had polycystic ovarian syndrome. She was perfect in every way and very much adored. The early days were tough, as with most newborns—sleepless nights, breastfeeding hurdles—the usual.

She was one of those babies you couldn't put down. At 6 weeks old she ended up sleeping in our bed full time, because it was the only way I could get any sleep. I'd tried to get her to sleep in the bassinet, but she would wake up crying 5 minutes after being put down, until finally we'd pass out together and she'd essentially use me as a pacifier. If I somehow moved and she could no longer access my breast, the crying would start again. I tried in vain to encourage a pacifier, which lasted about 5 minutes at a time and ended up being a chew toy when she got a little older. She ended up weaning at 1 and sleeping in her own bed at 2½. Naps ended before her first birthday, and the attempts to get her to sleep in a portable crib ended in a whole lot of screaming and flailing. She didn't sleep through the night until she was 5.

When she was about 6 months old, I read an article by Dr Sears about "high-needs babies," and several light bulbs went on. She was high needs, and that was okay—it just meant she needed a little extra support. So we slept together in bed, she breastfed—all night—and this went on, and on, and on. The Dr Sears article drifted into a vague memory until a few years later, when we were getting new labels from new doctors.

As an infant, my daughter was strangely fascinated by the curtains, or the curtain rod to be precise—or maybe it was the light that came from behind the curtains at the top. I was never quite sure what it was, but she would gaze, for a long time, at the top of the curtains. I called them "Habibi Curtains," which translates from Arabic to "Beloved Curtains." It was funny that I never thought much of it at the time. At that point, I knew nothing about autism, Asperger syndrome, or SPD.

As a toddler, she would scream and pull away if her father or anyone but me held her. It was heartbreaking to know that she loved her father but that she did not want him to hold her. I could only hold her in certain ways, and hugs were a rare and treasured event. Proper hugs still are. She was petrified of the doctor right from the start, and every time we visited, the doctor assured me, "It's normal—she won't do this next time you come in." But the doctors had stopped saying that by the time she was 5.

She started speaking at 10 months old, in full sentences by the time she was 1. She also started screaming. It became a daily, all-day thing, if anything—and I do mean anything—did not meet the standards of "Queen Muck," as we affectionately called her. My mother and I would joke that every time I had to say no, it was a decision to be made carefully. Was it, or was it not, worth the screaming? We couldn't have a 30-minute phone conversation without at least one screaming episode. Then there was the rice, all over the kitchen floor, whenever she was left alone with it. All of this was, of course, just the terrible twos.

At 2 years old, she got a little brother. She was somewhat indifferent to the baby before he came, interested in the belly but not really. She was only 2, we said. When her father brought her to the hospital to see the new baby, she stayed well away, not really interested in this new creature and don't-you-dare-try-to-bring-it-too-close. The photos we have of the first meeting show a terrified little girl being held much too close for comfort to this strange creature she wanted nothing to do with. It was 2 weeks before I got pictures of them sitting next to each other, and one picture shows her arched away from him, pressed against the other side of the chair with a nervous grin. During the first few weeks, she dared to peer over the top of the bassinet, but it took her several weeks to be comfortable enough to come a little closer at someone else's suggestion. It took her months to see the baby as another human being, but she eventually blossomed into a bossy big sister who tolerated her little brother and even—dare I say it—loved him. Still, they couldn't be left alone together when he was an infant, as she would hit, kick, and scream at him unprovoked and quite liked the look of him flinching away—but didn't so much like the loud crying that came next.

During our time apart, when I was in the hospital giving birth to her little brother, she finally bonded with her father. Not only did she bond, but she became extremely possessive of him and distanced herself from me. Her father "was not allowed to hold the baby," and if he did give any attention to the baby or show any affection for him, there was screaming and crying, and much drama ensued. On those precious nights when Queen Muck was finally asleep, I remember a father trying to steal a few moments to bond with his son and the difficulty of those first several months. Not knowing why she was reacting this way or what I could do about it still makes me tear up. It was bittersweet because she was finally bonding with her father, but at the expense of her little brother, who didn't really get to bond with his father until after he turned 2 years old.

My mother and I had started to talk about the multiple signs of something not being quite right. I used to say that my daughter was 2 years ahead intellectually, teaching herself to read and write by age 3, and 2 years behind emotionally. We'd talked of our concern at her lining things up, becoming obsessively attached to things, covering her ears at loud noises or the thought that something might make a loud noise, and the fact that you couldn't get through to her at those times and there was no convincing her that the blender was not plugged in or that the plunger did not make any noise. We discussed the chewing and the fact that she had never grown past the "mouthing everything" stage. The repetition. The unusual use of language. The fact that she assumed new names and characters regularly and was very serious and strict about being addressed accordingly. Our favorite name was "Grumbled-All-the-Way." And, of course, there was the screaming. The list was long, but we convinced ourselves that, for the most part, kids are just weird.

I tried offering alternatives for her to chew on, and it helped for only a short time. I was at a complete loss with the rest of it. I had little experience with typical development, and my older sister, who is an early-childhood teacher, was a virtual lifeline, offering me all the advice and ideas she had from the other side of the world...even showing my list to a special-education teacher and passing on her thoughts. My mom was my soundboard—we bounced ideas and concerns back and forth and talked each other down when we started to really worry. My younger sister was my moral support—she'd make me laugh when I was feeling like my hair would fall out. My husband was the counter voice. To him, there was no concern.

By the time my daughter was 3½, I had begun making a list of all of our concerns—the good, the bad, and the very worrying. I'd update this list every month or two. She'd made a relatively stable truce with her little brother, who was almost the complete opposite of her, adoring and forgiving of his big sister. He was truly a blessing—the easiest baby to take care of and a wonderful sleeper, allowing me the time to devote to trying to figure out his beautiful big sister and allowing her the time to learn how to interact appropriately with another person her size.

At her 4-year checkup, I mentioned some of my concerns to the doctor, and the doctor decided that those concerns, in conjunction with her advanced literary and artistic ability, were cause to look a bit closer. So the doctor and I met with a general psychologist, without my daughter. He listened to my concerns and asked me some questions. The conclusion of this appointment was that it was not worth pursuing further evaluation and that I simply needed to practice more "firm parenting."

I went away feeling somewhat defeated. I was raised to trust my intuition, but self-doubt is the natural state of a mother. I decided to soldier on. Maybe she would grow out of this after all—maybe I really did need to be more firm, and definitely more consistent. Maybe I was Googling too much, thinking too much, focusing too much. One thing you should know about me—I am one of the least worried parents you'll ever meet.

We continued trying new things, and nothing got better. I spoke to the doctor again, who told me that she supported me and would give me a referral if I insisted but that she didn't think it was necessary. She was a resident and admitted she had never met a child like my daughter before, and I deeply appreciate her honesty to this day and her support of my judgment as a parent. I decided we'd keep trying at home, until one day when my daughter was 4 and she chewed through an electrical wire—while it was plugged in. I almost spontaneously combusted, I was so angry because it scared me half to death. Not too long after that, she put a shard of glass in her mouth, and I had the same reaction. At that point, I decided enough was enough—I was going to find out what was going on with my daughter before it ended up harming her—or worse. The worst they could do was tell me that nothing was wrong, and I would just keep doing what I was doing and hope for the best.

We ended up at a children's hospital, where we saw a doctor who wasn't really an expert on autism or related issues, but she knew enough to do an assessment. I gave her my lists, which I'd kept updated every few months so I'd know how things progressed or regressed. She saw us several times. She said my daughter had pervasive developmental disorder—not otherwise specified and anxiety, and she seemed to suggest Asperger syndrome but said she wouldn't assign that kind of diagnosis to a 4-year-old. She told me to trust my intuition because I was right about my child and that I was doing a wonderful job, better than most parents she usually saw. I knew it—it wasn't my parenting after all. The sense of relief was somewhat more overwhelming than the sense of grief or shock at being told there was indeed "something unusual" about my child. This doctor was wonderful and trusted me as a parent and as the primary expert on my child. She insisted I take my daughter for further evaluation at an autism clinic in another hospital, where the services would suit her better.

After being on that waiting list for several months, my daughter turned 5 and we went in for a full evaluation. She was seen by a team of doctors over three appointments and assessed in all different areas—psychological assessment, speech, occupational and physical therapy evaluations, and I'm not sure what else. The final 10-page report said the diagnosis was Asperger syndrome and sensory regulatory disorder. She received this diagnosis about 6 months ago and has yet to seek the recommended therapies, owing to insurance hangups and waiting lists. Chewing is still an issue; however, we discovered a product called Kid Companions that offers several different chewing textures. It has been an amazing recourse for us and has helped our daughter to stop biting her nails and chewing furniture and other inappropriate things. The other issues also remain, but with her diagnosis, we've been able to work with her at home, and she has made some amazing progress and developed some wonderful self-coping tools, such as using breathing techniques and feelings charts.

After she got her diagnosis, we joked that at least my son was "normal," because that proved it really wasn't my parenting at fault. Once my son turned 3, however, he started flapping his hands regularly. He'd always done funny things with his hands, but I'd never noticed flapping like that before. He'd been lining things up for some time, as well as walking on his toes. He seems to seek sensory input in a great many ways and has a language delay. He's very shy and clumsy. I'm trying to decide whether to go ahead and get him evaluated. Unfortunately, this time around, even though my intuition has been supported before, the decision is no easier. And I have to wonder if there is a genetic component at play.

Emma Apple is a designer by day, a writer and advocate by night—or vice versa—and a mother of two children, an "Aspergirl" (that's her superhero name—otherwise, she goes by "Madam") and a Not Typical boy who would rather be a paleontologist than a superhero. Emma has had several pieces of creative writing published in anthologies in New Zealand and the United States. She founded MuslimasOasis.com, a collaborative magazine blog for and about Muslim women. Emma converted to Islam at age 17, became acquainted with autism when her daughter was 3, and recently married the two experiences with Blue Hijab Day, a yearly event for autism awareness in the Muslim community.

My Bubba

by Kristine M. Starks

This is Keagan's story. He's 5½ years old and the sweetest little guy you could ever meet, on a really good day. Most days, my sweet little boy is lost somewhere in a puzzle of sensory overload, social confusion, and a world of misunderstanding, and acting out as a result of these. My Keagan has Asperger syndrome, which is on the autism spectrum, and SPD.

Keagan was born 2½ weeks early, with a fairly traumatic birth. He was delivered via cesarean section, and because his umbilical cord was wrapped around his neck twice, it took him longer than normal to start breathing (it seemed like an eternity to me!). He was healthy, other than having some low-oxygen moments and jaundice that we watched closely, but we were sent home with a clean bill of health after 4 days. Since he was my first baby, I had nothing to compare him to, but he seemed to be "normal" and wonderful. He was breastfed exclusively until he was 6 months old, when solid food was introduced, and continued to be breastfed until he was 14 months old.

Starting when he was about a month old, however, Keagan developed reflux and would scream and throw up after he ate. He took medication for this until he started eating solid foods. Once he did start on solid foods, he instantly became chronically constipated and eventually had to take medication for that, because nothing that we tried with his diet worked. As he got older, we were able to wean him off the medication and substitute prune juice and Fibersure, and now we mostly just watch his diet. He endured many painful bowel movements and many, many suppositories during this time. Needless to say, he was *very* difficult to toilet train.

Regardless of these problems, he was a happy baby. Since our other two sons were older, aged 9 and 11, Keagan was doted on by all, and I was with him every minute of every day. He and I were very rarely apart, and to this day, we have a very powerful bond. Keagan always received what he needed; if he wanted to be held, he was held. If he wanted to be on the floor, he was on the floor. Starting at around 4 or 5 months old, he slept in bed with us because he was up quite a bit at night. I think because he was getting the sensory input he needed, he was not extremely fussy. He was a sweet, loving, beautiful boy. He was my bubba.

Looking back at the first couple of years, I remember things that I now understand to be "warning" signs: the reflux and constipation, not sleeping well at night, and instead of being calmed to sleep when I sang, he would wake up completely and watch me intently (I just thought my singing was really bad). I also noticed that he was very particular about having things in a certain order or making sure that similar things were grouped together. He was very timid and nervous about new things and almost scared at times.

Keagan took his time learning to crawl and walk, but he was not behind in typical development. Strangely, he learned to crawl backward first. He started walking at about 13 or 14 months. When he did start walking, he walked on his toes quite a bit and did not like to be barefoot on grass or sand or anything with different textures. He hated having dirty hands and became quite a picky eater at about 2 years of age.

Many things started happening around his 2nd birthday, and to this day, I do not know if some of his behavior was caused by our family situation or if it was just symptoms of the Asperger syndrome and SPD. His brother Patrick was born when Keagan was 2 months shy of his 2nd birthday, and this seemed to turn his world upside down. For the first time, I spent an extended period of time away from him—4 days—while I was in the hospital, and then for a couple of weeks after that he would go with friends for hours during the day so I could recover from another cesarean section and rest. Also, I was constantly feeding, holding, and changing another baby and not holding him. I was sleeping on a mattress in the living room instead of with him and Daddy in the bedroom. There were many big changes for my bubba.

In the months after Patrick was born, Keagan was dealt many traumatic blows to his little world: his big brothers left for the summer to visit family, Daddy moved away temporarily to Colorado to start a job and find us a house, and the kids and I moved in with a friend and then to another house…and then we made the big move to Colorado. On top of all that, I went through a severe bout of depression that lasted about 4 to 6 months, and I was not always mentally available to Keagan. It was after he turned 2, and during this time of huge changes, that he began to really act out and became very active (climbing, running, jumping off of things). He had temper tantrums, was difficult to get to sleep and did not sleep well, and became a very, very picky eater. He also started to become very violent toward his baby brother, and we could not leave them alone together for a second.

When Keagan turned 3, I enrolled him in Head Start, a terrific pre-school program. Although he enjoyed it at first, he had a very difficult time getting along with other kids and "listening." It was at this point that I really started to think that something else was going on and it wasn't just acting out because of being unhappy and confused. He would get lost in his own world, he was supersensitive to noise and hated having his hands or any part of his body dirty, and he would act out and have tantrums at times that just didn't make sense to me. He lashed out at other kids and played by himself a lot. He covered his ears with his hands if there was a lot of noise. He asked me if I heard a certain noise, and I wouldn't hear it for another couple of seconds if it was coming closer to us, or not at all if it was stationary. He had trouble with things that were not aligned perfectly and when he was not given enough time to complete something that he was working on to perfection. I would struggle with him for a long time each morning at school to get him to stick his name label on the board— the Velcro on the board was square, and the Velcro on the back of his label was a circle! It was so heartbreaking to watch my sweet little boy disappear more and more into himself.

I have always had trouble with sensory overload myself, and so I started mentioning to his teachers that I thought something was going on— maybe something similar to my sensory problems. I was brushed off as being overreactive and told on many occasions that he just needed to learn to obey. He was treated harshly at times and disciplined for things I now realize were out of his control. Other parents and teachers judged him as having "behavioral" problems, and I heard comments from time to time as such. He hated school. It was very difficult to get him out of bed, and he cried and begged me not to make him go to school that day. It was heart wrenching to make him go.

I switched him from a 2-day to a 4-day classroom (and different teachers) when he was 4, which unfortunately also contained many more kids, and then he really started getting aggressive. If someone was too close to him, if someone didn't do what he wanted, or if someone was too noisy, he lashed out. Again, I tried to talk to the teachers about SPD, and again, I was told that they didn't really see anything wrong and that he needed more discipline. He had consistently gotten worse at home, as well, and we were at our wits' end trying to figure out what to do. He was so aggressive toward his little brother, we were always afraid that he would really hurt him.

I decided to talk to our family doctor, who did listen to me and referred Keagan to an occupational therapist for evaluation and treatment. He received a diagnosis of SPD and started doing "heavy-work" exercises and working on the muscle tone in his hands (which explained why he hated writing). We had to pay for this out of our own pocket because the state insurance did not recognize SPD and would not pay for any treatment of it.

About the time that Keagan started in the 4-day classroom, the Head Start program started a new therapeutic classroom in the same building, which became a godsend for Keagan and our family. He started in the classroom in January, and by March, they told me that they were almost 100% positive he had Asperger syndrome. This threw me for a loop! At first I was skeptical, but the more I read, the more I knew deep down in my heart that this is what had been going on.

Having an answer is wonderful, but it does not automatically make everything all better. Yes, now there is an explanation for why he acts the way he does, but what do we do to help him? Insurance would not cover anything. He was still having major difficulties. In school, he was improving because of wonderful teachers and therapists, but he had a hard time focusing on what he was supposed to be doing—interacting with other children appropriately, transitioning, and regulating his behavior. And this was in a classroom that keeps the lights dimmed and very little on the walls, does heavy work on a regular basis, and has therapists and specially trained teachers. I was starting to really worry that he was not ready for kindergarten and all of the sensory input it would bring and that I would run into a wall again in my efforts to get him help.

Thank goodness I was wrong. The school's special-education team has listened to everything that I have to say and has done so much for Keagan.

Although he is not classified as requiring special education, he is receiving a lot of help. He has an aide that is with him almost every minute of the time he is in school, and he has recently started occupational therapy. He is doing very well and loves school, which is a nice change!

I am so happy that my son is getting what he needs from his school, but I am also so frustrated and angry with the system that we depend on to help us take care of our children. Keagan would benefit from more occupational therapy, including music therapy (which seemed to be working when we had to stop occupational therapy owing to lack of funds), muscle tone exercises, and social therapy. Until SPD and Asperger syndrome are more widely recognized and covered, additional therapies are not a possibility for him. And so, a young boy of 5 has to cope in a world that does not understand him and that he does not understand, because he cannot get all the help that he needs.

Please help my son and so many others to get the treatment they need…

Kristine M. Starks is a mommy to four boys, ages 16, 15, 6, and 4, which is the most wonderful, fulfilling, and difficult job she has ever had. Her kids are her life's work. She has a bachelor's degree in psychology, a master's degree in education, and a master's degree in accounting. She loves to travel, read, craft, quilt, and scrapbook. She aspires to have lots of grandbabies to spoil someday and also to be a successful forensic accountant.

Chapter 4

Siblings

The genetic link! There is nothing I love more than a good, old-fashioned "Aha" moment!

For the families in this section, that moment came when one of their children received a diagnosis of SPD—and it answered questions they had about their child's sibling, as well.

Oftentimes, in the process of learning about SPD, parents and families learn something about themselves and their other children, as well. When that first diagnosis of SPD comes in, it opens a door to a world of sensory learning. With a little education, it is not uncommon to find two kids in the same family whose sensory symptoms are virtually opposite of one another.

For these families, sensory diets and sensory accommodations are a way of life. They have learned both ends of the sensory spectrum and have kept their sense of humor along the way!

What could be more fun than a child with SPD? TWO!

The Same, but Different

by Sasha

When my son, "The Politician," started kindergarten in the fall, I was so excited for him. I remembered how much I learned in school, soaking up all the knowledge I could, and I just "knew" he'd be the same, because

Photo by
Trina Gibbins Photography

we share an awful lot of traits, both physically and personality-wise. We have the same wispy, thin, light-brown hair (although mine is high-lighted—ahem—bleach blonde), the same light olive, easily tanned skin, the same sense of humor, and the same slightly shy personality.

But kindergarten didn't turn out the same for him.

Not long into the school year, his teacher let me know that he was having trouble sitting still and keeping his hands to himself. In fact, he was so fidgety, he was actually falling out of his chair. Unable to sit still at "carpet time," he was rolling onto his back, kicking his legs in the air, and just generally being disruptive. His teacher observed that he seemed to be unable to control these behaviors, and when my husband and I spoke to him about his behavior, he was truly sad about his conduct and would say, "I just can't help it!"

You should know that I have a younger daughter, The Wild Child ("WC"), who received a diagnosis of SPD at age 2. Because of an ulcerated hemangioma she had as an infant, WC was in quite a bit of pain. At the time, we were unable to find anyone locally to help us figure out how to deal with her pain, so she was an upset baby who spent a lot of time raging.

Of course the hemangioma did eventually heal, but we were left with what we thought were behavioral issues. She became a biter (she bit others and even herself!) and was quite aggressive at 18 months of age—frequently hitting and kicking me to the point that I often felt beaten up. At times she seemed to "space out" and become unreachable, as if she were unable to hear. Because of her violent behavior, there was a 1-week suspension from daycare and many, many phone calls and meetings.

Right after her 2nd birthday, I stumbled into a biting workshop at our local county health department, and they mentioned that quite a few children with biting problems were actually seeking sensory input due to having SPD. It was like someone turned on a switch, and it all started to make sense. A child development specialist that I spoke to after the workshop offered to do some evaluations on WC, and it became apparent that she did in fact have SPD. She referred us to a wonderful occupational therapist, who finally helped us reach our beautiful girl and slowly get a handle on her treatment through the use of a listening therapy program.

Many, many books were recommended to me, but one that hit home on our journey was *The Out-of-Sync Child*. I checked it out from our local library and flipped through it on my way out the door. After a few seconds of flipping, I felt my eyes fill up with tears and I moved toward the wall so I could lean against it.

I had found it! I found a paragraph that I wanted to print out and give to everyone that knew WC. On page 193, it said:

> A mother wrote me this letter: "By the time Rob was two, I felt he had a special need, but I couldn't figure out what it was. He required constant attention. Time-outs didn't work because I couldn't contain him. He was defiant, disobedient, disrespectful, and demanding. He was always busy, always talking (great verbal skills!), strong willed, contrary, and easily frustrated. I felt blessed to have Rob and wouldn't trade him for the world, of course, but he constantly tested and rejected me."

And more on the next page.

> What was the reason for his behavior? How could I regain control? What method of discipline would get through to him? If his behavior was an attempt to get my attention, how could I supply it in a way that would satisfy him? How could I help a high-energy child channel his energy in a positive direction? I was desperate for answers.

Desperate for answers…yeah, that would be me! I devoured this book, seeking answers, information, hints, and tips—anything I could find to make life easier.

Things began to get better. Armed with the information I had gathered, I most likely drove our occupational therapist crazy with questions!

But she was wonderful and patient, and the listening therapy program she used with WC slowly began to work its magic. It was an amazing thing to watch. How could 30 minutes of special music twice a day make such a big change? Even my husband, who thought the listening therapy was a bit "hippie," was impressed.

Now, there were some hitches. WC wasn't able to complete the program because of some pretty intense reactions to the advanced CDs, and because of this, our occupational therapist suspected she may also have a central auditory processing disorder. But it's been about 2½ years since her diagnosis, and we've come a long way. We're still doing maintenance listening therapy and seeing a behavioral therapist that shares an office with our occupational therapist, and WC has become so much easier to be around. Her teachers even describe her as delightful at times!

So you'd think that treatment for a second child with SPD would be a breeze, right? Not exactly! Our son and WC couldn't be more different. Whereas WC's issues had to do with regulation, and she just seemed "off," his issues could be neatly fit into "seeking" and "avoiding" boxes. But, that made it an even bigger mystery to me. How do you get to the middle?

On the avoiding front, unlike most kids, our son had a strong aversion to temporary tattoos and stickers—we dared not even suggest it! Clothes were always hard—tags that you and I might not notice were like needles on his skin, and there were so many materials he didn't like. Showers and haircuts were a nightmare. And smells—he threw up when he smelled fruit, of all things—random, I know, but it was true, especially oranges and bananas. But then he started sensory-seeking—watching TV upside down, pushing his head around on the floor, touching everything, and falling out of chairs because he couldn't sit still. I was so confused.

Luckily, our occupational therapist was able to evaluate him, and sure enough, SPD was the culprit. The therapist explained to me that for some kids who are overresponsive to some things, in his case touch and smell, there can also be underresponsivity in other areas. What a puzzle! We were so fortunate to have a very understanding teacher who was willing to work with us on some modifications to help him succeed in school. A Disc 'O' Sit cushion placed in his chair helped provide him with the input he needed to sit still, and putting him at the edge of the group during carpet time helped him keep his hands to himself. The teacher also allowed him to return to his seat during carpet time if he felt that he couldn't control himself. Spending time away from the classroom, sometimes just in another classroom, helped him "reset" himself.

Luckily, the listening therapy program we completed this spring helped immensely. I am hopeful that his first-grade year will go well. So far, so good! His new teacher was willing to put the same modifications in place, and we used the Sensory Download from Hartley's Life with 3 Boys to map out our plan for the year. I am thankful every day for the Internet and the resources it provided to me in finding solutions for helping my two kids with SPD—who are the same, but oh so different!

Sasha lives in the Southwest with her husband and their son and daughter, who have both received diagnoses of SPD. Sasha works full time in the accounting field and blogs about her personal life at SashaSays.com. *In her spare time, Sasha loves to run and blogs about her obsession with nail polish at* ManicureMommas.com.

The Value of

True Sensory Therapy

by Patricia Porch Hooper

The past 5 years of my life have passed in a blur of ball pits, shaving cream, and dried beans. My family spends a great deal of time devising obstacle courses out of mini-trampolines, piles of blankets, and a plethora of cones and rings and plastic balls. We have purchased so many swings that we probably have more than some occupational-therapy clinics do.

My oldest son, Danny, received a diagnosis of SPD about 5 years ago. In that time, we have seen countless therapists, doctors, and experts. Danny has undergone speech therapy, swallowing therapy, and occupational, developmental, and physical therapy.

We have discovered that occupational therapy really works for Danny. He no longer has mind-numbing sensory meltdowns that nothing can calm. He no longer runs into other people, and he can speak now. I credit an amazing occupational therapist for that miracle.

While this is great news for us, there is a major drawback. We do not have a good occupational therapist who is qualified to treat SPD anywhere near our town. We have traveled to many cities within a couple of hours of our home, but most of the therapists we found didn't really understand the disorder. Many of them merely did sensory-diet exercises with Danny and never treated him with an actual sensory-based approach.

This is why we regularly travel 3 hours to Chicago to get the right treatment from a trained occupational therapist there. She set up a program for us to do at home and revises it every few weeks. Then, we come home and try to diligently do the exercises with Danny each night.

This has mostly worked for us, but it is definitely not ideal, at least not in my opinion. Yes, we have learned a great deal, and who better to help Danny than his parents? Still, I regularly wonder if Danny might not be making more progress if we had weekly access to a qualified occupational therapist.

Doing Danny's therapy with him is overwhelming, time consuming, and often very frustrating. I wonder on a weekly basis if I am doing the therapy correctly. Am I pushing Danny enough or too much? Do my personal feelings get in the way of doing things properly? Do I remember this exercise correctly? Could I possibly do damage to my son?

I lament the fact that we don't live closer to a decent therapist who understands SPD. A couple of years ago, I attended a conference at which Dr Lucy Jane Miller spoke. She outlined the research she has done on SPD and how she is proving that it exists and that it is different and distinct from attention-deficit/hyperactivity disorder. I sat there with tears streaming down my face and goose bumps all over my arms, because I knew she was working to educate therapists on SPD and proper therapy techniques. Here was an amazing woman who fights and works to help kids like my son and families like mine.

Later, I found myself looking in the mirror in the women's restroom and seeing Dr Miller washing her hands. I thanked her for all the research she has done and then asked if I could talk to her about a concern of mine. At that time, I was taking Danny to an occupational therapist closer to my home. This therapist was not really doing the kind of therapy that I expected. It was mostly using scissors and playing with putty. When she did have Danny swing, she did not have him doing any real exercises in the swing. She was not building his weak core muscles or helping him with his motor-planning problems.

I asked Dr Miller to confirm whether my suspicions were right, and she did. She absolutely agreed that just pushing a kid in a swing was *not* truly sensory-based therapy. She even went so far as to bring this topic up when the conference reconvened. She unequivocally told the therapists in the group that therapy with a sensory-based approach was much, much more than merely doing sensory-diet activities with children.

Though I wish I didn't have to spend hundreds of dollars in gas and spend hours upon hours driving, I am so grateful to have access to my son's occupational therapist. She really understands SPD and how to treat it.

It is because of research that Dr Miller has done, and others like her, that Danny's therapist knows how to help him. I am eternally grateful to Dr Miller and her colleagues for the research they do, for all the discoveries they have made, and for all the work they do to train occupational therapists in the best, most effective ways to conduct sensory-based therapy.

It is because of the research of therapists like Dr Miller that Danny can speak and that he has become a much happier and more well-adjusted little boy. Because of the work that the SPD Foundation does, I have access to the tools and knowledge that I need to help my son.

These therapists and researchers are doing amazing work. They have come so far in determining what treatment best helps children with SPD, but there is still so much work to be done. There are so many more discoveries that need to be made for kids like my son Danny.

And for kids like my daughter Charlotte, who just received a diagnosis of SPD 4 weeks ago.

We now have two children receiving therapy services in Chicago, and I am even more overwhelmed than before. Still, I hold out hope that someday there will be more occupational therapists who have a very firm grasp on what SPD is and how to treat it effectively. I believe that in the future, many more teachers and other kinds of therapists and pediatricians will be familiar with SPD, so they can help kids get the right diagnosis and treatment.

Patricia Porch Hooper is a former high-school teacher and mom to three young children, two of whom have received a diagnosis of SPD. She regularly blogs at www.pancakesgoneawry.blogspot.com and is a monthly contributor to ourjourneythruautism.com and hartleysboys.com.

New Adventures Every Day

by Jennifer Kaylor

There he was—my precious son, Joseph. So small, so perfect, and clearly asserting himself right from the get-go. Unbeknownst to me, SPD was making itself known in his little body at just 2 hours old, with tactile defensiveness. He wiggled, squirmed, and fussed until he had his arms free from my meticulous swaddling. I swaddled him again and again, and each time, Joseph wiggled his arms free and settled down in content. I finally let him be, cold arms and all.

Joseph was such a good baby—very alert and curious, he slept through the night at a couple of months old, and he never cried. Joseph loved to be swung around and upside down. When I say loved, that's an understatement. He would regularly flip himself backward while being held in someone's arms, then squeal with delight at the rush the movement gave him. He was the toughest kid I knew. To this day, Joseph has never cried about getting an immunization. He has always loved going to the doctor, no matter how invasive the examination or procedure. His curiosity continued to push him to explore the world around him, oftentimes resulting in injury. Still, he did not cry or fuss.

What seemed like a tough little kid to me was really underresponsivity to pain. A regular pastime was to flip himself off the arm of the sofa backward, landing on his head repeatedly. Or, climbing to the highest surface in the house and jumping off to enjoy the impact.

He was a very tidy child and eater. Joseph did not like to have dirty hands or a dirty face. He loved bath time and pouring water over his head. Riding his ATV was at the top of his list of fun things to do, being the thrill seeker he was—and still is.

My son was clearly a sensory seeker and was underresponsive to certain stimuli for the first couple of years of his life. Then, that all changed. He started to avoid loud sounds by cupping his ears, although he liked to make noise himself. He began to recoil when he was hugged or touched, which led to walking the perimeter of the room and avoiding large groups. The seemingly antisocial behaviors drew unwanted attention from family and friends. We began to suspect that something was wrong with his hearing, as he did not respond when people talked to him and he avoided eye contact. We were perplexed. What happened to our social and curious child, who stole the hearts of all who met him? All the forced conversations and hugs just sent him deeper and deeper into the shell he created to protect himself. He became a very picky eater, objecting to the color, smell, texture, and temperature of foods. They all had to be just right, or he couldn't get it past his lips. Putting clothing on him resulted in crying and writhing on the floor. Shoes were difficult to wear at best, and socks were entirely out of the question.

Although I expressed my concern for these odd behaviors and struggles, no one seemed to raise an eyebrow. Our well-meaning family and friends told me how to discipline my bratty child and not cater to him. At the top of the list was holding him accountable for his rudeness when pulling away from an unwanted hug and refusing to speak to guests. What we all didn't know was how their unexpected touch stung on his skin—for a few minutes up to a half-hour later. Their breath or perfume filled his nostrils at 100 times the strength it did ours.

The sensory-seeking and avoiding affected Joseph adversely at home, at school, and in social settings. It had a noticeable negative impact on him nearly every single second of the day. This left him a complete wreck and on the verge of a meltdown at any given moment, owing to the overwhelming information taken in by his senses every waking hour of his day. I felt completely lost and hopeless, as I had no idea what was going on. The moment Joseph's school psychologist and principal asked my permission to test him for sensory sensitivities, I began my quest for information on SPD.

My son was tested by an occupational therapist that was registered, licensed, and trained in sensory-based therapy. I read *The Out-of-Sync Child,* by Carol Stock Kranowitz, from cover to cover, before receiving the test results. I wanted to be as informed as possible. The results came in—and in the occupational therapist's words, my son was severely affected by his sensory issues, both in the classroom and at home. He had SPD. His behaviors and reactions were completely out of his control. He needed occupational therapy, classroom accommodations, and implementation of a sensory diet at home to help regulate his body. Now we had a clear understanding of what was going on with Joseph, why everyday life was so very difficult for him. The path we needed to travel was finally made known.

Our school was quick to implement the classroom accommodations Joseph needed. The occupational therapy that his school was able to provide only addressed classroom concerns. For the overall treatment of SPD, we sought help from a private occupational therapist, who designed his sensory diet for home and set up weekly therapy sessions.

Joseph was well on his way to learning how his body worked and didn't work at times. He learned what type of input he needed and when he needed it to calm his body down or wake it up. With his therapist's help, we worked on desensitization so that Joseph could better tolerate clothing and unexpected touch. We have noise-cancelling headphones for loud noise and a weighted blanket for deep pressure and calming. We use many methods and types of equipment to help regulate Joseph's body. Our sensory diet is designed for his specific needs and will not work for every child with SPD. In addition, our sensory diet changes as his sensory needs change.

Joseph was 8 years old and in the first grade by the time he received a diagnosis of SPD. So much time had passed—years from when we first noticed signs that something was off. With our second child, who is 5 years younger than Joseph, we were concerned that he too may be affected by SPD. We kept a watchful eye on Dash from the beginning. Dash's infancy was very different from Joseph's. He cried nonstop for the first 3 months of his life. He didn't like much of anything, from changing to feeding to sleeping. Dash did not sleep without waking every 2 hours until he was over 1 year old. He rocked in his highchair and playpen and even rocked so hard he shook the welded metal bars out of his crib. The rocking at night was almost violent on the days we went to stores. He rocked forcefully on his hands and knees, inadvertently banging his crib into the wall.

Dash was not the sensory seeker his brother was, nor was he curious about his environment. His environment scared him, and movement made him cling to us in terror. This child would not be flipping himself off the arm of the sofa anytime soon. Joseph was a seeker and spoke in complete sentences at 1 year old. Dash was an avoider and struggled with speech—at 2 years old, he only spoke about 10 words. He had great difficulty with communication, which resulted in daily frustration and severe meltdowns, with him slamming his body or face into walls or doors. He ate from the garbage obsessively and drank from the toilet, resulting in everything having to be locked down, it seemed. We decided not to wait to see if he would "catch up" or outgrow this possible "terrible two" stage. We had Dash tested for SPD, and just as we suspected, he too was affected by it enough to interfere with his daily life.

Recognizing and treating Dash's SPD at the age of 2 had a significant effect on him. He began to speak almost overnight. With the aid of picture cards, he could point to what he needed or wanted. Going to the grocery store no longer brought about raging screaming fits as we pulled into the parking lot. His occupational therapist had armed us with instructions on how to apply deep pressure appropriately to his joints and squeeze his muscles before leaving the house and in the car before entering a store. This input provided enough organizing information for his brain that he could tolerate the bright lights, loud sounds, and strong smells of the grocery store. What a life-changing difference just a few occupational therapy sessions made for Dash. In 6 months' time, he no longer struggled daily with SPD.

Joseph did not have the benefit of early intervention like Dash did. He had to cope for years, with great anxiety, in avoiding the things that bombarded his senses. Patterns of reacting and certain behaviors became automatic, and we still struggle with them from time to time. Because Dash got treatment so early, I haven't seen and don't expect to see the severity of anxiety and depression that we experienced with his brother surrounding his SPD.

What a roller coaster ride the past few years have been. I am not the scared, hopeless mother searching for answers and help that I was several years ago. Today, I am a loud and proud SPD mom, standing alongside her two boys, advocating for more awareness, greater understanding, and earlier intervention.

Jennifer Kaylor lives in the Seattle area with her husband Joe and their two sons, Joseph and Dash. She is a dedicated mother, advocate, and homeschooling teacher who is committed to raising awareness about and understanding of SPD. In sharing her story with others, she hopes to shed much-needed light on the struggles and triumphs that those living with SPD face every day.

Now There Are Two:

Raising More Than One

"Sensational" Kiddo

by Chynna Laird

I have a few gorgeous pictures of my son, Xander, sleeping that I love to gaze at from time to time. He looks so peaceful when he's sleeping. My favorite is the one we took mere hours after he was born. It's funny, but I knew, even then, that he needed me a bit more than my other children did, just as I had with his sister Jaimie. But it was different with Xander... it was much more intense. He cried continuously—so much so that the nurses politely came into my room in the middle of the night, asking, "Did you bring a pacifier for him?" He calmed the moment I wrapped him up tightly in his hospital blanket and held him close to me—quite the opposite of what happened with Jaimie.

He never ate well and constantly threw up after every feeding. And I don't mean those sweet little spit-ups, either. We're talking full-on, projectile vomit. When we brought him home, he screamed in his crib. We let him sleep in our bed, which we'd done with all four of our babies. (Jaimie was the only one who truly hated sleeping all together, feeling better in her own bed.) Xander needed to be rocked, and rocked, and rocked before he'd go to sleep. He couldn't stand being away from Mama. When he was around 1 year old, he stole my favorite sweatshirt—which he still uses as a blankie—and wouldn't go anywhere without it.

There are times when he's a happy, fun-loving boy. I wish I could hold onto those moments forever, because for most of the day, my sweet, beautiful little boy is crying, angry, upset, and screaming. He hurts himself and others, he calls us names, he yells at us, and it continues for hours. There seems to be no middle ground with him. He's either through the roof and extremely difficult to calm down or so low, we have to get right in his face, calling his name as he lies on the floor, running his cars in front of his face.

Early on, I knew something was amiss. I knew his nervous system was in trauma, but I also knew there were other things going on.

As he's gotten older, his struggles seem to have grown with him. We noticed his speech wasn't progressing as well as his sisters' had. In fact, we couldn't understand him at all. And he can be very aggressive when he's angry. We thought that it was his speech causing his behavioral problems; after all, it can be very frustrating to try to communicate with people when they don't understand you. But, he found other ways to communicate with us: pointing, gesturing, and making noises. At least we could get him what he wanted or needed without as much crying. The problem is that he hasn't gotten past that.

I knew that feeling weight on his body worked for him, and that swinging seemed to calm him. It wasn't enough, though. And when he turned 3, we knew we finally needed to get him some help. *We* needed help. During Jaimie's last round of occupational therapy, I discussed Xander's issues and how he and Jaimie fought like cats and dogs.

"It's like they're sensory polar opposites," I told the therapist. "She avoids touch, he can't get enough of it; he seeks movement, she avoids most of it—and the list goes on. And he just doesn't understand that it drives Jaimie to violence when he stands close to her or touches her or pats her on the back."

There were several visits where Jaimie's occupational therapist and I had to talk about Jaimie's reactions to Xander and how we could help her work things out with him in a calmer, less aggressive way. They are so much alike, yet so different. What amazed me was that it was actually Jaimie who suggested that Xander had SPD too. One afternoon, while Xander was going through a seemingly endless overload meltdown, Jaimie turned to me with her ears covered and said, "Mama? I think Xander has SPD too. He's mad because something hurt him."

A girl who can't even relate to other people on a social level most of the time picked up on *that!* Amazing.

So last summer, we finally got Xander in for his assessments with Jaimie's occupational therapist. If nothing else, we could rule out SPD and figure out another explanation. Yes, it was scary for me to have to start from square one again, but I couldn't just let him suffer anymore. It wasn't fair to him or to the rest of us to let him go on like he was. Xander went completely through the roof during the first assessment. He screamed, cried, and refused to look at anyone. After about half an hour, he hid under his blankie and shut down completely. His assigned occupational therapist, Misty, came into the room and squeezed his little arms and legs—just like I do at home. She talked to him softly, trying to coax him into the sensory gym. He wouldn't budge. I was ushered out to fill out my part of the assessment, and Misty still worked on connecting with Xander.

Just when I thought we'd have to leave and try again, I saw Misty carrying Xander—still hiding under his blankie—into the sensory gym. I heard her tell him he was on the platform swing and that she was going to swing him. I heard him giggle. They'd dimmed the lights and made the room calmer for him. For the remainder of the session (only about 20 minutes), he was like a different boy. He responded, tried to follow instructions, and did what he was supposed to do.

The next week was a little better. No tantrum. No crying. No hiding. He went right in the gym with Misty and participated. I did the rest of my paperwork and waited. At the end, Misty came out and said, "Now, you said to me last week that he spends most of his day the way he did last time, at the beginning. This time, he seemed so much happier. I'm just wondering what was different today?"

I couldn't give her a solid answer. "I think he was a bit more used to things," I said. "He thought his sisters were coming in with him last time, but when he realized he had to go alone, he panicked. He'd also had a very stressful day with Jaimie. He was tired. He didn't eat much for lunch that day."

"And today?" she asked.

"He's still really tired and fought with his sisters, but he spent a lot of time on our swing in the basement. We went for an hour-long walk, and he was speed-walking ahead of us the entire time. He ate a bit more today. I guess he's just…in the middle part of his cycle."

That's what I call what we'd been dealing with—cycles. It's almost an hourly thing. He starts each day not too badly, then gets more and more "up" until we can't bring him back down. He runs around laughing inappropriately, bumping into us and knocking baby Sophie over, squeezing too hard, and tackling us. He won't stop coming at you, no matter what you try to do to stop him. He won't look at you or seem to hear you—and then he crashes. One tiny thing will happen, and he throws himself on the ground or gets down on his hands and knees, running his head around the floor like he's a vacuum cleaner. He screams at us, calling us names or telling us we're bad. In addition to the screaming, he makes grunting noises and cries. It takes a long time to comfort him, too, because he doesn't want us to hold him. Heavy "lap cozies" or weighted blankets work, but not for very long. Then, when he finally stops crying, it starts all over again. And, of course, Jaimie feeds off of the "up" part, and then I have two kids that I can't calm down. It's exhausting.

After Xander's assessments, I met with the head occupational therapist and the team's psychologist. I wasn't nervous, because I already knew what the issue was—or at least part of it. What I wasn't ready for was to hear how severe my little guy's issues really are.

His scores were off the charts. In fact, he scored *much* higher than Jaimie on every level except "sedentary" (which is basically his ability to sit still or need to move; they need to do more testing with him in this area because he swings so widely from needing to move constantly to flopping on the ground, almost comatose). I burst into tears when I saw the results. I mean—you *know* it, right? You *know* when something is wrong. I had already gone through all of this with Jaimie, so my gut told me it was sensory based. I just wasn't prepared to see the extent to which he was affected.

They told me that Xander is *so* severely affected in *so many* different areas (eating, sleeping, speech, cognition, emotions, behavior, and sensory areas) that it was difficult to determine what the base of his issues are or even what is affecting what. He's so developmentally impaired that when he's melting down, I have to ask myself, "Is this from frustration with speech? Sensory issues? Not understanding the world around him? Or is it typical 3½-year-old behavior?"

"You have a long road ahead of you with little Xander," I was told. "He's going to need a lot of help. I am going to help with the sensory stuff. We can figure out how to regulate him, but he needs regulation in these other areas, too."

The psychologist further explained that with all of the issues he has, we need to "control for" his speech, his sensory issues, and the like, then take a look at the "real" Xander when all other factors are held constant (or regulated). If we can find the "real" Xander underneath of all of that, and he's *still* reacting the way he is to the world around him, then we'll have a better idea of what the next steps are. In other words, he can't be assessed for Asperger syndrome or autism spectrum disorder or mood disorders (we're worried that bipolar disorder may be in the mix, too) until we are able to "sift through" his other issues.

I'm tearing up while writing this, because I look at my little boy and I know who the "real" Xander is. He looks at me with his hazel eyes, his devious little smile, and his cute little cheeks, and I know. He bear-hugs me or rubs my cheeks between his palms, saying, "I love Mama!" and I know. He's my baby boy. Nothing will ever change that. A dear friend of mine reminded me that all of this therapy he needs won't change the core of who he is. It will give him the tools he needs to live in the world with us, but he'll always be *my Xander*.

Positive things came from all of this, though. Everything we'd gone through with Jaimie gave me the experience, knowledge, and resources I need to help Xander. I'm stronger than I was back then. And I will *not* sit back and wait for things to happen. It *will* happen. The other thing is that because of the level of severity of Xander's issues, and the fact that we have two severely affected children, we will finally get funding and access to the programs we need. It saddens me a bit to know that we couldn't get all of these things for Jaimie years ago. We kept hearing, "I empathize, but your daughter 'only has' sensory issues. We can't help you." Today, there is much more awareness for SPD, and we have a psychologist who not only "gets" SPD but fully supports our son in his efforts to get better. We are in a good place. I'm sorry that Jaimie had to suffer so much before we got the help we needed, but now I can help *both* of my children.

If you're reading this, I know you are going through something similar. You are on your own journey. Maybe you're in an "up" right now, where things are going well. Or maybe you've hit a bump and are in distress. Wherever you are right now...*please*...keep moving forward. The night after Xander received his diagnosis, I cried many tears, wondering why we were going through all of this again. Why did my kids have to suffer so much before people listened to us? I questioned whether I'm strong enough to deal with both Jaimie and Xander's issues while caring for another daughter with health issues and a feisty toddler. But God obviously thinks I'm a lot stronger than I believe I am.

Today, I'm filled with hope. God gave me these gorgeous children because they needed a person who could love them, care for them, and nurture them, despite their "high needs," and I was entrusted as the one who makes sure those needs were met. I'm still not sure whether I deserve that honor, but I'm going to step up to the challenge. And I ask the same of you.

Keep moving forward on your own journey. Never give up. Allow yourself to feel those emotions when you hit those bumps. And *always* trust your gut. We are all in this together, and, united, we'll help these children be everything they can possibly be.

Chynna Laird is a psychology student, freelance writer, and award-winning author who lives in Edmonton, Alberta, with her partner, Steve, and their three daughters (Jaimie [age 8], Jordhan [age 6], and baby Sophie [age 2]) and their son, Xander (age 4). Her passion is helping children and families living with SPD and other special needs. You'll find her work in many online and in-print parenting, inspirational, Christian, and writing publications in Canada, America, Australia, and Britain. In addition, she's authored an award-winning children's book (I'm Not Weird, I Have SPD), *two memoirs (the multiple award-winning,* Not Just Spirited: A Mom's Sensational Journey with SPD and White Elephants), *and a Young Adult novel* (Blackbird Flies), *and she's working on a follow-up book about her family's journey with SPD. Visit Chynna's Web site at* www.lilywolfwords.ca, *as well as her blogs at* www.the-gift-blog.com *and* www.seethewhiteelephants.com.

How I Learned What
"Special" and "Normal" Mean

by Ellie Giberson

When I was in college, I did my internship at a preschool that integrated children with a variety of special needs. I had never worked with children with any kind of disabilities before, and at this job I was introduced to children with physical, mental, and emotional challenges. It was an eye-opening experience, and I continued to work there for 2 years before moving on. In that time, I learned so much about the children I worked with and often wondered what it would be like to be the parent of one of these children. Quite honestly, I prayed that I would never find out.

When my husband and I decided to start our family, this earlier experience remained in the back of my mind. I believe there is a purpose behind every journey we take, and I couldn't help but wonder if God led me to this internship to prepare me for parenthood in some way. I prayed every day of my pregnancy that my children would be healthy and "normal."

Skye was born a few days after her due date, through a difficult and *long* labor. From the start, this child was hard. She cried all night. She would only sleep in my arms or in the swing. She slept an hour or two at a time, and then cried for hours more. She had trouble nursing for the first month. Somehow we survived the first month or two, but as soon as we resolved one difficult issue, another presented itself. As she got older, she screamed uncontrollably for hours on end, and any efforts to calm her would only make it worse. She refused a bottle or sippy cup and gagged on anything except the superstrained baby foods. She refused to be held by her daddy and would not let me put her down. Leaving the house guaranteed a screaming fit, so I stayed home a lot. She was scared of everything—loud noises, people getting too close to her, the changing table (aka fear of heights), and toys that moved or made noise. The first year was so tough. I told everyone who would listen that something was wrong—the doctors, our parents, our friends, her daycare teachers. Everyone said, "That's just how she is. She's fine." Those closest to me told me I was looking for problems where there weren't any. I wondered if they were right!

Eventually, we learned to get by with Skye, and we figured out little things that worked for her and big things that didn't. Some of those early difficulties became easier, and some just gave way to new issues. We learned to live with or work around a lot of things where Skye was concerned. We forged a life that worked for us, she learned to adapt to her sensitivities, and life went on. Even though in the back of my mind I still suspected something wasn't quite "normal," she was functioning well and seemed happy and well adjusted. So, I accepted that this was just her personality and tried to push my worries aside.

As the years went on, there were things that bothered me, but no one seemed to think they were significant enough to be concerned with. For example, potty-training was a nightmare, but she was wearing underwear before her 4th birthday. Eating issues abounded, but she loved fruits and vegetables and was gaining weight. She was strong-willed and stubborn, but so am I, so I figured it was just her personality shining through. She screamed and threw tantrums all the time, but everyone told me, "The threes are worse than the twos." Skye is so smart (her IQ is at the superior level) that I think she learned to adapt to her sensitivities as she grew. She did well in preschool and excelled later in kindergarten and first grade. I finally breathed a sigh of relief, thinking all my fears of having a "special needs" child were for nothing.

Then I was pregnant again, and I scared myself silly wondering how I would handle another baby if he was like Skye. Soon Seth was born, and he was perfect. We took him home, and immediately we knew that he was a completely different infant than Skye had been. He slept through the night. He hardly ever cried. He took a bottle or breastfed—he didn't care which. He was perfectly content to lie on the floor or sit in his swing or do just about anything we wanted him to do! I thought, "*This* is what a *normal* child looks like!"

Seth's issues started creeping up so slowly that I can't really tell when they started. I just know that we began noticing things that seemed a little "off." He was meeting all his milestones, but there were other problems. The temper tantrums—whoa! He could drop to the floor and scream for 30 minutes. A routine became more and more necessary with him, because doing something different triggered a meltdown. And there were the mood swings—he played happily one minute and screamed and threw his toys the next. At his 3-year-old checkup, I told the doctor my concerns. Once again, she said he was fine—he was just testing his limits. I called a behavioral therapist to observe him. She said he might have some sensory issues, but seemed fine.

For a year, I listened to everyone tell me he was fine and felt like I was a horrible parent because I couldn't get him to behave, until finally his preschool teacher mentioned SPD. As I researched it more, I realized that Seth definitely showed signs of this, but that Skye was a textbook case! She was coping so well, though, that we didn't feel the need to have her evaluated and formally diagnosed—it felt like we would just be slapping a label on her when we didn't need one. Seth, however, was barely functioning, and our family was suffering for it. So we focused on him.

Seth received a diagnosis of pervasive developmental disorder—not otherwise specified at age 4½. Though this diagnosis shocked us initially, we soon saw his many quirks as autistic characteristics. Seth is doing well today. He's 5½ and attends kindergarten in a special-education setting. As he has received occupational therapy and social work, many of his autistic qualities are fading into the background, and the sensory problems are coming to the forefront. We're focusing on these in therapy now. It's two steps forward, one step back most of the time, but that still puts us a step ahead of where we were a year ago.

Skye (now 8½) recently received a formal diagnosis of SPD and attention-deficit/hyperactivity disorder (ADHD). It was actually the suspicion of ADHD that prompted us to have her evaluated. She was starting to struggle with simple things—following oral directions, doing math worksheets, and finishing her homework. We knew she had SPD, but I was shocked to find out that the SPD seemed to be the *cause* of her ADHD. (She feels so unregulated all the time that she struggles to focus and pay attention to anything outside her body. She also has significant visual-motor delays, brought about by the SPD.) Skye also received a diagnosis of obsessive-compulsive disorder, a tic disorder, and depression—all exacerbated by an unregulated sensory system. All those years of people telling me she was "just fine" were wasted, when I could have been helping her. Perhaps she wouldn't have had to deal with all these other issues if she had been given the tools she needed early in life. I feel bad that so many years had to go by before we started to get her help. But, she is receiving occupational therapy now, and I have no doubt that she will improve rapidly.

I wish I had trusted my "mommy instinct" with both my children sooner. But, I refuse to be laden with guilt. I believe everything happens for a reason. Remember that internship? I ended up with "special" kids after all. I draw from that first job experience often and use many of the contacts I made there to help my children now. And despite my fervent prayers for a "normal" child, I have changed my view of normality. I would not trade the beautiful children I was given for any other kids in the world.

Ellie Giberson is the mother of two very special and mostly normal children. Ellie blogs about her journey through SPD and autism at www.tastingthecolors. com *and at the SPD Bloggers Network. As an early-childhood educator, she is an advocate for early intervention in her community and at her school and leads workshops on special needs for early-childhood teachers.*

$(Autism + SPD)^2 =$
Double the Pleasure, Squared

by Angela Fish

Eight years ago, I became a mom for the first time. Back then, I had no idea what my journey as a parent would be, and I can tell you it's quite different than I expected. Having kids is wonderful, but it's certainly no picnic! Looking back, all of my preconceived notions of parenting seem to be figments of my imagination. That wishful reality never quite materialized in the way I expected. If only I could go back and share knowledge and words of advice with my former self, preparing her for the road ahead and saving her from her own ignorance and worry.

The chaos in our household magnified after I had my second son, Kyle, who was born when his older brother Ryan was 2 years old. I certainly wasn't naïve about the responsibilities that come with having more than one child, but for some reason it seemed exponentially more difficult in reality. My boys are complete opposites and had vastly different experiences as they grew from babies to toddlers and beyond. Little did I know that they would both end up with the same diagnosis.

When Ryan was 3, his preschool teacher told me how he was incapable of sitting down during circle time, instead choosing to run laps around the room. She thought he could have some issues related to hyperactivity or that he was possibly bored, owing to a gifted intellect. At any rate, she suggested that I consider getting him assessed through our school district.

Many moms I know would likely have been put off of by such a statement, aghast at the suggestion that something could be wrong with their child. Me? I called the school district the second I got home. My husband and I had been noticing that he was having some difficulties in preschool, and we weren't sure why. We also saw some peculiarities, like how he was unable to touch a car door handle that was wet with rain. He also hated being dirty and immediately started to cry until we changed his "dirty" clothes, even if the "dirt" was only a drop of condensation from a drinking glass. And there were other things, too. However, we were also proud and amazed by his intensity and attention to detail when we saw him line up toys across the room or stack blocks in a single tower as high as he could reach. His teacher's comments were the nudge we needed to try to learn more about him.

I had no idea that a simple conversation with a concerned and observant preschool teacher would be such a pivotal moment in my life as a parent. It opened up a door I didn't even know was there. That door was eventually labeled autism spectrum disorder and SPD…times two.

While seeking a diagnosis beyond developmental delay, I became an autism expert almost overnight. I would convince myself that Ryan was fine and didn't have autism, and the next day I would see symptoms that fit into all of the little checkboxes on the list. We were impatient in wanting answers, but the waiting lists were long. As we filled out loads of paperwork, it became evident that a diagnosis was needed not only for Ryan, but also for Kyle. At that time, I really had no idea what SPD was, nor did I know how intertwined its symptoms could be with autism and how commonly the conditions occur together. Although my sons are vastly different, the diagnosis for both of them was the same.

They both have pervasive developmental disorder—not otherwise specified, which is found on the higher-functioning end of the autism spectrum. Autism is also known as pervasive developmental disorder. My boys fell into the "not otherwise specified" category because they didn't fit into all of the classic diagnostic boxes in the "normal" way but still had enough symptoms to be placed on the spectrum. As we worked with a team of speech, occupational, and physical therapists, I learned what SPD was and how it manifested differently in each of my boys. I also began to understand what the causes were for some of their behaviors and how I could work with various tools to develop a sensory diet to help manage those behaviors.

If one of my boys could be labeled a sensory kiddo, it is most definitely Kyle. He is a huge sensory seeker but can also be sensory averse. He craves intense proprioceptive input to his body almost all of the time. He satisfies this need through things like biting his lips, grinding his teeth, crashing onto his knees, jumping, and head-butting. He calms down with vestibular activities, like swinging. And the only way he is able to sleep through the night is with a weighted blanket on him to keep his body calm.

Prior to Kyle's diagnosis, he was nonverbal and violent. He had frequent meltdowns—usually several each day—often triggered by some sort of transition or perceived sensory assault. He had a diminished sense of pain and wouldn't cry out when he hurt himself. I would find small injuries on his body without knowing what caused them. One time he had a strange red mark on his neck. I found him the next day holding a string from a lacing toy, rubbing it back and forth on his neck like he was cutting a tree down with a two-handled saw.

Almost every time we went out in public, it triggered a meltdown. Walking into a store, Kyle immediately started getting out of control. There was a time when we were waiting in line for about a minute to return something at a department store, and he started to scream so loudly I actually heard his voice echo off the walls. He began to fight with me, struggling to get away. In response, my grip got tighter on his hand. When he started to flail wildly, I wrapped my arms around him from behind in an attempt to keep him from hurting me or others around us. This only escalated his meltdown. I was completely mortified and barely able to maintain composure, silently praying for the cashier to finish my transaction. All I wanted was to bolt out the door with my screaming and squirming son as fast as humanly possible.

It was at this time that a picture schedule became a very important tool for us. Kids on the autism spectrum crave order because their world is often overwhelming. The picture board helped Kyle maintain a sense of schedule and order, which kept him calmer. Both boys loved the picture board. I had one board for home, one for the car, and one for preschool. When Kyle woke up in the morning, I handed him the board with our morning schedule ready to go, and he carried it around with him as we went about our day. I broke up our routine into segments so that the schedule wouldn't be too much for him to handle. With the board in hand, my son felt some control over his world, which lessened the frequency of meltdowns.

What we learned from our occupational therapist was that Kyle was in fight-or-flight mode whenever we went out. We hadn't considered some things before, like multiple sounds bouncing off of hard surfaces and flickering fluorescent lights. He needed to have several sensory tools at his disposal to be out in public successfully. To facilitate (or at least attempt) a meltdown-free experience while outside our home, we needed the following things:

- SPIO suit—a full-body compression garment made of Lycra material that goes from neck to wrists to ankles
- Weighted vest—with weights concentrated on his shoulders to provide maximum input, whether sitting or standing

- Baseball hat—pulled down low on his brow, it helped to create a more enclosed view of his surroundings
- Sunglasses—to filter the light
- Earmuffs—to muffle sounds
- Picture board—used to prepare him for the outing, reinforce each step as we go, and maintain a sense of calm and order during the entire process
- Chewy Tube—to provide oral-motor input, a major sensory need
- Kids' fanny pack or backpack filled with various fidget toys and the like—things like a squishy or textured ball or a spinning/vibrating/lighted toy provide additional sensory input and also serve to distract and redirect when needed

We got a lot of interesting looks from people, especially when he was wearing fuzzy earmuffs in the heat of summer. But, this is how he learned to cope with the world. As time went on, it got easier for Kyle to manage all of the sensory input that assaulted his body. Some of the same tools also helped Ryan learn to cope. With these strategies, both boys drastically improved their ability to self-regulate.

Now we are able to go out and run errands without needing a litany of tools. We are meltdown-free most of the time. My boys still struggle with tactile defensiveness, auditory sensitivities, and other things. But, those issues are all pretty minor compared to what they once were.

SPD and autism spectrum disorder have practically merged into one thing in my mind. The lines are blurry. Symptoms of autism can exacerbate symptoms of SPD, and vice versa. As far as I'm concerned, all of their symptoms have simply become part of who my boys are. They are improving every day—and they're double the pleasure!

Angela Fish lives in the Tacoma, Washington, area with her husband and two boys, who are on the autism spectrum and also have SPD and multiple food allergies. She founded a support group for special-needs families and loves to connect local people with all kinds of resources. When she's not chasing her kids around, you can typically find her blogging, hanging out on Facebook, reading, or making a mess in the kitchen.

Chapter 5

Domestic Adoption

Many children who have been adopted through the foster-care system have sensory issues. Research suggests that this could be caused by many factors, including neglect, abuse, and drug and/or alcohol exposure in utero.

For a child's nervous system to develop correctly, it requires sensory stimulation—being held and allowed to explore the surrounding environment, being sung to, rocked, and given tons of interaction. Babies that are neglected are less likely to get these crucial forms of sensory input early on and are therefore more likely to have sensory issues as they get older.

These stories highlight families who have adopted a child that did not receive appropriate early care and sensory stimulation and is now actively seeking it—requiring his or her adopted parents to learn the ins and outs of SPD along the way.

Early Neglect and SPD

by Kristen Howerton

We adopted our first child, Jafta, from the foster-care system at 6 months of age. We really didn't know much about his life prior to coming to us, nor did we understand the impact that those few short months could have on his development. On Jafta's first night home, he slept through the night, and we found him lying quietly in his crib at 9 AM the next morning. We thought we had hit the parenting jackpot with a quiet baby. Little did we know that this baby had just decided to stop crying after months of no one responding to his distress.

It's safe to say that Jafta's life before coming to us was one of neglect. He lived with his birth mother for a few months, a woman who had previously lost seven other children to the foster-care system after failing to parent them properly. After he was removed from her home, he was placed in the care of a well-meaning but very elderly foster mom, who quieted his cries by giving him bottle after bottle of milk or rice cereal. She would cut large holes in the baby bottle so he could drink his rice cereal propped up in his crib, without anyone having to hold him. At 6 months, Jafta could hold the bottle himself and was severely overweight from having food offered as comfort instead of loving arms.

We began to put the puzzle pieces together in terms of our son's neglect as an infant, but we were still lacking education in terms of how this could have affected his neurological development. He seemed like a relatively typical baby. He learned to walk a bit late, but by and large he met his milestones on time.

Looking back, there were some clues that he had sensory issues. He was excessively clumsy as a baby—always bumping into things. Once he learned to walk, he seemed to barrel into furniture and people. We chalked this up to his size. He also had the habit of rocking himself when he was tired or excited. We called it the "wild man dance." And then there was the drool. Oh, the drool. Jafta left puddles of drool in his path. It seemed like he struggled to hold his mouth closed. He wore a bib until he was 2, just to try to keep him from soaking through his shirts with slobber.

It wasn't until Jafta was about 18 months old that we had some concerns about his development, and it was the speech delay that had us worried. He was doing well with the baby signs we taught him, but he still couldn't say many words. He was struggling to point, which seemed to be an important milestone, and his eye contact was very poor. When we relayed these concerns to our local early-intervention team, they assessed him and put him into speech and occupational therapy.

As Jafta grew, his sensory-seeking became more pronounced. He was a crasher, a banger, and a hugger. He loved to run into our arms, or have us smoosh him into the sofa. He had trouble with peers because he assumed that others would want the same brutish affection that he craved. He loved to stand on toys just to experience the feeling on his feet. He excelled at gross-motor activities, learning to ride his bike and scooter at an early age. Still, we had no idea that these could be symptoms of SPD.

I was actually familiar with SPD because a close friend had a daughter with the disorder. But where Jafta was a sensory seeker, her daughter was a sensory avoider. She couldn't stand the feel of sand on her feet, or the texture of most foods, or the feeling of rough fabric on her skin. Conversely, Jafta seemed to prefer these things. Never in a million years did I think he could have the same disorder, because he seemed to be the *opposite* of the only child I knew with SPD.

The one diagnosis I was concerned about, though, was autism. I had worked with autistic children in college, and many of Jafta's sensory-seeking behaviors looked like self-stimulation to me. That, coupled with his speech delays and poor eye contact, had me very worried.

These worries were further stoked when Jafta was placed in an autism program by his early-intervention team. I was devastated, but at the same time, I figured that the combination of speech delay and poor eye contact was a sign that he was on the spectrum. He was never given a diagnosis, but in conversations with his therapists it was clear that this was their suspicion, as well.

Unfortunately, throughout his time in early intervention, no one ever questioned us about Jafta's early months of life. We are a transracial family, so Jafta's adoption was apparent to his therapists. Still, no one asked about attachment issues or his history of neglect—probably because the unfortunate truth is that most therapists are not trained in attachment and how it affects neurology. It would be 3 years later when I would first learn of the well-documented link between adopted children and SPD.

We trudged along in therapy, and Jafta's sensory-seeking behaviors increased. As he learned to feed himself, he frequently overstuffed his mouth. He had trouble chewing his food, and he had trouble sitting still. He craved spicy, sour, and salty foods. He would eat just about anything. He was constantly moving or making noise. He loved to play the drums just for the noise. He didn't seem to notice when he was dirty or messy—in fact, he seemed to like it. He preferred to upend his toy box and then walk through the toys instead of playing with them. He loved to spin himself in circles. He was a happy, bright, and socially engaged child, but he was like a bull in a china shop. We called him our "Tasmanian devil" because he never stopped moving.

His fine-motor delays also became more pronounced. His occupational therapists pointed out his oral-motor difficulties, which resulted in the drooling, the difficulty chewing, and the hard time he had forming his words. Slowly, his therapists began to conceptualize his speech problems as a fine-motor issue rather than a communication issue. They also determined that his difficulty in pointing was also a fine-motor issue. Jafta was great at big motor tasks, but he really struggled with getting the smaller muscles to cooperate.

Finally, when Jafta was about 2½ years old, he was removed from the autism program and placed into more sensory-specific occupational therapy. Someone recommended the book *The Out-of-Sync Child* to me, and it all clicked into place. My son was a textbook sensory seeker. Armed with this knowledge, I felt so much more empowered to help him. We understood that he needed sensory input, and we made it our goal to make sure he was getting it, both in occupational therapy and at home.

After Jafta turned 3, he "graduated" from early intervention and had to be assessed by the Department of Education to see if he was eligible for continued services. I am sure this will come as no surprise to other families of children with SPD, but he was denied services because they deemed that his sensory issues would not interfere with academic learning. This could not be further from the truth—he struggles very much with sitting still and with the fine-motor tasks involved in handwriting. And yet, every year, we go back on his birthday seeking services and are denied, even though they acknowledge that he has severe sensory issues.

Our private insurance does not cover occupational therapy, either. While I believe Jafta made huge strides in occupational therapy, I also think that many of the things they did there were things that we could implement at home. We decided not to pay out-of-pocket for the very expensive therapy appointments, especially because the benefits from each appointment only seemed to last for the day of the session. He needs therapeutic sensory input every day, so we took it upon ourselves to develop a sensory lifestyle, instead of viewing it as something to address only in weekly appointments. We have found that a day filled with riding bikes, wrestling, and jumping on the trampoline does as much good as an expensive hour of occupational therapy.

Jafta is now 6 years old, and it wasn't until earlier this year that I learned about the connection between adopted children and sensory disregulation. It makes perfect sense to me...children who lack sensory stimulation in their early years will struggle with it later. I now understand the way inadequate nurturing can affect the development of neural pathways.

I consider myself someone who is well educated on adoption and child development. I am a family therapist, and I had read many adoption books to prepare for parenting our son...and yet, I had no clue about the connection between adoption and SPD. We also saw many, many specialists in the first years of my son's life, and I remember asking repeatedly about whether or not my son's adoption could be a factor in his symptoms. This question was always met with disregard—it seems the professionals were not aware of the connection, either.

My hope is that both adoptive parents and occupational therapists can be better educated in SPD, so that we can better serve the kids who are affected. I also hope that parents can seek support. Raising a child with SPD can be very isolating. The child may look completely normal, but life with a sensory seeker can be exhausting. I don't think I realized how challenging my son was until I had three other children who were more "sensory typical." I am thankful for the online support I have gotten from other parents who help me feel less isolated as a parent of a child with these unique behaviors.

Kristen Howerton is a mom via birth and adoption and lives in southern California with her husband and four children. She is a freelance writer and an adjunct professor of psychology. She blogs about her life at RageAgainstTheMinivan.com.

Charlie

by Christina Morris

Life is an accumulation of what you do. Mick Jagger said, "It's all right letting yourself go, as long as you can get yourself back." Doing what you want is a strong impulse, made even more difficult when you have a neurological disorder. The story of Charlie has been one of trying to find balance. We know Charlie is very bright, but we have been so worried about his education because of his SPD. We have thought, "Only a very special teacher will be able to help him." So far, he has only had us, and we make progress most of the time, but it's not always pretty.

Charlie is our 5-year-old middle child. He has an older brother, Cameron, who is gifted and kind, and a younger sister by 7 months, Coco, who is showing signs of being advanced. We adopted Charlie when I had just become pregnant after a few years of trying.

Early on, we suspected that schooling would be an issue for Charlie—he was so fast, he had to touch everything, and nothing could satisfy his curiosity for long. One minute he was up on the counter with a butcher knife, and seconds later he was on the carpet, prying open a can of soda with a screwdriver. We had to keep everything away from him. I can even make an alphabetical list! A—Appliances: Refrigerator, oven, and microwave locked, and toaster unplugged. (Yes, even the toaster.) B—Bathroom: Door locked, to prevent splash time in the toilet and rolls of unspooled toilet paper all over. C—Cat: Poor, poor kitty. You get the picture. Charlie reveled in the way things smelled and felt. He luxuriated in it. I marveled at his reaction to a bubble bath, carefully picking up the bubbles, slowly putting them to his nose, and then inhaling deeply before his hand got too close and he smashed the bubbles on his face.

We made a few trips to the emergency room because of Charlie's tendency to eat lotion. I think we have since surmised that he didn't mean to eat it so much as smell it and feel it. We made sure to visit the park daily, bathe frequently, and always have chew toys and pacifiers on hand. While he was always looking for input, he also fought us for space. There were a few people, me included, who leaned in for a kiss and instead got a fist in the kisser. It was hard to communicate with him. He didn't often hear and/or understand "no." I remember becoming the mom who yells and spanks. When he got out of control, I got out of control. When the house was calm, we were on eggshells to keep it that way.

At 2 years old, Charlie wanted to follow his brother to school. He got a backpack, filled it with toys, and walked around the house wearing it, waiting impatiently to be taken to school. When we found a preschool for him, the reports from his teachers weren't particularly complimentary: "He doesn't stop." "He can really keep you on your toes." "He took off his own dirty diaper and gleefully ran around the classroom with it in his hand." Because of a personnel switch, they changed the class routine—something that really bothered him. He began to fight and cry when we dropped him off. We pulled him out of preschool.

That was probably one of the hardest times for us. We knew he couldn't control himself, but we were without a definitive answer or plan. Our family and friends and teachers acted like they knew exactly what to do. "Make him listen." "Put him in time-out." "Spank him." "That child needs to be on medication." "He's so smart, he's playing you. You're a fool if you don't see it." My husband and I were, for the first time in our marriage, at odds with each other. We were constantly unhappy and bickering, exhausted, and frustrated. We would blame each other for the kids' behavior or for not handling conflict correctly. We were second-guessing each other, angry, and generally unhappy. I felt miserable. I don't believe that kids who are 2 years old consciously manipulate anyone; I believe they are just trying to express something. He agreed with me. But the stress was overwhelming. We were both feeling judged.

When Charlie was about to turn 3, we tried another school. Being the sensory shark that he is, he was in time-out on the first day for going into the teacher's purse, and then later finding and squeezing the paints. He was in time-out on the second day for pushing another child. We began to hang our heads again. We didn't want to be the parents of "that kid." We didn't want him to be "that kid."

It was around this time that I heard of SPD. I recognized some of the symptoms, and a light went on. I wasn't crazy! I knew there was something wrong, something he couldn't control, something that we could and needed to address to get Charlie ready for school and—eventually—life.

Although the school was willing to let Charlie stay, we decided to pull him out. We were just beginning our journey with SPD and wanted to make sure he had a positive start to his school experience. We were worried that he would spend most of his days in time-out for doing things that were beyond his control. We needed to understand what was going on before we dropped him off at school and hoped for the best.

Our first experience with an occupational therapist was not exactly satisfying. She confirmed our suspicions of SPD but seemed distant. While she recommended therapy, she never seemed very firm about the diagnosis or positive about the outcome. "Yep, that's Charlie," she would say when I commented on some behavior. It felt like any time I asked for advice, there was nothing more than agreement about the situation.

When we first realized that Charlie had SPD, we began to notice the unique difficulties he had with balance, like his posture when he sat in a swing or the way he fell down, even from a sitting position. Before learning about SPD, he moved so quickly all the time that we didn't have the inclination to identify his differences; we were just keeping up—barely—and were very frustrated. He wasn't listening, and his curiosity always seemed to lead him to the most dangerous and/or maddening activities. While I was cleaning up paints, he would be squeezing lotion or getting into prescriptions. He required vigilance, not just supervision. While occupational therapy helped us identify some of these issues, we still had other, bigger issues with controlling his behavior.

After looking for more information, I found a school that I thought would be great. It was a school in an occupational therapy gym, and I thought that I had found "it!" They worked on transitions, behavior, and more. We stopped going to occupational therapy after being enrolled at the new school for a few weeks, and for a while, it was really good. Then, they had a huge turnover in personnel and kids. His teacher was fired because she disagreed so vocally with the director after the director therapeutically "held" Charlie in class one day after an aggressive outburst. The changes were ruinous for him. Within 4 months, they were managing him, not helping him.

Not long after, we found our occupational therapist, Diane, who has been so helpful to us. We wanted to approach Charlie's differences intensively. We researched Dr Lucy Jane Miller and considered going to her clinic in Denver, but we decided we could get many of the same benefits by treating Charlie twice a week over a longer period of time. Diane tested

Charlie and gave us actual details about Charlie's deficiencies in years and months, in terms we could understand. She helped us to see what he was missing, recommended specific activities for us to try at home, and set goals so that we could recognize his successes. His tests revealed that he was almost 2 years behind in his gross-motor development and a little over a year behind in his fine-motor development. Our goal was simply to close the gap.

We also consulted with a developmental pediatrician who recommended medication after meeting with Charlie for 1 hour. I was devastated. Medication is the absolute last resort for me. On the advice of Diane, we had him tested by a neuropsychologist. She diagnosed his condition as attention-deficit/hyperactivity disorder (ADHD), as well as SPD. She also proposed medication but gave us an alternative recommendation of neurofeedback therapy (a type of "brainwave training," with sensors placed on the head). We did the neurofeedback therapy three times a week and occupational therapy twice a week for about 3 months. We were very busy, and while Charlie enjoyed occupational therapy, he detested neurofeedback. He got candy for doing well in occupational therapy, but he upped the ante for neurofeedback. We were at the hobby store once a week, buying models.

All that we have done so far seems to have worked for us. Charlie is less oppositional today, he doesn't have bad days at therapy anymore, his balance and gross-motor skills have improved by more than a year, developmentally speaking, and he is almost up to average for his age group. Because of our intensive approach, I think we have progressed. But is it measurable? If he can stay in school and remain happy, that would mean success.

It has been a little over a year since we have had Charlie in school. Four different schools have told us that he isn't welcome. One of them is specifically for kids with sensory and ADHD issues. "He doesn't listen." "He doesn't focus." "He isn't mature enough." "We can't handle him." Without recognition, he will fall through the cracks. He doesn't "qualify" for services because he is incredibly intelligent and well spoken. Although he can't read or write or even color, he is gifted in other ways. For example, he has a talent for tools—recently he unscrewed the hinges on the door to the laundry room. We discovered it when the door fell on my husband.

It is obvious that our journey with Charlie and SPD is just beginning. He just had his 5th birthday. He delights us with his knowledge of ships, pirates, and sea creatures. He maddens us when he uses my very expensive cosmetic products and bug spray in his experiments of mixing liquids. He is unique and beautiful, and I can't imagine my life without him. Cameron, his older brother, helps him build Legos one minute and fights with him for breaking them the next. Coco, his younger sister, is either conspiring with him to get my attention or crying because they have come to fisticuffs again.

My husband and I now build each other up, rather than knock each other down. That is what education about SPD has done for us. We are the special teachers, and we are being specially taught. We are a family, true and whole. I know that we all love each other very much, and that won't stop. Yes, I am still worried about school. Yes, I am still explaining SPD to friends and family. But look what learning about it did for us! I am hopeful and happy, and I can think of no better way to live.

Christina Morris is a work-at-home mom who lives with her work-at-home husband, Chris, and three very different children, one of whom has SPD. She began her blog, sensingmadness. com, *to document the outcome of the treatments for her middle son, and it has evolved into a blog about family. She enjoys writing prose and code until her kids come home from school, and then she enjoys* them.

Forever Family

by Kimberly S.

After several years of trying unsuccessfully to conceive, we made the decision to take a little break and provide a safe home for a few kids out there in foster care. We would help out for a couple years, hopefully make some small difference for a child, and then maybe, magically, everything would fix itself and we'd be able to get pregnant.

We'd never been parents before, and with both of us working full time, even though we finally had that foster-care license in hand, we couldn't be those amazing foster parents that sign up for anything. We could only take in a child that was a right fit for us. After weeks of call after call, it was Friday at 5 PM, and I was about to walk out the office door when the phone rang. It was our private agency, and they had a 7-week-old baby boy that had just been dropped off on the porch of the local Department of Social and Health Services office. I went through my list of 20 questions (which is hilarious now, after eventually having 15 other kids in and out of our home over the next several years), and of course she couldn't answer any of them, as she really knew nothing about this child. She said the only thing she knew was that he was born addicted to cocaine and that he needed a home *now*. So, this was it! We agreed to meet.

When I got home with this beautiful little 9-lb baby boy, my husband and I couldn't take a bite of dinner. We couldn't believe this was finally happening. Maybe it was just for the weekend, maybe it was only for a month, but for now—we had a baby! When I introduced the baby to a dear friend the following week, she looked at him, and she looked at me and said, "This is your Forever Child. He's yours, I just *know* it." I thought she was crazy, really.

Other than one incident at daycare, when they'd given him a peanut butter and jelly sandwich at 10 months old and we had to call 911 (obviously we found another daycare) and later finding out that he had a life-threatening nut allergy, everything was great. He was kind of a sick baby—never anything major, but just always had something. We went through the disclosure step and learned that he had been prenatally exposed to cigarettes, alcohol, and countless drugs by both biological parents and that his birth mother had had no prenatal care. But, he was perfect!

They told us it was still early, and that complications could still arise with his development later. They gave an example that everything could be fine for years, and then one day he could get into kindergarten and suddenly struggle with reading or something. So that was kind of…like worst-case scenario to us.

At 21 months old, our dear friend was right, and we became a Forever Family on National Adoption Day. The entire adoption process had gone through without a hiccup, and we had no idea at the time how incredibly rare that is. He was ours, and everything was perfect. We had fallen in love with being foster parents and would never go back to trying to have our own—we knew that with everything we had. We were meant to be foster parents. In the meantime, the state asked us to adopt a little girl that we'd been fostering, and we moved forward, full steam ahead. Our son had his own big sister, and we had a family. We finally had a family.

Six months later, 6 days before our little girl's case was transferred to the adoption social worker, another couple stepped up and wanted to adopt her and her biological siblings together. We spent the next 9 months fighting to keep her, and somewhere in all of that, our son started to fall apart. He got out of control at home and at daycare. He ran laps around the room, threw anything he could get his hands on, and climbed up high and jumped down. Nothing could hurt him. We received countless phone calls at work and a whole stack of "naughty notes" over the following months. One day, the little girl that had been our daughter for the past 23½ months was taken away and shipped off across the country. The following morning, we got a call from our son's daycare, saying they'd had enough and he was being kicked out. They gave us a very strong recommendation to have him treated for attention-deficit/hyperactivity disorder (ADHD). I got up off the couch in my sweats, with no makeup on and my eyes puffy (as you might imagine), and went on the hunt for a new daycare that would take our behaviorally challenged 3-year-old son and our foster children (not an easy task!).

We had our son screened for ADHD, in a one-on-one setting in a gray, plain room, and they sent us home, saying, "Absolutely not—I think you just need to find a new daycare. He's 'fine.'"

The new daycare lasted 4 months, and after an incident where he stabbed another child in the eye and then stomped on a smaller child, we moved on to the next facility. That one lasted 2 weeks, and we were told there had to be something wrong with him and it was highly recommended we get a second opinion on the ADHD. We had no doubt about it—it wasn't ADHD. He could sit and work with us on a project *forever*. However, it seemed like the minute things got "too busy" around him, he went into overdrive. We didn't know what was wrong, but it wasn't that. The fifth daycare had their first incident about a month in, when the children were sitting perfectly at the breakfast table and a little girl got up to clean her plate. As she walked back behind our son, he jumped up, turned around, and stabbed her in the eye with his fork, breaking the skin open. He was suspended. I can't begin to explain how horrifying it is to get phone calls about your child doing things like this to other children. We hadn't done anything "wrong" as parents—there was never domestic violence in our home, he'd never seen a bad movie, and he'd been in our home since he was an infant. Where in the world was he getting this from?

We took him to the pediatrician, which led to seeing a long string of specialists. Our son received a diagnosis of a severe level of impulse-control disorder and a severe level of fetal cocaine exposure. It was not ADHD, and we were told that had we treated him for ADHD, it would have had the opposite effect on him. We were instructed to get him onto a seizure medication immediately and to never take him off of it. His blood would need to be monitored monthly, as the drug was known to cause liver damage and nobody knew what the future held for him. Two electroencephalogram tests were done, the results of which both came back normal—no seizures. Shortly after, our son stabbed a child in the back, and then there was another stabbing in the eye. That was it—we got the dreaded warning that we were now looking at termination from the daycare. We were still working full time through all of this, and it was a disaster. We were doing everything we could. They had increased the dosage of his medicine, and then increased it and increased it again. No matter whom I called, no matter what we did, there was no hope, because the many services out there all required you to be low-income. There was nothing for us. We took him back to his pediatrician, who explained that he hadn't seen anything this severe in a child so young, and he recommended that we go back for a second screening to the place that had said he was fine, that they could really help if we could just get approved. Now we had a stack of incident reports from multiple daycares, official diagnoses, and a letter stating that he was permanently disabled, which *would* affect him behaviorally and academically for the rest of his life. The pediatrician refused to sign off on the behavioral plan to keep our son in daycare.

I finally got in touch with a place that could do a psychological evaluation, but the waitlist had nearly 60 children on it. I told the receptionist our story and begged for something that wouldn't take 6 months to get in. We were falling apart. I had just accepted a new position in a line of work where I felt that I could better help people and make a difference, and my husband's job was up in the air with the floundering economy. We could not keep doing this. She apologized and said the need was just too great. She put us on the list and gave me another number I could try. I called the other number, but the receptionist was out of the office, so I just started telling our story to the lady who answered the phone. I put it all out there, and I wasn't going to stop—somebody had to help us. She said she couldn't get us in right away but that she'd see what she could do to at least get us an evaluation and figure out if this was the path we needed to look into. She said she would try to squeeze us in somehow, because she was the owner. I cried. Finally! We got a call the following week, and we took our son in for an evaluation. They told us he had six subtypes of SPD.

Shortly after that, the receptionist from the first facility called me back, saying she was calling to schedule our evaluation. How could this be? I told her I had just called last week and there were something like 56 children on the list ahead of us, and was she sure?! Her tone was short, and she said she didn't know what happened but we were at the top of the list and what day would work best for us. Wow.

Our son started occupational therapy. We created a therapeutic environment for him at home and found a nanny that had previous experience with a child with Asperger syndrome and was familiar with occupational therapy. His grandma made him a weighted blanket, Daddy built a Lycra swing in his bedroom, and we did everything else we could possibly think of.

We also relinquished our foster-care license.

Being foster parents was our passion, and it is something we hope and pray to one day go back and do again, but for now, our little man has been through enough, he has been judged enough, he has had enough beloved foster siblings come and go in his life, and it is time to give him all we have. We still don't know what's going on. We're still waiting for our second evaluation from the place that sent him home, saying he was "just fine"…the place that meets with the child one-on-one, in the plain, gray, very-sensory-friendly room, where they evaluate these behaviorally challenged children. Apparently it's a lot of work to convince them, but this time, I am going in prepared. There *is* something wrong, and we *do* need help, and I am not taking no for an answer.

Some others think it's a type of posttraumatic stress disorder that originated after losing his big sister (and Mommy and Daddy, emotionally, there for some time, too). Some feel that it's the effects of the drugs. Some think it's going to eventually turn out to be mental illness. But, everyone sees and knows now that it is all stemming from SPD.

Sometimes, I feel anger start to creep up, and it can be easy to feel upset with my son's biological parents that they did this to him. How could they put him through all of that, and diminish his chances of having a full life because of their thoughtless acts? How could they hurt him like that? And then I remember… they gave him life. No matter what, they are a part of him, and he is here because of them. He is as handsome as he is because of them. We must be thankful, because as incredibly sad as some of it is, they gave him life.

So, as they say…some people come and go in our lives. And some stay forever. *We are a Forever Family.*

Kimberly S. is Mommy to a very handsome, hilarious, and incredibly smart toddler with SPD, severe impulse-control disorder—not otherwise specified, and severe fetal cocaine exposure. She is married to her very best friend of 8 years. Everyone told them over and over again that if they'd just stop "trying" to get pregnant and not think so much about it, they would finally be able to create the family they wanted. As it turns out, they were absolutely right. Kimberly and her husband could not have dreamed of a more perfect ending to their story of becoming a Forever Family.

Chapter 6

International Adoption

Children adopted from overseas often have sensory issues. The reasons are similar to those with domestically adopted children, and can include abuse, neglect, and substance abuse. However, many of the children adopted overseas come from orphanages, which are a different scenario altogether. Although orphanages vary greatly from country to country, most of them are low on staff and funding, making that crucial one-on-one attention between caregiver and baby almost impossible.

Because of this, children often do not get the attention and sensory stimulation they need. Children can spend too much time in cribs or alone and are not given adequate time to explore their environments or receive the physical care they require, like rocking and singing, which helps a child's sensory system develop. Additionally, many infants that are placed in orphanages have been born prematurely or have other health issues.

The families in this section have each adopted a child internationally—from Russia, China, or South Korea. These stories highlight a diverse group of adorable kids who all have SPD.

Hello, World— It's Me, Kaia

by Karla Fitch

On a November morning, the double doors from the international security area at the Detroit International Airport opened, and three escorts pushed three identical strollers with a baby girl in each into the waiting area. One of those little girls was my daughter, Kaia. Amid tears, hugs, kisses, and photos, we welcomed Kaia to the United States and into her new family.

Kaia was born near Seoul, South Korea, in late February and joined our family a short 10 months later, with a world of experiences I can only imagine. By the time she arrived in the states, she had lived with three different Korean families and in the Korean Social Services orphanage. We knew bits and pieces about her life in Korea from the occasional reports we received via the adoption agency. Her referral described her as a healthy child, within normal ranges for height and weight. Photos that we received from the adoption agency showed a sleepy-eyed infant girl who reportedly loved to cuddle with her foster mom. The final instructions from her foster family that arrived with her on her trip home said that she liked "every kind of fruit" and would also eat "rice soup and bread."

We began almost immediately with what we had been taught in our adoption training. Kaia was fed from a bottle to foster attachment. We also used skin-to-skin contact (such as infant massage) to build a connection with her and spent a lot of time snuggling on the sofa and trying to make eye contact while talking to Kaia in soothing tones. She was very shy when it came to eye contact, but with that one exception, we felt that attachment was going pretty well. My husband and I were on cloud nine, and everyone in the family adored our new addition.

After taking a few weeks to get Kaia somewhat settled, we started taking her to various specialists to ensure that the health information we had received from Korea was accurate. Our pediatrician and adoption agency referred us to an adoption clinic for babies, where we met with a doctor who specialized in international adoption. The doctor noted that by her current age (Kaia was then about 11 months old), she should have been sitting independently and perhaps even crawling. The doctor referred us to an early-intervention team and suggested that we find out whether we could get Kaia into physical therapy.

Our training had prepared us for the developmental delays that are often seen in adoption, and we were keen to cite the statistic that "for every 3 months a child is in [orphanage] care, he or she will lose 1 month of development." It seemed only natural to us that our 11-month-old was functioning at a 7-month-old level.

But at the same time, Kaia had these "idiosyncrasies." For example, she loved to "scritch." By that I mean she would take a fingernail and scratch her finger on a surface—the bumpier, the better. I can distinctly recall her sitting in her ExerSaucer, ignoring all the toys and scritch, scritch, scritching at the plastic support ring—or lying on her play mat and scritching on the plastic/nylon edges.

Kaia has also always loved to do sit-ups. To do a "Kaia sit-up" properly, you have to position yourself on the lap of the most convenient parent or grandparent, lock your legs just around the person's waist, grab their hands, and toss your body backward over the their knees. You can pull up immediately (and repeatedly), or just hang out there until everyone in the room is afraid you're going to pass out from the blood rushing to your head. Kaia could do these sit-ups *forever*. The longest any one of us has gone with her is about an hour—and then she proceeds to the next available person, assumes the position, and tries to start again. She is literally tireless when it comes to this activity.

More worrisome than her scritching and sit-ups was Kaia's refusal to eat. Shortly after we were assured that the attachment process was going well, we were encouraged by our pediatrician to start feeding Kaia pureed baby foods. We eagerly stocked up on infant spoons and tore the wrapping from those special thermal bowls we had received in our adoption shower. I researched the best baby foods and selected some fruits I thought she'd like (after all, her foster mom had left instructions that she liked all kinds of fruit), and we sat down for our first feeding. But Kaia was not having any of that.

There was screaming. There were tears. There was food everywhere—

except inside her tummy. My mom assured me that this was normal for some kids and that I just needed to keep trying. She even shared that she used to sneak the spoon into my mouth between sobs just to get food into me. So, I dug in my heels and kept trying. I even managed to have a few successes with my mom's trick of sticking the spoon into Kaia's mouth between sobs—until she learned to cry with her mouth closed.

Weeks went by. We tried different foods…different spoons. Nothing worked. This was definitely not normal.

Meanwhile, Kaia was becoming more active and growing, yet not gaining any weight. The chubby baby legs we remembered when we received her from the escort back at the airport had almost melted away. We were "spiking" her bottles with pureed foods and rice cereals just to get some calories into her, and on the advice of the pediatrician, she began seeing an occupational therapist to help us to work on our "feeding issues."

Our first occupational therapist introduced us to therapeutic brushing, joint compressions, facial toweling, Nuk brushes, and Maroon Spoons. She told us that Kaia did not like the sensation of the spoon in her mouth or the pureed foods and that these exercises and tools would help to desensitize her. But she never told us why Kaia had developed the intolerance in the first place. We diligently went along with our therapies, believing that the oral sensitivities had developed because we switched Kaia back to the bottle (for attachment) when she was developmentally ready to start eating purees with a spoon. We convinced ourselves that Kaia's problems were our fault.

Kaia continued to make progress with feeding—slowly. After moving to the other side of town, we started seeing different occupational and physical therapists. Our new therapists made great strides with Kaia, but we still wondered why she wasn't gaining any ground. She was in a loving home and getting plenty of attention. She had weekly therapy sessions, encounters with early-intervention specialists, a playgroup for children with developmental delays, and "mainstream" activities like Gymboree, where she could have positive peer role models. She was eating better (well, better *for Kaia*), and we were supplementing the calories she wasn't getting through her regular diet with PediaSure. But, by 21 months she still wasn't walking, her language development was closer to the 12-month level, her self-help skills were nonexistent, and she was showing more and more idiosyncrasies.

We began to resign ourselves to the possibility that Kaia was just always going to be a little behind and that we would never really know why, when the behavioral problems started showing up. Kaia was always stubborn and tended to have a short fuse, but as she approached 2½ years of age, behavioral problems that we were able to deal with in the past started to intensify. She started hitting and biting kids in her playgroup, the early-intervention staff members and her therapists, and me and my husband. When we tried to discipline her, Kaia would laugh wildly and throw her body around or hit and bite more. Dinnertime became the time of day that the entire family dreaded because she would demand to be released from her high chair and then immediately engage the nearest person to do sit-ups with her—whether that person was finished eating or not. When she was refused, the meltdowns would begin.

I was at my wits' end a few months ago, when I Googled "behavioral problems in toddlers." Whether by luck or the grace of God, the first thing that came up was a Web site on SPD. And then things began to fall into place.

I went through the red flags on the SPD Foundation Web site and couldn't believe how many sounded like Kaia. I got books from the library and scoured blogs on SPD, and I watched in disbelief as Kaia's idiosyncrasies painted a more and more detailed picture—not of a little girl whose development was affected purely by the circumstances of adoption—but of a little girl whose senses contributed to a virtual traffic jam of information inside her head.

We now know that Kaia experiences several forms of SPD. She has sensory modulation problems with oral hyperresponsivity, along with hyporesponsivity and sensory-seeking behaviors with her auditory and vestibular senses. She is also affected by sensory-based motor disorder and continues to lag behind her peers in gross- and fine-motor milestones.

At this point, I feel like we have a long road ahead of us. But, unlike before, that road has a name—SPD. Armed with that information, we can begin to learn more, educate others, and join in the growing community of families who support each other with tools, ideas, and a listening ear. I feel like we are ready to face the world together.

So, say "hello," world. And get ready for Kaia.

Karla Fitch is a writer, crochet designer, and mother to a beautiful, energetic little girl who also happens to have SPD. She and her husband are also adoption advocates who treasure every adventure with their sensational daughter.

Scenes from a Sensory Life

by Terri Mauro

When we first met our son, he was 18 months old, and his world had been limited to a playpen in a Russian orphanage. His chief mode of entertainment was swinging his head back and forth. The workers at the orphanage rarely let him out, and we soon saw why. When he was released from those wooden walls, he zipped away on all fours, at the speed of light, from one corner of the playroom to the other. He loved to be picked up and removed from that pen, but as soon as he was free, the last thing he wanted was to be held. Only once did he consent to be cuddled, and the warm, emotional moment was quickly followed by a warm, wet sensation on my lap. Having relieved himself through the rags used as diapers at the orphanage, he was off and crawling again.

We came home to the USA. With early-intervention help, our son learned to walk—and then there were so many things to run into at full speed and hit with his head and his face. Walls. Table edges. The feet of his sister as she played on the backyard swings. Rear-view mirrors on the car. Doors as he compulsively opened and shut them. I lived in fear of people noticing the cuts and bruises on his eyes and nose and chin and coming to horrible and completely understandable conclusions, for which I had no explanation other than the accurate but totally lame, "No, really, he just walks into things!"

Confined to the relative safety of his crib, he rocked back and forth so violently he knocked a hole in the wall and slightly "singed" the back of his hair (the friction of the rubbing caused his hair to be thinner in the back). His official diagnosis was fetal alcohol effects, but the neurologist also mentioned "sensory integration," words I'd heard from fellow adoptive parents on an e-mail list. I started reading up.

A year later, my son was still not in favor of being held. His school physical therapist suggested starting small: Instead of trying to hug his whole, wriggly body, just try holding his little foot. Casually, as we sat on the couch, reading a book, my hand would creep toward his toes. I would touch his foot. Then I grabbed his foot and gave it a squeeze. To my delight, no flight ensued. Little by little, slowly but surely, his tolerance grew for allowing me to give his limbs a squeeze. I become skillful at sitting him on my lap to watch TV and stealthily sneaking my arms around him. Barney the purple dinosaur became my ally in focusing his attention away from the dreaded closeness of another person. In small increments, my no-hug boy became my cuddlebug. I loved him, and he loved me. We were a happy family.

The following year, we got the chance to have our son evaluated by an expert on sensory-based therapy, Sharon Cermak, who was evaluating children adopted from Russia. She tried to interest him in doing specific things with toys, but he preferred to examine the spot where a video camera was plugged into the wall. She tried to get him onto a platform swing, but he didn't think that was such a good idea. I mentioned that he would do pretty much anything if you let him play with keys, and she tossed my keys onto the platform swing. Up he went. It was good to know that perseverance trumped his sensory trepidation. We came away with a confirmation that sensory issues were a problem for him, some suggestions for his teachers and therapists, and a videotape of the session that still makes me smile.

When my son got a little older, we attended orientation day for a pricey special-needs summer camp. We moved from station to station, learning about the camp's activities. At one station, a counselor brought out an enormous drum and encouraged the kids to bang on it. My son was "in the zone," loving the feeling of hitting that bouncy, loud surface. Another camper screamed at the noise, his sensory sensitivities on red alert. The counselor told my son to stop. With his sensory-seeking compulsions fully activated, he didn't want to stop. This was treated as a behavioral offense. Note to self: A camp that doesn't offer full sympathy to both ends of the sensory spectrum is not a camp in which my son is going to succeed! Note to camp: Don't pull out a big drum and then tell a child not to beat it.

As far as school goes, we were lucky. His special-education teachers and school occupational therapists were interested in administering sensory-based therapies, and we were able to keep his mixed bag of overresponsivity and sensory-seeking behaviors in context. We doubled up on therapy, seeing a private occupational therapist specifically for sensory-based therapy. I found books on sensory issues and read everything I could get my hands on. I found catalogs full of sensory tools and bought up anything that I thought might work. We tried brushing. Joint compression. Weighted vests. Weighted shoes. Weighted lap animals. Weighted blankets. Weighted wristbands. Body Sox. He had a rubber band around his desk to press his feet against. He wore big boots to keep him anchored to the ground. His teachers gave him heavy things to carry. He was discouraged from pushing people and encouraged to walk on balance beams and crawl through scary tunnels. He could go to the park and swing forever, higher and higher, zoning out in the joy of flight, but he clutched the top of the slide in fear and refused to go down. He was getting better. He was staying the same. He was exchanging one sensory weirdness for another. He was getting older. And he was what he was.

My son is 17 years old now. He is tall. Sturdy. Hairy. And completely cured of his sensory-processing problems. Ha! No. It doesn't work that way—not for us, and not for him. The problems change; they lessen—they mutate. They don't go away. They are a part of him. He does not, thank goodness, walk into things anymore. He no longer leads with his face. He does still chew on his shirts and suck his fingers. He does still jump in place to remind himself that gravity is in effect and that the floor is down there. He still rocks himself to sleep some nights—not hard enough to damage the wall, just hard enough to make me wonder what the heck that sound is? He tolerates car alarms and thunder in a way he once could not, but he's developed a fear of going down stairs. Hugs do not bother him, but his inability to modulate his own strength and squeezing mean that the hugs now hurt me. Tags and seams do not bother him now. Neither do bunched up socks in sneakers he has jammed on his feet, something that we wish he really would find uncomfortable. For years we bypassed his dislike of hair-combing by giving him a buzz cut. This year, he wants to grow it longer again. We'll see if combing is another sensory road-marker he's now able to pass.

I'd love to say that sensory-based therapy worked miracles for my child. I'm a true believer in SPD. I've written articles and blog posts galore, and I've even written a book on the subject. I don't want to give any ammunition to those who think that all this sensory stuff is just another scam that desperate parents throw their money and hope at. All the therapy helped in cutting the sharp edges off his sensory needs and pulling him in from the dangerous extremes. Age and maturity helped, too. But what helped the most was having a framework for understanding his behaviors and permission to not take them personally. Just as understanding a child's blindness or deafness gives you tools to help her cope and grow and thrive while not actually delivering a cure, understanding the role of all the senses and the way sensory-processing problems can affect all areas of functioning gives you the power to help your child and respect his strengths and special needs. Who wouldn't want to know that? What strikes me most about my son's growing up is the way in which the thoughtful and creative responses of clued-in adults made bad situations better. Awareness is vital. Spread the word.

Terri Mauro has been working as a writer for more than 30 years. After she and her husband adopted two children with special needs from Russia, she began writing about her parenting experience, first on her personal site, Mothers with Attitude, and now as the About.com *guide to Parenting Special Needs Children. She is the author of* The Everything Parent's Guide to Sensory Integration Disorder *and* 50 Ways to Support Your Child's Special Education.

Emergence

by Judy M. Miller

Her cries and screams occurred without warning, often over a dozen times each day, expressing an inability to connect and her fathomless grief. My daughter was trying, but her sensory-processing system was not integrated. I didn't know how to help her, other than to snuggle her up as close to me as I possibly could, often skin-to-skin in an attempt to absorb the demons that chased her.

Years later, I came to understand the magnitude of the cards she'd been dealt by losing her birth mother and by being adopted. I, mother to this precious soul, was ripped open. My daughter's SPD and grief connected us on the deepest level imaginable. She felt safe with me and shared every bit of what she felt. Her disorder made me look deeper at another aspect of adoption—loss.

My daughter joined us at 13 months old, broken in spirit and disconnected. I sensed this in her referral pictures and felt it as soon as she arrived in the large meeting room at the Ministry's office in China. I stepped forward to take her when her name was called. She didn't cry—she smiled (this would be the only one for several days). Her smile was unexpected, and although it registered somewhere in the back of my mind, I ignored that warning of things to come.

She scooted up on my shoulder. Dark hair grew out of her shaved little head, bug bites covered her pale face, and the stink of polluted water permeated her faded and ratty orphanage clothing. She promptly stuck her thumb in her mouth and fell asleep. I had to bat one official's hand away when she tried to take my daughter's thumb out of her mouth.

"Bu (no)," I said. She was comforted by her thumb. Let it be.

My girl was a sad baby those first days in China. She would sit folded in half, her chest flat against the short-piled carpet of the hotel room, pressed in between her splayed-out legs as she sucked her thumb—one, two, three, four, rest...one, two, three, four, rest. The rhythm soothed her, and in the months and years to come I would find myself putting her thumb into her mouth to settle her.

My husband and I were rewarded with another smile 2 days later, and a few days after that, she began to sit up without assistance. Within the second week, she was walking while holding onto our hands. We were thrilled with her progress and believed that love and attention were working to bring this gorgeous baby girl around.

Upon arriving home, we warned our other kids not to take anything from her. In China, we had noticed that she ate off the outside of her closed chubby fists—grinding them into her food and then carefully sucking the food off of her right hand. When she cleaned it off, she would carefully open her fingers to suck what food had made it into the crevices between her fingers. She kept her left hand tucked behind her, hiding what little food there was in that hand. We had made the mistake in China of cleaning the left hand before giving her more food to hold in her right. Never again. She was still in survival mode.

Her adjustment seemed to be going well. She enjoyed being with her brother and sister. She smiled and cooed a lot, but still, something seemed "off." Within months, I began to notice other things. She was content to be still—not a normal activity for a toddler. My daughter could hear me, but she wouldn't respond. She would fall and not react. I received blank looks when trying to engage her in "follow me" games. I had her assessed by development therapists. They said my daughter was in the lower range of normal. She was a late walker, and her gait was "odd." We had her hips x-rayed. They appeared to be just fine.

Everything looked fine, and it didn't. Time passed, and I asked for another assessment. The findings were that she was slightly delayed and would catch up soon.

My niggling feeling grew into fear and then panic when it all began to escalate—the screams, the crying, the throwing herself on hard surfaces (like concrete) without any warnings or triggers. As I held her sleeping, rung-out-from-her-tantrum body one afternoon, I began to cry. She was so beautiful and in peace as she slept. I wanted her to feel peaceful all of the time. I ached with her pain. While she slept, I made phone calls and found an assessment group that could see us the next day.

The hour-long assessment turned into 3½ hours. Multiple therapists went over our daughter with a fine-toothed comb and then met with me and went over my notes. She received a diagnosis of something I had never heard of, and it required a lot of therapy—it was SPD.

SPD is a disorder that can affect all of the far and near senses. It can affect children who have been institutionalized, like my daughter. Proper integration of the senses involves the neurological processing of information that is received by an individual's body about his or her environment. SPD occurs when the brain cannot modulate the reciprocal process of intake, organization, and output of the sensory information that it is receiving—and therefore regulate the body's activity level.

My daughter exhibited difficulties with the tactile, vestibular (movement), and proprioceptive (positioning) senses and was responding with a combination of over- and underresponsivity. Her prognosis was good because she was healthy and very young. The recommendation was that she should begin occupational, speech, and physical therapy as soon as possible.

The improvements that occurred within a matter of weeks were miraculous. My daughter began talking and processing. Her tantrums decreased. Her need to throw herself on the floor for input disappeared. Her gait became normal. She attended a developmental preschool program and graduated in a year.

As my daughter began to "heal," she began to process her losses and grieve openly about the loss of her birth mother, being given up, not being loved enough by her birth mother, and not growing up in China. Her grief was triggered annually by her birthday. I began to understand that her SPD was not only tied to being in the orphanage, but to her personal losses, as well. Her neurological system, which had been severely stressed by being separated from her birth mother, continued to shut down as she lived in the welfare institute, with little stimulation and nurturing.

We've made a great deal of headway over the past years. My daughter calls on her coping skills when she feels out of sync. She grieves less about what she sees as the injustice of adoption, of her being our daughter. She knows there is nothing she can do to make me stop loving her. Knowing that I will love her no matter what has given her the permission she needed to open up, talk about adoption, and find some resolution.

And that thumb? Well, now it's painted wild and funky colors.

Judy M. Miller coordinates and teaches parent-preparation education and transracial parenting to parents in the adoption process. She also works as a support specialist, equipping parents with new techniques and information and encouraging and empowering adoptive families through difficult times. Her essays and articles appear in adoption and parenting magazines and in A Cup of Comfort for Adoptive Families *(Adams Media),* Pieces of Me: Who Do I Want to Be? *(EMK Press), and* Chicken Soup for the Soul: Thanks Mom *(Chicken Soup for the Soul). You can find out more about Judy at* judymmiller.com.

Chapter 7

Preemies

When a baby is in the womb, its nervous system is developing thousands of connections, all of which will help him or her cope with the much brighter, much louder outside world after birth. When a baby is born prematurely, that process isn't complete, and the result is a sensory system that is overwhelmed by the world.

For babies that have SPD because of their immature and underdeveloped nervous systems, life can be overwhelming! The bright lights of the hospital, the wind on their skin while being carried to the car, and all of the sensory smells, sights, sounds, and movement involved in life outside the womb can really be too much.

The families in this section have been through the stress and emotional turmoil of giving birth before they were full term—and they are open to sharing their story with you.

Our Incredible Journey (That's Only Begun!)

by Heather Bergemann

My son Eli was born at 34 weeks' gestation, weighing 5 lbs 8 oz. He was very healthy and needed no time in the neonatal intensive care unit. He was able to come home from the hospital with us.

Eli was always a very good eater. When it was time to introduce solid foods, it went off without a hitch. He begged for more and was ecstatic when he was able to eat table food. He did like to chew on things a lot, but he was teething, right? He always liked to be rocked to sleep and had difficulty falling asleep if he wasn't rocked. I didn't mind, because it was special time that we got to share together.

Eli hated being on his belly when he was a baby. Bummer for him that he has a developmental specialist for a mommy! He was "forced" to do tummy time every day. He fought it hard and consequently didn't roll over until he was 6 months old. He didn't crawl until he was almost 8 months old and started walking at 9 months.

As he got a little older, I started to notice that there were noises he didn't like. He would cry if I turned on the hair dryer or the vacuum. We dealt with this easily—I closed the bathroom door when the hair dryer was in use. We kept him out of the room when it was time to vacuum. Family events never seemed to bother him. He mostly slept through them.

We went through our lives for the next 3½ years, constantly amazed by our little boy. He talked at a young age—with full sentences by the time he was 18 months old. He asked questions at 2 years old, like "How did God make me?". We were thrilled at all he was learning.

One month before he turned 4, we put Eli into a preschool program in our local school district. It is a fabulous program that has a good child-teacher ratio (12 children to two teachers). There are children with delays and children that are developing typically. We were excited to have someone else answer his questions for a change. He was beginning to challenge us with all of his thoughts and ideas!

About 2 months into the school year, we began to see some changes in Eli. He was hyper when he got home from school—so much so that he couldn't calm down at all. He started to do some vocal stimming—making noises just to make noises. He started to hide when there were a lot of people around. He threw temper tantrums that lasted 30-45 minutes. He stopped sleeping through the night.

When I look back, I can see the signs that were there the whole time. The auditory sensitivities. The weaker muscle tone that contributed to the vestibular and proprioceptive issues. The shutting down in a crowd. It all led up to the chaos that erupted when he started preschool.

I recognized the signs and symptoms during that first preschool year and knew what I needed to do. I called my dear friend, who also happens to be a pediatric occupational therapist and the owner of her own business. I told her what I was seeing, and she asked me to bring Eli in for an evaluation.

I completed a sensory profile for her, and the evaluation began. At first she didn't see what I was seeing. He was incredibly cooperative. There were no tantrums; there was no hyperactivity. I pulled her aside and asked her to stop letting him have his way—to challenge him. I shared with her some of the things that he has a tendency to avoid. The moment she changed her methods, the entire evaluation changed. Like magic, the little boy I was so very worried about suddenly appeared. She got the full story.

She immediately went to work on putting together a treatment plan for him. He started therapy with her every week for 1 hour. She started by addressing his poor muscle tone and challenging his vestibular and proprioceptive systems. She introduced therapeutic listening to him and set us up with the program at home.

All of this went along fabulously for about 6 months. We were amazed by the outcomes. He was throwing fewer tantrums. He wasn't as hyper coming home from school. We seemed to be getting back to "normal."

Then something changed. Later on, we realized exactly how sensitive he is to extreme changes in weather. At that time, though, we went right back into mass chaos. Eli started having emotional meltdowns that lasted at least an hour whenever we did his therapeutic listening. His occupational therapist tried changing the CDs, introducing them at different times of the day, and trying everything she could think of. In the end, we decided as a team to just take a break. Almost immediately, things got better. He continued his weekly occupational therapy sessions, and his therapist went back to the drawing board.

Through all of this, we never noticed a change in Eli's sleeping habits. He was still waking throughout the night and had a lot of difficulty falling asleep. We introduced a weighted blanket, which seemed to address the issues he had with falling asleep. There was still no relief for the constant waking at night.

My partner and I racked our brains night after night, wondering what to do. We sat on couches across from each other, coming at the issue from every angle possible. The night the "light" came on was the night that I was coming at things from a developmental-specialist standpoint, and she was coming at it from a sleep-specialist standpoint. We realized that we needed to get an ear, nose, and throat physician involved, because it was likely that our little boy was not sleeping well owing to his snoring through the night. And, as my partner put it, there's nothing normal about a 4-year-old who snores.

We met with our pediatrician, who is so incredibly supportive. He didn't see a cause for concern but didn't want to deter us from checking into it further. We saw the ear, nose, and throat specialist, who said that our son's tonsils and adenoids needed to come out. We scheduled the surgery, and I'm happy to report that Eli has slept through the night ever since.

Meanwhile, our occupational therapist was still trying to figure our little Eli out. She started noticing other children in her practice who had similar concerns. She asked if he could join a group that she was thinking about putting together. I was open to anything that would help him, so I gladly said "yes."

Eli started attending this group every other week. It was amazing. Suddenly, his lack of progress had turned around again! He was being challenged by other children—children who didn't give in. Children who couldn't be persuaded by his clever little antics. Children who had minds of their own. This was the best thing to ever happen to him. He was suddenly able to function better in groups. And, when he did have difficulty, he was developing coping skills.

Eli was evaluated for special-education services last September. He did not qualify because "he's too smart to have an Individualized Education Program." SPD was not enough to be recognized as something that would impair his ability to be educated.

I started hearing the buzz from his occupational therapist that SPD was being looked at as a diagnosis to add to the *Diagnostic and Statistical Manual of Mental Disorders*. I wondered immediately what I could do. The possibility that the manual would recognize this diagnosis could open up a world of assistance for so many children. Perhaps that would mean that my intelligent little boy would qualify for the educational services he so desperately needs! That he would continue to be able to advance his knowledge and not be terribly hindered by the "out-of-control" aspects of his body and mind.

We are by no means out of the woods with SPD. Eli rhymes or does math problems when he's nervous. He acts out and throws tantrums when he's unsure about something. He still shuts down in crowds. He was the only child at T-ball who needed to move constantly when standing in the outfield. He has difficulty carrying on a conversation with someone who doesn't want to talk about his topic of choice (usually Lego Star Wars or his favorite Wii game). He chews on his clothes or toys when he is overwhelmed. But now we are armed, and so is he, with tactics to help him get through the day.

Heather Bergemann is the mom of two amazing boys, the oldest of which has pervasive developmental disorder—not otherwise specified, anxiety disorder, and SPD. She lives and works in Ohio and is a developmental specialist for children under the age of 3. She enjoys leisure time with her family at their family cabin in northern Michigan.

Can't Hardly Wait: The Story of Jax's Prematurity

by Ember Walker

When I was asked to write about having a premature child, I have to admit, I got a bit emotional. I can handle two special-needs children and talking about every aspect of their lives, their care, their struggles, their achievements, their joys and frustrations, and their futures. Ask me about having a baby a little over a month early, and I'm never prepared for how emotional I still get.

As a mother, you know that the longer your baby is inside your womb, the safer it is for him and the more likely it is that he will have a "normal" life. As a pregnant mom in general, though, no one wants to think about having a premature baby at all. So, do I tell you that there were about 543,000 babies born prematurely last year? That's about one in eight! A rise of 30% in the past 30 years! Do I tell you that the number-one killer of newborns is being born too early? Do I spout the total cost of caring for a premature baby and how it is 10 times that of caring for a healthy baby? Do I say that a premature baby comes with a higher-than-normal risk for cerebral palsy, gross- and fine-motor skill delays, and speech delays? Would these statistics mean anything?

Do I talk about how you blame yourself for not being able to keep your baby in your womb long enough to give him or her a fighting chance at coming out "normally"? How, even though I fell into the 40% of women who gave birth preterm for some unknown reason, I still can't stop wondering about what I could have done differently—had I just ingested more water, eaten fewer preservatives, exercised more, stressed less, or didn't lie on my back so much, would I have been able to keep my son in my womb full term?

There is really so much to say on the subject—but, all I can do is share my story.

The day that Jax was born, I'd not been feeling well. I'd had Braxton-Hicks contractions all weekend and was still trying to figure out how to prepare my oldest son for the big transition that was about to befall him. As a child who needs structure and transitional warnings and doesn't handle unexpected change well, this weighed heavily on my mind.

I had seen my obstetrician that afternoon for a regular checkup. He looked a bit alarmed and was concerned at how low the baby was positioned. With a little over a month to go, though, I was not worried and even laughed off his concerns and his attempt to give me his after-hours number. I mean, this was my second child—I would know if I was going to go into labor. I hadn't lost my mucous plug, my contractions were irregular and inconsistent, and, again, I still had a month to go.

At home, not even 5 minutes after I arrived, I was in the kitchen telling my mother how the appointment went and thanking her for watching my son, when it happened. I remember thinking I had wet myself—only I knew I didn't. A little over a month to go before my due date, my son was coming—and he was coming that day!

It's a weird thing to have happen. You're excited because it's happening, but then reality sets in, and you realize he's coming too soon. Then, every worry I'd suppressed from my first son and whether his issues would happen to this baby hit me like a bug on a windshield. I knew that whatever was about to happen, it was not going to be good.

Since I could not have a vaginal delivery, an emergency cesarean section was ordered. While I lay there on the table with the sheet pulled up so I couldn't see anything, I prayed and prayed and prayed. I begged and pleaded. I bargained. You name it, I did it. Then I waited to feel that final bit of pressure and the tug I knew would precede the delivery of my son.

When I felt it, I vaguely heard the congratulations of the doctors and nurses gathered around me. Instead, I focused on the tiny sound I prayed so desperately to hear. I waited and listened. I kept listening. I didn't hear it—no whimper, no cry—just silence. I remember barely being able to speak, asking, "Why isn't he crying?"

Thinking no one had heard me, I asked again—louder. Then louder. I kept asking, louder and louder each time. No one would really answer me. I looked at the anesthesiologist for some sign, and his averted gaze told me everything. I began to get hysterical, in spite of myself. I began begging and crying to know what was wrong.

The last thing I remember is my husband going over to our son. Apparently I was getting hysterical enough to raise my blood pressure and "bleed out," so they felt it best to give me something to relax. When I "came to" again, my son was in the neonatal intensive care unit (NICU), my husband was with him, and I was in a white room with a bunch of masked strangers who would tell me nothing of my son, except that he was being looked after in the NICU.

Knowing the drill, when I awoke in recovery, the first thing I did was work on moving my toes, then my feet, then my legs, and so on. I knew there was no way that they would let me see my son if I couldn't move.

Having a cesarean section is a weird experience, but—throw in having a premature baby in the NICU—and it becomes even more numbing. With both of those experiences, you are robbed of the basic thing every mother wants, even deserves: the right to hold your child after birth. I know that you do get to eventually, but, the time when you most want to, most need to, you're not allowed to. This is something that, to this day, still hurts.

When I was finally able to "see" my son in the NICU, it was 1 AM. They wheeled me in and there he was, in the dimly lit NICU, behind a wall of plastic. A little hole was opened up for me to be able to reach in and touch him. To just touch a leg…just a leg!

I remember a nurse almost running over to me to actually stop me from touching him. I was horrified, but she explained that he was super-sensitive to touch, to movement, and to light, and that any "disruption" to his status quo was very upsetting to him. His oxygen and carbon dioxide stats would change, and he'd become upset. So, she asked me to be very gentle. I think that is the thing that hurt the worst—this nurse I didn't know, who was a stranger, really, knew more about my son than I did. I remember just crying.

After a few days of fighting for his life, my son's oxygen levels stabilized enough that they removed him from the Isolette and put him into a normal crib in the NICU. I got to hold him for the first time that day. I remember unwrapping him and putting him up against my chest, feeling his warmth and listening to him breathe. His softness against me was the most reassuring thing I'd felt in a long time. I quite literally counted his tiny toes and looked at his premature fingers, which were very skeleton-like. I looked at his button nose and his gummy little mouth. He was a big baby for a preemie, but it was very easy to see that he was premature. Every part of him was almost miniature in relation to what it should've been. I cried then, thinking of what could've happened, at how my body wouldn't keep him inside, safe and warm. I cried at all the "what ifs," knowing what a premature birth could mean long-term. The thought of it all was almost overwhelming. I do know the one thing I was sure of that day—that no matter what, he would be loved and cherished, just as we loved and cherished his big brother.

Jax, now 2 years old, is healthy for the most part. He is intolerant to milk and soy protein, something he shares in common with a lot of other babies, as well as his big brother. He has childhood apraxia of speech, and, like his big brother, he has SPD. To simply look at him, though, you'd never know it. He is one of the happiest toddlers I've ever seen! You can tell he was born prematurely because he lags behind his peers in almost everything, from gross- and fine-motor skills to just "catching on" sometimes. His size tells another story, though. He is twice the size and height of a normal 2-year-old! It's hard to believe he was premature. He has come with his own unique sets of issues and challenges, but, at every turn, his sheer determination and pure joy at reaching his milestones affects us in so many positive ways.

The truth is, I know that we are very lucky—even blessed. Our story could've gone much worse, as with so many families I've heard from over the years. There are some whose babies never made it, and some whose children are still at the hospital years (yes, years) later. Some premature children are wheelchair bound and have cerebral palsy. Those families, and their stories, I will never forget. It is a reminder of how truly blessed we are.

Ember Walker is a thirty-something mother of two special-needs boys and runs an online support group for mothers of children with Tourette syndrome. She is an advocate for SPD, and you can find her blogging at My Two Hearts: janddsmom.blogspot.com.

JT's Story

by Laura Petersen

My son JT was born 9 weeks early. He had a very rough start, but considering that we were told he would only live for about an hour, I think it has gone incredibly well!

We were told about 6 weeks prior to this (about 25 weeks into the pregnancy) that our son had "posterior urethral valves." This blocks the bladder from being able to empty, so our son's bladder was over full-capacity by the time they caught it. They did a bladder tap (performed like an amniocentesis) on my son several times during that 6 weeks to clear the urine before he was born. The reason for the dire outlook was the possible irreversible damage to his kidneys. The doctors expected full kidney failure very shortly after he was born.

He was born at 5 lbs 8 oz, but after he was completely drained of urine, his lowest weight was 3 lbs 15 oz. He continued to grow and gain some weight for the 8 weeks he was in the hospital.

Looking back, there were signs of irregularities in his behavior, but at the time, I just thought he was a very good baby. He would not cry at times that you would expect him to, like when getting shots and when he was hungry. He cried very little during several procedures that he had.

We did the normal birth-to-3 follow-ups for preemies, but other than some muscle weakness, not much was noted. It wasn't until he was about 4 years old that things started getting difficult.

The problem for us at the time was that there were several factors going on that at least partially explained the issues. His dad and I had split up and were getting divorced. We had moved two times. He had lost his best friend (since they had been in the neonatal intensive care unit together as babies) to cancer. It was a hard year, so the fact that he was having separation anxiety and meltdowns didn't seem to unexpected…at first.

I asked the school district to come and test him before kindergarten, so we would know what we were up against. They did find that he had problems with handling more than one task at a time. They asked me to keep my voice calm and ask him to do one task at a time. This did seem to help tremendously in my dealings with him, but trying to explain it to any caretakers was very difficult. They always said that he was just willfully disobeying.

He was placed in developmental kindergarten and his homeschool kindergarten class. He was bussed to the different schools and then back to daycare. This worked well for the kindergarten year, and then he graduated out of developmental kindergarten at the end of the year.

The following year, things went bad quickly. It was apparent that not only was his first-grade teacher not a good fit, but his anxiety had gone through the roof and I didn't know why. Just getting him to go to school was difficult, then getting him out of the car, then getting him to class... well, you see where this is going. Not to mention *keeping* him in class. The two worst examples I have of his school day was the day he pushed a child into a brick wall because the child had "hit" him (the child had actually just bumped up against him) and the day he actually left the school grounds... he was 6 years old! He told the principal that he was going home. We lived about 3 miles away.

That was the scariest day of my life—the day I realized he wasn't safe anymore. I always watched my kids closely, but JT needed to be watched even closer. His thought process was different, and his fear threshold was different. Things were just different, and I didn't understand why! (I found out later that these things that scared me so badly ended up being great assets when he got a little older.)

I went to doctor after doctor, trying to get help. I finally made an appointment with a physician who told me that JT did not have autism but he had "all the flavors of it." This meant that although he did not meet the criteria for autism, like lack of imaginary play, he did have the rigid thinking (no inferences and or joking or sarcasm) and an inability to transition from one activity to another. He was very literal and usually took everything you said seriously. He didn't understand words with double meanings. For example, when people used the word "but" in a sentence, it confused him because he only knew the word "butt" as his backside. If you think about it, you can start to understand why school was not a friendly place for my 6-year-old.

The physician we saw recommended that I take JT to a neurological developmental center at the children's hospital. Things have changed greatly at that hospital concerning sensory issues in the past 8 years, but back then, it wasn't a good fit for us. They gave me a very long list of things to try and people to see—sleep studies, nutritionists, behavioral specialists, and physical therapists. We did everything on the list with no luck, except for physical therapy. That was the last thing I tried because I couldn't see how physical therapy was going to help with the problems JT was having at school. How wrong I was!

When we arrived at the physical therapist's office, we went in and she asked a few questions while she played with JT. I knew very quickly that the questions she was asking were some that no one else had asked. I got anxious very quickly, because I started to realize that she "got him." She understood him. Like, in a way that I didn't and no one else had. I wanted to know what she knew, and I wanted to know it *now!* I probably seemed a little crazy to her that day, but she was very professional and answered any questions that she could.

She then asked me to fill out a few questionnaires while she played with JT. In the process, I also found out that he had very poor muscle tone in his legs, and that, yes, he did need physical therapy! Go figure. But, more importantly, he scored very high on *all* of the sensory question-naires that they gave me. She was going to put him at the top of the list to receive occupational therapy with their best therapist (OK, that might just be my opinion) as soon as possible. In the meantime, we could continue to see her, and she would incorporate sensory activities into his physical therapy. We were so lucky! I have known people since that have had to wait 6 months just to be evaluated. We were in and evaluated and seeing a therapist within a couple of weeks. (But, it had been 2 years now since this all began.)

We found out that his sensitivity to sounds and light and food and smells was completely overwhelming him. It is really hard to focus on anything when your senses are that out of control. I asked him one day to close his eyes and tell me everything that he could hear. He gave me a list of things, and most of them I wouldn't have heard right off the bat. I could hear them when he brought my attention to them, but not before that. The thing that really opened my eyes was after he got done listing the things he could hear—and he started listing all the things he could smell. I hadn't even considered that being a problem in the classroom. Then, when you think about visual sensitivities…well, if you're anything like me, your anxiety level is probably going up just reading this. Imagine being 6 years old in a classroom with all of this sensory overload going on, and you are being asked to pay attention!

I have been very fortunate since then that JT continued to improve. School has continued to be difficult for him, but we have worked hard with the schools to get them to understand why his meltdowns happen. In the beginning, they would say, "Well what if he takes advantage of it?" in response to a proposed accommodation. My answer would be, "Can we try it and see if it helps, and *then* find out if he tries to take advantage?" He never did. At one point, I just asked if he could have a safe place to go to, in the resource room, when he was having a hard time. They started with 10 minutes, three times a day, at specific times. I then asked them to give him three times a day whenever he needed it. He rarely used it after that. He just needed to know that there was somewhere safe he could go, and that alone lessened his anxiety enough to be able to get through the day. That safe spot morphed into just being able to go to the resource room when he was having a hard time. It became his safe place. He would take his homework and just go in there to get it done.

In my experience, kids with sensory issues really do just need to feel safe, and then they can get on with learning. If they can't get to feeling safe, they aren't ever going to be able to reach their true potential. My favorite saying that has come out of all of this is that "Kids will learn if they can." If they can't, it is our job as adults to figure out why!

I asked so many questions about him being a preemie and about the amount of stress he had been under. Did these factors cause his sensory issues, or was it the other way around? I wanted answers, and unfortunately, I could get opinions but not true answers. It has been very frustrating. As parents, we just need to know what we can do, and we will do it. Our problem was that I couldn't even find out what to do for a very long time. During that time, people seemed to want to blame me and my child for his behavior.

I still don't know whether JT would still have sensory issues had he not been a preemie, but I do know that a large percentage of preemies have them. To what extent, and if those sensory issues impede their ability to live life—those are the unanswered questions.

Today, I have a happy, healthy 14-year-old. In the first quarter of 8th grade, he was on the honor roll! After that, he started pushing back, saying that he didn't want any of his accommodations and that he just wanted to be like the other kids. His grades dropped almost immediately. I think he finally understands that the accommodations are there to help him and not just to point him out to the other kids as being different.

He and I had a conversation the other night after watching the TV show "Parenthood." The boy in the show had just received a diagnosis of Asperger syndrome—and his parents had not told him. My son said, "Why didn't he know?" I replied that his parents were trying to protect him. My son was very confused. He didn't understand how not telling a child about his own diagnosis was protecting him. I found that very telling. We need to be honest with our kids. They are very intelligent, and they deserve to know what they are dealing with.

My son has always been very proud of having SPD and will tell you all the great parts of having this disorder. He is very strong and can hear and see things that others don't. It is all about looking on the bright side of things.

To any parents who are just starting this journey, always remember that it *will* get better!

Laura Petersen has three kids and lives in the Seattle area. She is passionate about helping other parents of children with SPD, and if she is lucky enough to get some free time, she enjoys watching football and NASCAR.

Chapter 8

Infertility

The stories of these women and their journeys to become mothers are truly moving. Most of us take for granted the ability to get pregnant and carry a baby to full term. Not these women.

These moms endured a long journey of doctors, specialists, medications, and emotional struggles long before they had a child with SPD. Experiencing the ups and downs of failed attempts to get pregnant, multiple miscarriages, and fragile pregnancies, resulting often in weeks upon weeks of bed rest—these are stories that go beyond the typical.

For those of you who have followed in these footsteps, or are doing so right now, you will immediately connect to the pain and struggle that these women went through to find their way to motherhood. Those that contributed to this section were brave enough to discuss that pain and the difficulty of raising a sensational child in the hopes of connecting with other families who are going through the same thing.

And for that, I thank them.

From Infertility to SPD—Our Journey in the Trenches of Intervention

by Kristin M. Wentz-Krumwiede

Long before I was ready to become a mom, I knew that it was going to be a struggle. When I was 15, I got cancer, and one of the side effects of the treatment was infertility.

I knew that infertility would affect not only me, but my future spouse, as well. When I entered into my first serious adult relationship, it was very clear to me that he would not be able to handle not having biological children…and as much as I cared about him, I knew that not having children would eventually tear us apart.

When I started dating again after the pain of ending that previous relationship, I was very up-front with my possible infertility issues sooner in the relationship than I probably would have been, but only because I didn't want to "waste anyone's time." I knew from experience that some men could handle my circumstances and that some could not.

My husband, Chad, was one of those that could handle it. I will never forget him saying to me, "I am OK with possibly never being a dad. What I am not OK with is possibly not being with you." That is the moment when I knew he was kind of amazing.

We started trying to have a family as soon as we were married. Because of our ages (I was 21 and he was 25), we knew that the medical community was going to make us follow all the unspoken rules when it came to trying to conceive. We tried month after month with no success. We did become pregnant twice, but sadly, both of those pregnancies ended in miscarriages.

Finally, we were able to see a specialist. After meeting with the doctor and divulging our medical histories, several tests were run on both me and my husband. We learned that I had polycystic ovarian syndrome, and I was prescribed medications to help regulate my hormones. A month later, we learned we were pregnant again, and this time, because of the blood work that had been performed at the beginning of my cycle, the doctors knew that I'd need additional medications throughout my pregnancy to remain pregnant. In late November, we welcomed our daughter, Delainey, who was born early but healthy. We were over the moon…and we knew that we wanted more children as soon as possible. Because I was nursing Delainey, we were limited with just how far we could go with the help of medications, so we agreed to try naturally until Delainey was a year old. We tried for those 12 months, and each month ended in heartbreak. Sometimes it was harder than others because we were able to get pregnant—we just weren't able to stay pregnant.

Once we were able to begin using medications to assist in ovulation, we did not get pregnant again, so our doctors asked us to try stronger medications. In April of that year, we began the cycle with this new medication. On May 11, we learned that we were pregnant, and on June 6, we learned that we were in fact expecting twins.

It was a relatively normal pregnancy, with only a few of your typical "multiples" pregnancy problems. The pregnancy continued with few real complications until the 34th week, when I became very ill. Our daughters, Shelby and Avery, were born at 34 weeks' gestation and spent 11 days in the neonatal intensive care unit.

Our girls came home, and our life was good. We adjusted to the life of having three children aged 2 and under. We knew that as much as we would love to welcome more children into our family, we also wanted to be the best parents to the ones we had, so we decided to stop pursuing infertility treatments. If we were able to get pregnant naturally—awesome. If not, we were OK with that, too.

We struggled, but we thought we were experiencing typical "multiples" struggles. Avery had acid reflux and constant ear infections. Shelby had difficulties eating, sleeping, and growing. Shelby was constantly "on edge" and was a roller coaster kind of baby. She was either super happy and involved or distant and withdrawn; there was no happy medium for her. She would startle at the slightest noise and cry with the smallest change of light. She loved constant motion, and if she could have, she would have lived in our infant swing. Thank goodness for the invention of plug-in swings, or we would have gone broke buying batteries! Shelby struggled with sleep, and even at only 3 months of age, she had to be swaddled tightly so she wouldn't startle herself awake.

Shelby struggled with meeting her milestones. At 4 months old, she was still having trouble holding up her head and hadn't begun to babble or coo as her sister had. I knew that the girls were different individuals and would develop at their own pace and on their own time, but it was hard not to compare Shelby to other babies her age…especially her sister.

We were lucky that our hospital had put us in contact with a program for early intervention in our town. Every few months, a person would come and reevaluate the girls. Each time, Shelby would score "low" but not low enough to qualify for services. Avery began rolling at 9 weeks, and Shelby stayed put. Avery began crawling at 6 months…and Shelby stayed put.

At the girls' 6-month visit with their pediatrician, I asked for an occupational- and/or physical-therapy screening. Both of the girls were behind in their fine- and gross-motor–skill development…but Shelby more so than Avery. The therapists were confused by how Shelby, a child with such "loose" muscles and tendons, could be so tense and tight. At 10 months of age, Avery began to walk. Shelby had just begun to roll. At 12 months, Avery was speaking in three-word sentences, and Shelby had just begun to babble.

The girls were in therapy for almost 6 months. They were both discharged from therapy—Avery had met all of her goals, and Shelby was no longer "far enough" behind to qualify for services any longer. This was the first time I was hit by the "she's behind, but not behind enough" phenomenon. My husband and I figured that we could do for her what others couldn't. We began working with her even more at home on our own, and just days after her first birthday, she crawled for the first time.

At the girls' 12-month visit with their pediatrician, I expressed my concerns with Shelby's delays and both the girls' lack of growth. Our pediatrician was on board for some testing, and—trust me—we tested everything. We were assured that both of our girls were perfectly healthy, and that there was no medical, genetic, or metabolic reason that they were both so small (both weighed less than 15 lbs at 1 year of age), nor was there a "reason" for Shelby's lack of development in other areas.

After this round of tests, my husband said that maybe I was looking for something that wasn't there. We both knew that Shelby did things in her own time, when she was ready to do them. So, we relaxed a bit and just did our own versions of therapy at home. We tried to help her along and build her muscles and her strength. We busted our butts working with her, but we were able to make it fun for our other children, too.

While in the trenches of our challenges with Shelby, we learned that we were pregnant again. We couldn't have been happier…we also couldn't have been more confused and torn. We still did not know what was going on with Shelby, and now we were going to have four children 4 years of age and under. It took a while to adjust to this…but by the time Brody joined our family in December, we knew we could handle it.

It was during a screening with Brody through the early-intervention program that it became obvious that Shelby may again need more therapy. Brody had begun to do things that Shelby couldn't…and he was a full 2 years younger than she was. We asked for another evaluation at our hospital, since the early-intervention examiner again found no need for therapy for Shelby. We were quickly approved for therapy.

It was during her second stint in the land of constant occupational- and physical-therapy visits that I started searching the Internet for more information. I have always been a person who needs to know the "why" of things. In the early hours of the morning, I sat at the computer and typed all of Shelby's "quirks" into the search engine—hypotonia, tactile defensiveness, fine-motor delays, oral sensitivities, sensory-seeking, high energy and lethargy, feeding issues, and so on. When I hit the search button, a Web site came up for the Sensory Processing Disorder Resource Guide.

I read through the information and went through the symptoms checklist. I must have spent hours on that site. It was like the heavens opened, trumpets played, and the angels began to sing…I had finally found out what was "wrong" with my little girl. I printed off all the material I had found. I scoured the Internet and bookstores looking for information, all of it explaining Shelby more and more.

I gathered up all the information I had found and brought it to our next occupational therapy visit. I handed it to the therapist and said, "This is Shelby...now let's finally help her." Our amazing occupational therapist and our pediatric rehab/physical medicine doctor agreed with us completely. We all hit the books. We learned together. We shared information, and we put our heads together to set a "treatment" plan in motion.

Shelby was finally assigned a diagnosis of SPD when she was 3 years old. We have been on the bumpy ride of this disorder ever since. We have learned from others, and others have learned from us. Our occupational therapists have been the backbone of our treatment schedules and planning, and without them, we would be completely lost in this journey.

Shelby has come so far, but I'll be honest—it's still a challenge. We are still constantly living the one-step-forward, two-steps-back lifestyle, but we have come to celebrate the times we move forward and don't worry about the steps back, because we know that in the end, there will always be another step forward. Shelby is going to be fine, she's going to be great... because Shelby is sensational, and we are one sensational family.

Kristin M. Wentz-Krumwiede and her husband, Chad, are parents to four amazing children—daughters Delainey (age 7), Shelby (age 5), and Avery (age 5), and son Brody (age 3). They reside in Bismarck, North Dakota. In addition to being a stay-at-home mom, Kristin is also a full-time college student, majoring in social work and psychology. She is very active in local groups, such as the North Dakota Autism Connection and the March of Dimes, and is president of her local MOMS Club International Chapter. Since her daughter Shelby's diagnosis of SPD at age 3, Kristin has become dedicated to educating people and families about SPD.

From "Cyster" to "Sensational"

by Deanna Pace

"If you just relax, it will happen." "Have you thought of adopting?" These phrases made me cringe every time I explained our struggle to conceive. Seven months after we were married, my husband and I started trying to get pregnant. Not long afterward, I underwent treatment to remove precancerous cells found during a regular "Pap" test. Irregular periods and hair growth, weight issues, skin issues, and episodes of hypoglycemia led me to an endocrinologist, who diagnosed polycystic ovarian syndrome. The syndrome interferes with hormones and can cause cysts on your ovaries, making it difficult to ovulate. Once I had a name for my condition, I began researching it in my quest to find treatment. I discovered an online community, a "cysterhood" of women who understood what I was going through. I became a "cyster" and found support and comfort when my husband and I weren't able to get pregnant on our own. We learned a whole new language, an alphabet soup of acronyms for the infertile—HSG (hysterosalpingogram), SA (semen analysis), IUI (intrauterine insemination), and IVF (in vitro fertilization). Further testing revealed that I had a blocked fallopian tube and that my husband had some issues, as well. Our combined conditions meant that it would be next to impossible for us to have a child without medical intervention.

Worn out from tests and bad news, we stopped our intense efforts to have a child. But, I continued to yearn for a child of my own. Every time someone I knew got pregnant, the heartache came back. Every baby shower was another reminder of our failure to fulfill a basic biological function. Every month I continued to hope that by some miracle, I would get pregnant, only to be disappointed time and again.

And then, more than 8 years later, I got pregnant. To say that we were shocked was an understatement. But the shock was quickly replaced by excitement and then worry. I began bleeding on and off for several weeks. An ultrasound showed the placenta implanted close to my cervix, a condition known as placenta previa. As the baby grew, the placenta moved away from my cervix, and we began to relax. My husband and I began working on decorating the nursery, buying furniture, and picking out paint colors and toys. Then, at 26 weeks, I felt a soreness in my stomach, like I had done about 200 crunches in a row. I brought it up at my next doctor visit. An exam and another ultrasound revealed that my cervix had dilated and effaced, and I was having contractions. The procedure they used to remove the precancerous cells in my cervix 8 years before had left it weakened and unable to support the weight of the baby. I was dispatched from our local hospital by ambulance to another facility that had a neonatal intensive care unit. I spent a week on medication and in the Trendelenburg position (with my feet above my chest) to stop the labor. After another week of monitoring, I was allowed to go home, but I had to remain on strict bed rest.

For the next 8 weeks, it was just me and my little girl, hanging out for most of the day. I enjoyed her regular movement and kicks. Keeping track of her and talking to her helped pass the time. I was allowed out of the house once a week to travel 40 minutes to the hospital for more monitoring and checkups. When I started having contractions, I drank more water in case they were caused by dehydration, and then laid on my left side. Each week of bed rest was a step toward the goal of keeping the baby cooking until 36 weeks, the earliest I could deliver at the hospital closest to home. Exactly 8 weeks later, at 36 weeks, I went into labor. It was long and difficult and ended in an emergency cesarean section. Exhausted and worn out, I was still thrilled to meet my little girl—my own miracle—who had kept me on my toes from conception, it seemed. She was perfect, with 10 tiny fingers and toes and a head full of dark hair. My husband and I were over the moon for her.

After we got home from the hospital, life with our little miracle got rough. Any attempts to swaddle her were a nightmare. She struggled and cried until she got herself out of the blanket. She would only sleep if she was being held or was right next to me. Naps were infrequent and short. The slightest noise would wake her. We tried every trick in every book to get her to sleep on her own and stay asleep. I spent 2 months in a daze before I finally gave up and let her come into our bed with us, because that was the only way I could get any rest.

She wanted to nurse very frequently, and when she had a growth spurt, it was even more challenging. As much as she liked to nurse, she refused any kind of pacifier. When I returned to work, she would only take one type of bottle. She ate well at daycare, yet continued to wake and nurse multiple times throughout the night. During the day, she was happiest if I was right next to her or holding her. She protested at being left to play on her own for even a few minutes. She didn't like the swing my mother gave us. My best friend and I went to the store and tested out every model of swing they had before we finally found one she tolerated for more than a minute or two.

When she started walking, the real fun began. She spent most of the day running, moving from activity to activity. She was fearless and unafraid. When she wasn't climbing, running, or crawling around and under anything she could, she insisted on being held. She would wriggle, turn, kick, and climb in our laps and refuse to get down.

When I asked for advice on her behavior, I heard, "It's her age, she will grow out of it." "All toddlers do that." "She just has her own quirks." And because I had never spent a lot of time around other children her age and had not seen her interact with other kids for long periods of time, I didn't realize just how different she was.

At 2 years of age, she wasn't talking well, and we were referred for early intervention. During the intake process, the caseworker suggested testing by an occupational therapist for possible "sensory issues." Testing revealed she did have some delays in her speech and fine- and gross-motor skills, but not enough to warrant receipt of services. They encouraged us to call if she didn't improve in her speech or had other delays in her development.

When our daughter was almost 4, I called to have her tested again for speech issues. She had developed a stutter and was very difficult to understand. Because she was now old enough for preschool, we were referred to our local school district. A date was set for her to be evaluated by a speech pathologist and school psychologist. This time, there was no denying her need for speech therapy. The psychologist recommended testing for "sensory issues" again. So, another evaluation was set up with an occupational therapist. At that session, I found out that our daughter had SPD. Specifically, she was a sensory seeker. And so we began to learn another new language, another alphabet soup of conditions and treatments, such as sensory diet, SMD (sensory modulation disorder), SS (sensory seeking), IEP (Individualized Education Program), and LRE (least restrictive environment). Again, I began doing whatever I could to help treat her symptoms. I went online and discovered a community—a "sensory network"—filled with parents of "sensational" kids like mine.

Since we began working with her therapists and teachers at Head Start, we have seen great improvement in our daughter. Her fine-motor skills are coming along nicely, and her speech is vastly improved. But we still struggle. It's a challenge to get her to be able to sit for more than 5 minutes, much less chew her food and not stuff her mouth during meals. At school, she has difficulty with following directions and completing a task if there are any other children around. She can't seem to focus, and her eyes are constantly moving, tracking for what is going on and unable to filter out the things around her.

Although she now starts out each night in her own bed, sleep remains elusive. On a good night, our daughter will fall asleep in less than an hour and only wake once. On a bad night, it can take 2 to 3 hours to get her to fall asleep, only to have her awaken multiple times. There are days when I wonder if the few glasses of wine I drank before I knew I was pregnant caused this. I wonder if treatments to stop preterm labor had an effect, or if the infection in my amniotic fluid was to blame. I question if holding her skin-to-skin immediately after birth would have helped rewire her brain. Maybe I should have pushed harder to carry her to term instead of being thankful that the hardship was over at 36 weeks. I wonder, and worry, and feel guilt. But then, I see my little girl smile at me. I feel her squeeze me tight. I hear her say she loves me. And I am thankful for this gift and my new identity as a "sensational" mom.

Deanna Pace lives in central New York with her husband, daughter, and the family cat. Her adventures as the mom of a "sensational" superstar means that life is never boring! She has a BA in secondary education and worked in the history-museum world for more than 12 years before switching careers and becoming a certified lactation counselor.

Infertility and SPD

by Y'vonne Marie Ormond

My journey with infertility started over a decade ago, when I was in my mid-20s. I remember fondly the day I was sitting in a doctor's office after being told that I needed to accept the fact I may never have children. That was *not okay!* Five doctors, multiple procedures, and two miscarriages later, I gave birth to my first son, Aidan, a month prior to my 30th birthday. *Success!*

My second journey into fertility was even harder. I was a bit older, and the age gap between my boys was 4½ years. I thought that the process would be easier the second time around, but it was much harder. This is the journey that led us down the path of SPD. My story will discuss how our infertility led to finding out that Roan had SPD and what I believe the connection to be between the two.

When we decided to get pregnant with our second son, Roan, we used the familiar route of the same doctor and treatments as before, but I had challenges getting pregnant. When I did become pregnant, I ended up miscarrying. This was so difficult for me to handle. The process was talking a toll on my heart and my body. The doctor and methods that were used to get pregnant with my first son, Aidan, just weren't working, so I made a hard decision to switch doctors. I sought out the best clinic I could find in San Diego County and went for a consultation.

The initial consultation process at the fertility clinic was interesting. It was much different than seeing a doctor that dealt with infertility issues in an obstetric practice. It was like a business. They brought you in, talked about their practice, drew on the white board as they explained their "business model," and handed you a bunch of brochures and paperwork to read. They weren't concerned about your past history, because they were going to figure out what the issues were and proceed straight to the appropriate treatment plan. It's their business model, and they do this very successfully, as is evident by the pictures of newborns posted all over the office walls, accompanied by letters from successful patients.

The doctor walked through my medical history and talked to me about my "challenges." A lot of notes were taken. The doctor then explained what to expect as part of the process and went through the materials in the pamphlets he handed out earlier. The next steps were to sign their waiver, saying I "understand that 20% of babies are born with some kind of issues, problems, or birth defects, due to the unnatural intervention of the creation of the fetus" or something to that effect. This made me stop in my tracks and almost walk out of the clinic. Thinking back now, I wonder if this "unnatural intervention" could be related to my son developing sensory issues and SPD. Lastly, they gave me a list of tests to be undertaken by both me and my husband.

Most of the tests were done on me, since I was clearly the one with the issue, based on my medical history. However, my husband did have to do the dreaded semen analysis. He was such a good sport, though, as he'd been through this before. After all the results came back, they talked to me about our issues, and we were given a treatment plan. I was going to start immediately with progesterone suppositories, blood monitoring every few days, fertility drug injections, human chorionic gonadotropin injections, and intrauterine insemination. We crossed our fingers for a hopeful pregnancy.

During my first cycle, I produced 21 healthy-looking follicles. Follicles are what are produced that may or may not turn into eggs. They have to mature in size to 18 or 30 mm to become a successful, possible ripe egg that the sperm can enter. I ended up having only three. I didn't get pregnant this cycle.

During my second cycle, I had produced eight healthy-looking follicles. I ended up having only two. I didn't get pregnant this cycle, either.

In my third cycle, I produced one healthy-looking follicle that resulted in one healthy egg. I cried and cried that month, believing I would not get pregnant. There was no way. This was the last month we would be doing intrauterine insemination, and we would then move on to in vitro fertilization, which is a much more intrusive and difficult procedure, where they would have to physically remove the eggs from my body.

I got the dreaded monthly call while I was at work. I picked up the phone, and the woman on the other end asked me if I was sitting down. I said I already knew what she was going to tell me—and she said, "Great, then you already know you're *pregnant* then!" I screamed with joy. It was a miracle! My one miraculous follicle had turned into a little baby.

The next 9½ months were long and not enjoyable. This was not surprising, because my first pregnancy had been very hard, as well. I had a difficult pregnancy, ridden with preterm labor since my 13th week (I was taking terbutaline), slight diabetes, placenta previa, and bed rest. I went on maternity leave from work 2 full months early, on disability for complete bed rest, until Roan arrived.

I underwent a scheduled cesarean section on November 28, 10 days prior to my due date because of the placement of my placenta. I could not have a natural birth, as I had hoped. Roan was 7 lbs 5 oz and was 19 inches long, with an Apgar score of 9/9 (generally normal). He was a healthy little guy.

Roan was a beautiful baby, and we were so happy to have him. It was so refreshing to have a "healthy" baby, since our first son Aidan had so many health challenges in his first 4½ years of life. We were blessed with and welcomed an easier child. Little did we know that our life was about to be turned upside down in a different way.

From the time we brought Roan home from the hospital, he never liked to be swaddled in a blanket. He would find his way out of it quickly. He'd kick all his blankets off at night, even in the freezing cold. I'd have to layer his clothes and put him in blanket sleepers to keep him warm at night in the winter.

Roan didn't meet his first milestone of rolling over at 4 months or even at 6 months, like his brother Aidan did. We didn't think too much of it, because he was a very chunky baby. We thought, "Oh, he'll do it in time…let's not compare him to his brother. He's much chunkier, and his brother was much more advanced at everything." By the time 6 months came around, Roan wasn't rolling, sitting up, crawling, pulling up, walking, or even doing much on his own. He would sit if we put him in a sitting position; however, he fell over if he giggled or tried to reach for something. He also wasn't cooing or making any noises. As a mommy, my intuition started to kick in that something wasn't right.

I took my concerns to Roan's pediatrician, and he agreed that there was an issue. Roan had poor muscle tone in his trunk area and poor motor-planning skills. He was referred to a physical therapist and started therapy immediately. He began sitting, rolling, pulling up, kneeling, and walking by the time he was 13 months old.

As I reflect back, based on what I know now, this was really when his SPD journey began. However, I think he started exhibiting symptoms pretty early on as an infant, judging by the way he disliked swaddling and overstimulation from touch and sounds.

Between 1 and 2 years of age, Roan struggled with motor-planning and coordination skills. He was very clumsy, fell a lot, and had difficulties with what was going on in the space around him. His occupational therapist referred to it as "special awareness." He had good balance but lacked awareness of how close or far away objects were from him. This resulted in many little accidents. In addition, his speech and hearing seemed obsolete. We used sign language with him, but he would not speak or babble.

At Roan's 2-year checkup, his pediatrician referred us to see a speech therapist. The waiting list for an assessment was 6-8 months. So, I called our local state-run services center and had him assessed in the spring, after his winter birthday. They observed that he had some speech, auditory, and sensory issues, but he fell just below the 40% threshold to be able to utilize their services. What they did do was arm us with a lot of great information and places where we could seek private care, and they put us on the 3-month prevention plan where they follow up every quarter until his 3rd birthday. The next couple of times they met with us, they identified the same things. However, right before his 3rd birthday, they told us he should really see an occupational therapist, and they believed he had something called "SPD". I had never heard of this.

Roan is a little over 3 years old now and has been in therapy for 8 months (speech and occupational). I'd say that he is severely affected by SPD and that there is possibly something not yet diagnosed that we have yet to discover. He demonstrates attributes of all three types of SPD. We have some big things to figure out with upcoming physiological testing in the next few months.

When I found out Roan had SPD, I went searching for many answers. I needed to understand what it was. How did he get this disorder? What did I do wrong? I found some very interesting connections as I looked at my own story and his, and I'd like to highlight them here:

What I believe *may* be some of the causes of SPD for us:

- Problems with my placenta during pregnancy
- My extreme stress levels when pregnant
- The fertility procedures we underwent to get pregnant

- The terbutaline I took to reduce preterm labor contractions

While nobody really knows for sure what factors lead to developing SPD, I hope that my story brings some kind of awareness or education or makes your heart feel "familiar" in some way. I will continue to advocate for my son and others with special needs. My husband and I will also continue to try to find out what we can do to help make his life healthier and to provide a more balanced emotional environment for him as he grows and discovers his own unique strengths.

Y'vonne Marie Ormond is a full-time mom who balances life with her two young sons and working in the corporate world. She has been married to her husband Ned for over a decade. They live in San Diego and enjoy advocating for their son's individual needs (Aidan has asthma, allergies, and anaphylaxis, and Roan has SPD) and spending quality time with their family.

Hopes, Dreams, Infertility, Polycystic Ovarian Syndrome, and SPD

by Joanne Wells

I had been told at an early age that I needed to be "more careful" than others, as my biological mother was 16 when she gave me up for adoption. So you can imagine the thoughts engrained in me at an early age that I would obviously *never* have any issues when I finally wanted to become pregnant.

My adoptive sisters are a bit older than me, and I was raised around many nieces and nephews that were more like brothers and sisters because of our closeness in age. I was an aunt when I was 2 years old! I saw how much work raising a child was at an early age, and I didn't think I was ready for all it entailed. I also had a degree in elementary and special education (which would come in handy later in life!) and dealt with other people's children 8 hours a day. So, I knew that I wanted to wait until I was 30 to begin to have children.

When I turned 30 and decided to stop taking birth control, I was *shocked* that I didn't get a period for over a year. A whole year! After the first few months, I went to my gynecologist's office, demanding answers and medicine to help me along. I was told, "Honey, nothing's wrong with you. It just takes time." Well, I know that making a baby can take time for some, but I remembered what my mom always used to say. "You need to be more careful than others, dear." I now know this was just her silly attempt to keep me scared out of my mind about getting pregnant at a young age. I have since found out that my birth mother was 20, not 16. Still young—but not 16.

When my doctor told me it would just take time, I couldn't help but wonder if she had the whole picture. I knew things would take time, but I wasn't even getting a period! How could I get pregnant if I couldn't even tell when the beginning of a cycle was? To this day, I still laugh when I hear someone say, "Oh, I have *no* idea how I got pregnant!" or, my favorite, "I'm always like clockwork—28 days!" I faithfully did *everything* the doctor told me to do and began clomiphene treatments. In fact, I took so much clomiphene that it did the reverse of what it should have! My body completely shut down. And the only answer my doctor offered was, "Keep trying—it takes time."

A dear friend of mine finally pulled me aside after a year and asked me if I had ever thought I might have what she had—polycystic ovarian syndrome (PCOS). Me? Poly what? No (shaking my head). My biological mom had given birth to me at 16 (or so I thought), and what in the world is PCOS?

I gathered up enough courage to approach my doctor and just ask. She didn't like that! But, she did send me for an ultrasound to check. And, the results indicated that I didn't have it. So I quizzed her again at my next appointment. By this time, I had armed myself with information on PCOS. I had a lot of the symptoms. She got angry and asked me why I thought I had it. I told her the reasons, and she got angrier and pulled out my ultrasound results and even a display she had on PCOS. I touched a medical-school nerve! She wasn't having it! She upped my clomiphene one more time, and off she sent me. This time, though, at my friend's recommendation, I made an appointment with a reproductive specialist. I told them what my doctor had explained to me and detailed my medical background.

They took one look with their own, in-house ultrasound machine, began to almost smirk, and said, "See that oval? That is your ovary. See the small ring of pearls around the outer edge of the ovary? That's called PCOS. On a scale of 1 to 10, you are about a 9." Are you kidding me?

I was told that my gynecologist didn't diagnose it because an ultrasound is only as good as the person performing it, and the ones doing it before weren't specialists. I was also informed that I had endometriosis. The next 4 years were spent going from specialist to specialist, in hopes of one day being able to get pregnant and create a little person in my life that looked like me and had the same mannerisms as me—to create a little piece of me. Please understand that not all adoptees feel this way, but I did. I spent most of the equity of my home chasing after that dream—the dream I *never* thought I would have trouble obtaining. I had many issues in my life, but my fertility was never one that I thought would get in my way. I spent thousands and thousands of dollars on six artificial inseminations (all with injectable medications), two in vitro fertilizations with injectable medications, and a frozen embryo transfer. I became a pincushion! The last time I counted, I had been stuck with more than 700 needles. After that I lost count.

When nothing worked, and my husband and I had very little left in the bank, I approached him about pursuing adoption. He agreed, and we went to the agency where I had been adopted. I guess you could call that a full circle. I looked around the room at all the other couples and knew that the odds someone would become pregnant were high—but that it wouldn't be me. I had never been pregnant before, so it wasn't going to be me for sure! I began working on my birth-mother book, and I felt like the weight was lifted off my shoulders. Then I became that story you always hear about. I got pregnant. And it took. There was a strong heartbeat. It was a beautiful, normal pregnancy, until 36 weeks.

My beautiful daughter, Emily (ironically born the day Hurricane Emily was formed), entered the world at 36 weeks and 1 day. I was told that every extra day counts at that stage! My water broke at 2 AM, and boom—she was on her way. She was healthy in every way (or so I thought). Because of my PCOS, I didn't make breast milk, so I was unable to nurse her. She took to the bottle, instead. Around the 2-week mark, however, I noticed that she wasn't a happy baby anymore. I was told not to worry, that all babies "wake up" around 2 weeks.

I didn't realize that "wake up" meant *never* sleeping and crying *all the time!* We tried formula after formula and any and all medications. I was desperate. I remember going into the pediatrician in tears, begging for help. I told him I had tried to have a baby for so, so long, and now that I had one, I didn't think she liked me. Thank goodness he had a sense of humor. He asked me, "Kind of makes you feel like punting her across the room, huh?" Oh my goodness—I would never do that, but it did make me laugh and cry at the same time. He gave me some prescription reflux medicine, and the crying did get better. At least now we could sleep a little. But, I always noticed that she had to be positioned at the right angle, or in the right chair, or at just the right temperature, with the right light, or with the right "kind" of noise. If it all wasn't just right—forget it! Bath time, fingernail-trimming, and new foods made us all break out in sweats. I noticed she didn't like to be touched. It was almost like she wanted you to pick her up, but then she fought you after you did. Any unexpected noise, loud or soft, brought on hysterical cries. And don't even mention changing our routine. Having a new place to go meant a new level of tears for us all. Then we began to notice she wasn't speaking. She was crying, but not speaking. She seemed to want to talk, but she couldn't quite move her mouth in the way she needed to to be able to form words. At the age of 2, at the prompting of my friend, I called our local state-run early-intervention program. Just for a screening. What harm could that do? My daughter screamed in the kitchen with her hand up in the air for an *entire* hour while the intake coordinator took down notes. She asked if I knew what SPD was. Sadly, I have a degree in learning and behavioral disorders, but I only vaguely remember reading a paragraph in one college textbook about it. Sensory what?

Well, that day, my world became SPD. Everything finally made sense— her cries, covering her ears, picky eating, not being able to stand in one spot for more than a second, never wanting to be held, aversion to noises, anxiety of the unknown, delay in speech, late walking, and the list goes on. This little miracle was given to me for a reason. I had *no* idea back in college and when I was teaching that my degree would come in so handy!

I am the best advocate for my daughter. And I will continue to do so for her entire life. I had no idea that the reason then I picked my degree was to be able to help my own children. Yes, that's children—plural.

I was blessed with a son, Jake, several years later, who also received a diagnosis of SPD. He has many of the same sensory issues as his sister, but some are different. Our days can be crazy around here. I'm still making payments on that last tube of frozen embryos I never used. I haven't come to terms yet with what to do with them. My husband is finished having kids! But I'm still lingering. After all that struggling, how can I just let them go? But, after having two of my own, and they both have SPD, how could I bring another child into this world knowing the odds are high that he or she too would have SPD. Passing something on to an unborn child that I know he or she would struggle with would be cruel. So, for now, they sit in a lab. And I keep paying my storage fee. One day, I will make a decision about what to do with them. For now, though, I know that I have been blessed beyond belief. I have two little miracles to show for it, sensory issues and all. Take that, SPD! You can't knock us down! HA! We may have a quirky family, but we *are* a family. And in the end, that's all I ever wanted.

Joanne Wells is a native Kentuckian who currently resides in the Atlanta area with her husband and two children. She is a stay-at-home mom to two wonderful kiddos with SPD and two furry golden retrievers. In her former life, she was a special-education teacher, which has come in handy. When not engulfed by getting rid of flying bugs, finding just the right food her kids will actually eat, and reading princess stories, she enjoys cooking, watching a good television show, and doing anything that makes her laugh—because what every sensory mom needs a GOOD laugh!

The Journey
for Jack

by Allison Whitford Campbell

After a few years of marriage, my husband, Steve, and I decided to start a family. We tried for a few years to get pregnant, to no avail. My primary-care doctor put me in touch with a reproductive endocrinologist, who ran tests on both of us. We found out that I had polycystic ovarian syndrome (PCOS), as well as type-2 diabetes. In addition, our reproductive endocrinologist found nine polyps on my uterus that had to be removed and some other issues that required a dilation and curettage ("D&C"). Still, after addressing these issues, I was unable to get pregnant. We tried a round of clomiphene, but nothing happened. At this point, there was a huge upheaval within our extended family, and we decided to wait a bit longer before we tried again.

That June, after all the drama had calmed down, we decided to take a vacation (our first one since our honeymoon!), and when we returned, we again embarked on our journey to start a family. We tried clomiphene again, along with a human chorionic gonadotropin (HCG) shot to help boost my progesterone levels. Our doctor had warned that if this round of HCG didn't work, we would need to move on to the next level, which meant injectable medications. We kept a daily log, followed our instructions to the letter, and on July 20, we found out we were pregnant!

My pregnancy was high risk because of my hypertension (prior to pregnancy) and my type-2 diabetes. I was monitored very closely by my obstetrician and by an endocrinologist to ensure that the baby and I were healthy.

Labor and delivery were rough. I was in labor for 22 hours, before being wheeled into the operating room for an emergency cesarean section. The baby was in distress. Things moved quickly, and at 6:23 PM on March 16, Jack was born.

When he emerged, he was in distress and not breathing. I didn't hear him crying, but I did hear someone from the neonatal intensive care unit say, "Come on, baby—breathe." Tears flowed down my face. I had worked so hard to get him, I had done everything I had been told, and yet I still might lose him. After what seemed like an eternity, he finally started breathing. He still never cried.

He was finally stable enough for Steve and my dad to hold him. Then he was sent back to the nursery for more evaluation, as well as a bath. During his bath, Jack went into respiratory distress and was admitted into the neonatal intensive care unit. They administered oxygen and started running tests. It was determined that his sodium levels were low, which was easily fixed. The first time I held him, I felt a completeness that I had never known.

Looking back, things were always "off" with Jack. Several nurses commented that Jack never cried when they were trying to find a good vein to place an intravenous line. He barely cried when he was circumcised.

I spent the first 3 weeks holding him at night because he would not sleep in his crib. Finally, our pediatrician suggested that we swaddle him and put him in a bassinet in our room. He slept! For more than 4 hours in a row! So, we continued to swaddle him until he was almost 9 months old. We had to stop because he kicked out of his blankets and then woke up crying several times during the night. It took about 2 weeks of him waking and crying in the middle of the night for him to finally be able to sleep without being swaddled.

Bath time was an absolute nightmare. We had gotten an infant seat for the tub, but Jack screamed and screamed when we put him in there. Steve had to get into the tub and hold him for me to be able to get him bathed. Still, Jack got upset and cried when his hair was washed and his face got wet.

Chronic ear infections plagued Jack. I never really knew there was a problem until he got a high fever and his babysitter insisted on a doctor visit. He never acted like his ears hurt. He just didn't eat well. He eventually had two sets of tubes placed in his ears to relieve the infections. After the first set of tubes was placed at 14 months, Jack finally started to walk. Within a few months, we noticed that he was walking on his tiptoes. My mom had walked on her toes until she was about 3, so it didn't concern me or the pediatricians.

I missed a lot of signs that Jack had SPD early on. He was my first, and I thought that his behaviors were those of a typical child and that we weren't doing an effective job of parenting. It wasn't until he stopped eating foods he usually ate that I began to worry. Jack was already an *extremely* picky eater. His food repertoire is mostly meatless, with the exception of chicken nuggets (sometimes), bacon, and ham. He doesn't eat veggies but will eat just about any fruit you put down in front of him.

When I finally realized there might be an issue, Jack had only been eating yogurt and granola bars for 2 weeks. I'm not sure I really noticed that he was just eating that until I picked him up one day and he was a lot lighter than I had remembered. I weighed him, and he had lost 2 lbs. For a tall, underweight 5-year-old, that was a lot! I was at my wits' end and started scouring the Internet for ways to deal with a picky eater. I stumbled upon a Web site about SPD.

I read the symptoms. It was as if they knew Jack and had written all about him. Life with Jack finally made sense.

Everything was listed. He absolutely hates getting his hands dirty. He continued to walk on his toes, even though he had casts placed on his legs twice to correct the problem. He spins, he flaps, and he's always in motion.

I seemed to be the only one to think that there was a real issue. I didn't feel supported by my family. So, I sat on the information, and I prayed. I finally got the nerve to call the pediatrician to ask for a referral. There was an opening that afternoon if I wanted it. Of course I did. The pediatrician listened to me (!), looked over the paperwork I brought, and excused himself to find someone more knowledgeable than him. He returned a few minutes later with his wife (she was the assistant to the psychologist on staff). I went through all of my concerns with her. She agreed that a consultation was warranted, and within a few weeks, we had an appointment.

During our initial meeting with the psychologist, I requested a comprehensive evaluation, so that we could see where we were and determine if there were any developmental delays. Jack was himself during the consultation, couldn't sit still, and moved from activity to activity. She met with him in 2-hour sessions. After 8 hours of testing (four sessions), she felt she had the information she needed. I had filled out page after page of forms, detailing everything I could from birth and all of Jack's major milestones.

A few weeks after the evaluation, we finally got the diagnosis I had been expecting: SPD. What I wasn't expecting was a diagnosis of Asperger syndrome, as well. I was so glad to have a name for his "behavioral" issues, and therefore a more effective way to manage them. Not only did the psychologist spell everything out about the "whys," but she also detailed what we needed to do to help Jack. She gave me specific names to call and had already started the referral process for occupational therapy, physical therapy, behavioral therapy, and case-management services. I was very relieved that we were on a path that would get us help.

We have learned quite a bit since Jack's diagnosis. We understand that when he acts out, it's because his body is out of sorts and that we need to act quickly.

We are still learning what works and what doesn't. One thing is certain—this has been a roller coaster of a journey. The journey for Jack.

Allison Whitford Campbell lives in eastern North Carolina with her husband, Steve, and her two boys, Jack and Henry. Jack is now 6 and has received a diagnosis of Asperger syndrome and SPD. Henry is 4 and has very poor muscle tone and a speech delay. Allison is a stay-at-home mom and spends most days in and out of therapy lobbies, usually with a crochet hook and yarn in her hands. She also enjoys cooking and listening to music.

The Wood Family

by Michelle Wood

By the time my son was 2 weeks old, he had already survived a traumatic birth, brought a veteran lactation consultant to tears, bewildered his poor father, and reduced his indomitable mother to a pathetic puddle of defeat. He was the child who shrieked with hunger but would not eat. He wailed from exhaustion but would not sleep. His name is Alex, but that doesn't matter—because one night, in the wee, horrid hours of postpartum hormonal hell, I looked into those newborn azure eyes, and he was my Bear.

He'll tell you, too. In his greatest moments of 2-year-old righteous independence, He Who Has No Need for Pronouns will puff up and firmly announce, "*Bears* do." I have 8 months of speech therapy to thank for that.

In the beginning, I told my husband repeatedly that it wasn't supposed to be like this. And I wanted to strangle the people who came at me with variations on the "clueless new mom" theme. Because after 7 years of infertility, I was *ready*. And none of the regular baby stuff—like poopsplosions and sleep deprivation—bothered me. It was the other stuff. The stuff you couldn't put your finger on. The stuff that made it *so very hard*.

It's easy now for the specialists to say that an inability to coordinate the suck-swallow-breathe sequence is common in infants with SPD. Just like it was easy for people to say that my nonverbal son, who was rapidly approaching his 2nd birthday, would talk "when he was ready."

Nothing about Bear is easy. And the 2 years before his diagnosis were the hardest of my life. It challenged my marriage, my mental health, and my physical well-being. On a good day, I didn't break down sobbing until at least dinnertime.

Bear was 5 months old when someone outside the family finally noticed a peculiar behavior: He would shake his head as hard as he could. Repeatedly. For no apparent reason. And when he graduated from baby food to solids, he regressed dramatically in the variety of foods he would accept and had difficulty eating in general. He gnawed at even the softest foods before spitting them out in frustration.

Thankfully, these were red flags to my best friend—a former daycare teacher who was experienced in dealing with infants and toddlers. She felt from the start that something was off, and she kept me sane when I had nowhere else to turn.

As Bear bulldozed his way through infancy into toddlerhood, she made a profound observation that perfectly expressed what I couldn't admit. She said it felt like there was a wall around him. You didn't play "with" Alex—you were just along for the Alex ride. It was a gut punch, because I knew she was right. I was deeply ashamed that my child seemed disconnected and desperately unhappy. As he grew, the atypical behaviors—and my worries—grew with him.

His desire to be in motion was apparent from the beginning. As a baby, we couldn't put him down. Not even to use the bathroom. He was walking by 9 months and running by 10. Mobility created new outlets for increasingly disturbing behaviors. He started spinning and body-slamming. I'll never forget his utter joy the day he first stood on his head. It was cute, but I wondered how many bedtime rituals involved toddlers spinning in circles on their heads?

This was also about the time he started stuffing his mouth, which was terrifying. He'd squirrel his little cheeks full and run, laughing, in circles around the house while we tried to stop him. We lost count of the times he started choking. My husband and I got certified in infant cardiopulmonary resuscitation.

Bear got bigger and wilder. I often had scratches and bruises and spent a year wearing wrist braces to mitigate the tendinitis pain caused by trying to manage him. And then there was the noise. Oh my God, *the noise*. The endless, droning, half-screaming, whining, did-you-swallow-an-electric-kazoo *Dear-God-Someone-Take-His-Batteries-Out-Already* NOISE.

The food aversions piled up. *Everything* was too hot. He couldn't touch different textures. He occasionally tasted new foods, but this resulted in vomiting so often that he started refusing anything new. He was also oblivious to his own safety. From the deep end of the pool to the tallest slide at the park, he was "all in." I joked that if I hadn't spent the previous 3 years training for triathlons, I couldn't have kept up. My best friend told me that an hour alone with him was more exhausting than spending 10 hours in a classroom with eight toddlers. From everyone else in my world, the refrain became, "He's just a healthy, active boy."

I screwed up my courage and voiced my concerns to our pediatrician at Bear's 12-month visit. She literally blurted out, "But he's an easy baby!" I responded, "He is a *healthy* baby. That's not the same as *easy*." I was devastated, because it hit me then how hard it was going to be to get help.

As we worked our way through his 2nd year, I heard about the things others moms were doing with their toddlers but couldn't imagine doing them with Bear. Attending something like story time at the library was inconceivable. It felt like I was failing him. I couldn't help thinking that if I were doing it right, he'd be doing normal kid things.

Life with Bear was like tap-dancing on eggshells. Unless he was getting my undivided attention in some activity invariably judged too vigorous for his age, he cried and whined and clawed at me endlessly. At bedtime, he screamed in his crib for hours, working up such a sweat I'd have to change his sheets and pajamas before trying yet again to rock him to sleep. I did try reaching out to other moms for support but quickly discovered they couldn't relate. I fell deeper into social and emotional isolation.

A helpful comment on a desperate blog post I wrote when Bear was about 18 months old led me to read *The Late Talker*. There was one short section that seemed applicable, but it was specific to children with a "self-regulatory disorder." I remember thinking, "but Bear doesn't have that." I made the naïve assumption that his pediatrician would have noticed it if he had. But it was my first glimmer of hope. *Because it was in a book.*

That was also the summer my best friend brought me an autism checklist and insisted I go to our pediatrician with my concerns. She was worried about upsetting me, but by this time, Bear's behavior had even prompted a stranger at the park to ask if he was autistic. We called his doctor. To my relief, she supported my concerns and told us it was time to consult a pediatric neurologist. Bear was 21 months old.

We found our first neurologist. He laughed off autism, diagnosed a 45% speech delay, and referred us to early intervention. That was it—appointment over. I was frantic, practically begging him to listen. Because the *not talking* seemed like it had to be part of a bigger problem. It *had* to be, because this thing everyone kept telling me I was imagining made life with our long-awaited miracle baby a living hell. But no. He brushed me off.

I called the early-intervention people right away, because regardless of what else was going on, Bear clearly needed help talking. I pushed the issue at the intake interview, and for the first time...*someone listened and took me seriously.* So much so that the coordinator promised a full multi-disciplinary evaluation.

Bear met the early-intervention occupational therapy evaluator shortly before his 2nd birthday. She observed him for about 5 minutes before she started asking pointed questions. It was a "hallelujah" moment, when my answer to everything was, "YES! He *totally* does that!" That day, I heard the term "sensory modulation" for the first time. Before she left, I understood that his problem was a neurological one and was given clear instructions to read about sensory integration and to start him on something called a "sensory diet." Services were recommended four times a week.

And with that...the roller coaster left the station. I grieved at first. That gave way to relief. I decided I didn't care what it was—just that it had a name. A diagnosis meant I wasn't crazy, I wasn't bad mother, and I wasn't alone anymore. It had a name, and there were people out there who knew how to help my Bear. And help us they did. Even though it turned our world upside down, I rolled with it. Because I finally got to meet my son. Occupational therapy broke down the wall, and Bear finally reached out to us. He started signing and interacting and—eventually—talking. He was 27 months old the first time he called me "Mama." And it was worth the wait.

Epilogue: After the initial SPD diagnosis and starting treatment through early intervention, we found a fantastic pediatric neurologist who takes our son's case seriously. Not only did he concur with the occupational therapist's diagnosis of SPD, he also diagnosed speech and language processing disorder and nonepileptic seizure disorder. Autism was on the table for the better part of a year, but after careful observation of his progress, the doctor cautiously ruled it out near Bear's 3rd birthday. The doctor is also considering diagnoses of attention-deficit/hyperactivity disorder and auditory processing disorder, but Bear is not yet old enough to make that determination.

Michelle Wood *is a business writer who lives in Chicagoland with her husband and preschool-aged son, who has SPD. She tries to find the humor in life with SPD at ShesAlwaysWrite.com and has been a regular guest contributor to the well-known SPD resource site, HartleysBoys.com. Michelle's goal is to use her professional communication resources to share information about SPD in the hope of helping other families.*

When the Time Is Right

by Lindsay Fallen

Two years. Two long years. Two long, hard, gut-wrenching years. My body didn't work. But I was a woman! And women are *made* to have babies! But not me—because my body didn't work.

I already had a gorgeous daughter, who was conceived easily and, actually, quite by surprise. She was wonderful. She made me want another baby, so bad. Right before she turned 1 year old, we started trying. And trying. And trying some more.

I had also put on a lot of weight. More weight than when I was pregnant. And I knew why. I had polycystic ovarian syndrome (PCOS). My older sister has it, too, so I was familiar with the symptoms. I went to my doctor to be tested, just to be sure. I was right. An internal ultrasound showed that my ovaries were completely covered in cysts. They surrounded my ovaries like horrible pearl bracelets.

"You're overweight," the doctor said bluntly. "*Thanks a lot, Genius,*" I thought to myself. "*Glad I'm paying you to tell me what my tight pants already have!*"

"Eat less and exercise more," the doctor told me, as if I hadn't thought of this.

"If I eat any less, I will pass out during all that exercise!" I snapped back, this time out loud.

I switched doctors immediately—a few times, actually—before finding one I liked. She was a new mother and a fellow PCOS-er. She *got* what I was going through. It was 6 months before I could start fertility medicine. My ovaries were just too covered in cysts. If we tried to force ovulation, it could result in more cysts. More cysts could cause my ovaries to become too heavy, causing them to shift and become even more useless.

I was 20 when my husband and I started trying. My age was a real hang-up of mine. I had never paid much attention to my age before then. My husband was 7 years older, and most of my friends were 5 to 15 years older. But my age mocked me. Twenty years old, and I was not able to get pregnant. And I was gaining so much weight, no matter how I tried to control it!

Six months of taking clomiphene made me a still-not-pregnant hormonal mess. Eventually, I was sent to a reproductive endocrinologist. I needed medicine to start my cycle, then we had to give the clomiphene one last go. Our next step was injections and intrauterine insemination. On the highest dose of clomiphene, taken for 10 days instead of 5, I did it. Finally, I got pregnant!

For 2 years, I had thought up all sorts of cute and creative ways to tell my husband we would finally be having another baby. Instead, I walked out of the bathroom, shoved a pregnancy test in his face, and blurted out, "How does it feel, knowing you are going to be a father of two?" Then I started blubbering, which I'm sure looked lovely with my "pregnancy glow."

Brennan was born via an emergency cesarean section on Mother's Day. He was the perfect present, and big at 9 lbs 3 oz. The cesarean section didn't bother me as much as I always thought it would. I was scared for him, panicked that we had gotten so far and that the worst would happen. But it was fine. I had gotten to experience my water breaking the night before on its own, and the feeling of going into labor on my own, so the surgery itself wasn't too much of a problem for me.

Through the countless evaluations that were to come, I was often asked when I knew something was wrong. I always want to say, "the day he was born." I thought maybe it was because of the exhaustion. Maybe it was the shock of having to have a cesarean section. But something felt "off." I tried to brush it off, but the nagging feeling persisted.

No one saw it but me. I kept quiet, hoping I was just being paranoid. When Brennan was about a month old, I finally told my husband I thought something was wrong. We went to the beach for a boat parade, and it was loud. Someone was shooting a pretend cannon that was so loud it hurt *my* ears. But Brennan slept through it and didn't wake up. He didn't even startle. Nothing. The next night we saw fireworks, and the same thing happened. They were so loud, but he had no reaction.

I brought Brennan to the doctor and was immediately dismissed. Brennan passed his hearing test at the hospital, and some babies sleep through anything, I was told. A couple of weeks later, on the Fourth of July, he startled during the fireworks. I was thrilled. But that night was when I put it together.

"It isn't that he can't hear," I told my husband. "He can't see!"

Sure enough, I took Brennan to the eye doctor, who said that he showed no signs of being able to see. The doctor wanted to give it a couple of weeks, just to be sure, before sending us to a specialist far away. At around 4 months old, something clicked, and Brennan started tracking with his eyes. He started looking *at* you, not *through* you. It was wonderful. I thought that was the end of his issues, but…it wasn't.

As Brennan got older, it became more obvious that he wasn't "typical." He didn't answer to his name. He didn't babble. He didn't seem happy or excited, angry, or frustrated. He seemed sad—blah, even. He was just… there. Going with the flow. He didn't play. He just snuggled.

The turning point seemed to be when he started walking. After that, we couldn't stop him. He still didn't play. He just walked—from one wall to the other—or he did laps around the room. He shut down if you got in his way, pushing against you as if he could magically walk through you.

No one believed us. He was adorable, and no one else thought there was anything wrong. He still wasn't babbling, but "boys talk later." Not to mention, he had a very talkative older sister. We were dismissed. He was still young. But we knew that there was something different about him.

At 11 months, he had horrible febrile seizures—intense ones, which didn't fit the "typical" pattern of febrile seizures. I chuckle slightly at that now, since there is just so little about him that has ever been "typical." Because of the atypical seizures, nighttime shaking and jerking, and staring spells, he was sent to a neurologist. Our concerns about his development were still dismissed, but we pushed. We were finally told to contact early intervention, although it was "doubtful" he would even qualify.

He did, of course. His cognitive skills were mildly delayed. His language skills were significantly delayed. We started special education once a week at 15 months. We added speech therapy at 19 months. As his language skills developed, his quirks got worse. Things that people said would stop once he could say more words either continued or got increasingly more pronounced.

We were sent to a developmental center when things hadn't improved. "He isn't autistic. He is strong willed, with a severe language delay." We were sent on our way with the recommendation to have him see a behavioral therapist. We knew he wasn't autistic—he was very social when he wanted to be. No one had any answers for us about why he walked in circles, why he insisted on having something in each hand, why he still wasn't playing *with* his toys, or why his face would go blank and he would attack his older sister for no reason at all.

It wasn't until a friend had mentioned his sensory issues that we got answers. I looked up SPD online, and it explained so much. He was a classic "seeker"—he overstuffed his mouth, wanted spicy foods, felt an undersensitivity to pain (he didn't even flinch at a blood draw!), and was constantly moving. Because of occupational therapists being in such high demand, we waited a long while before we were finally able to have him evaluated. But in the end, it was worth it to finally have answers.

My son has SPD. He still has a lot of comprehension issues that we just have to see if he outgrows. I am thankful I trusted my "mommy instinct" and got him evaluated so early. People tried to talk me out of it. He is a boy, after all, and boys tend to talk later. And some kids are just late talkers. But it was never just the speech. It was the quirks. The lack of comprehension. Something was different about my child, and I needed to know what it was and how to fix it.

Brennan just started occupational therapy. It will take some time to figure out what works for him. Along with his SPD, he is showing very early but very severe signs of obsessive compulsive disorder. His speech has improved so much, which I think goes to show how much more there is to his quirks then just a simple language delay. We still are on the hunt for more answers about the health issues he has, but we are making progress.

In many ways, I am grateful it took so long to get pregnant. When people told me it would "happen when the time is right" when I was trying, I wanted to rip their eyes out. But—and I truly hate to admit this—they were right. Midpregnancy, my husband left his stressful job for a regular 8-5. We moved 7 hours away from our home, back to where my family was. Our daughter was 3½ when Brennan was born and started preschool a few months after. Had we gotten pregnant right away, there would have been so much strain and stress. It is because of my husband, and his constant support, that I still have hair on my head today!

Lindsay Fallen is a stay-at-home mom to two children—a little girl and a boy, Brennan, who has SPD. A resident of upstate New York, she likes her coffee iced, her rock music loud, and her eyes heavily mascara'd. She spends most of her day in her rockin' minivan, shuttling her kids around and cursing the price of gas. Her free time is normally spent blogging, tweeting, cooking, or playing addictive Facebook games. She blogs at Mama on the Move at onthemooovc.blogspot.com/.

Chapter 9

Early Intervention

One cannot say enough good things about early intervention, can they?

We all know that getting our children into therapy and working on their developmental challenges as soon as possible is ideal. But, the roads many of us have to take to get there are challenging—professionals discount our concerns, and friends and family insist our child will "outgrow" their issues, or—even worse—that they just need more discipline. Add to those voices doctors who are uneducated about SPD, and the road to diagnosis and ultimately getting help can be long.

For the families in this section, that hasn't been the case. The children in these families have received early intervention as early as 8 months old and are a testament to how essential it is to get our kids help as early as possible!

The Sleepy Little Wizard

by Christian Vindinge Rasmussen and Pernille Isabell Kray Rasmussen

This is the tale of our son, Sixten. Sixten was born on September 30—almost 17 days after his original delivery date. The pregnancy was normal until the end, where we felt something was wrong—it seemed like the baby wasn't kicking around that much anymore. The doctors told us they wouldn't interfere with the pregnancy until at least day 16 to day 18 after the delivery date and that the reduced kicking could be quite normal, as the available space inside my wife's belly got smaller and smaller. But, finally, after pressuring the doctors, they started the birth process by injecting a hormone on the 17th day after his due date.

My wife quickly dilated to 8 cm just 50 minutes after getting the hormone, which was a short but painful hour, and that's when problems started showing up. The amniotic sac wouldn't break by itself, so the doctors decided to do it, and out came thick green water—which is clearly a bad sign of infection and stress to the baby.

The contractions started getting stronger and stronger, and the doctors decided to put a heartbeat monitor on the skull of the baby to follow it more closely. I can still hear that sound today, when his heartbeat went down to zero for the first time... "Biiiiiip"—then they yelled "Breathe, Pernille, *breathe!*" several times. After several drops in the heartbeat and no further dilation, they checked the baby's skull and found that he had turned the wrong way—Sixten was a stargazer.

An emergency caesarean was called for, and after 20 minutes, Sixten was born with an Apgar score of 1/1 (critically low) at 1 and 5 minutes after birth. Sixten was approximately 23 inches long, with a weight of 11 lbs, and his head was nearly 12 inches around. As one doctor said shortly after the operation, "He would never have been able to come out normally." Since the birth was characterized as "traumatic," we were moved to the neonatal intensive care unit for further monitoring.

Sixten is our second child, and after just 2 days in the neonatal unit, we realized something about Sixten was not like many other children—he wouldn't sleep unless he was sitting up with my wife. This situation was repeated again and again—and the nurses couldn't get him to breastfeed, as he rejected having anything in his mouth.

After more than 2 weeks of hard work with two breast pumps and intensive training with Sixten, we finally got him to breastfeed. As with most misunderstood children with SPD, we simply tried to force Sixten into of those "normal baby" boxes.

The first months at home were really hard. Sixten wouldn't sleep unless you jumped around with him, swung him vigorously in the cradle, or sat him up with Mommy—and only Mommy would do. Essentially, we had to be awake, whether sitting up, walking around, or bouncing with him on an inflatable stability ball. Sixten would also scream a lot during these months, and he would only take small snacks while breastfeeding—meaning he spent a lot of time eating. So when Sixten wasn't sleeping, he was breastfeeding, and the result was that we had to be awake 24-7 to nurse him.

In Denmark, you get a personal nurse to track your baby's progress during the first 8 months. She will visit once a month, depending on the complexity of the child, the family, and the experience of the parents. Our nurse had never experienced such a restless child before, so together with her, we tried a lot of different things from the beginning. We tried taking him to a chiropractor first, as Sixten had a little trouble turning his head to the left after being so big at birth. After nine treatments with the best specialist we could find, he simply gave up and told us that Sixten had troubles beyond his knowledge.

We then tried a reflexologist for six treatments, until she gave up with the same answer: "Sixten has some troubles that lie beyond my capabilities." However, we did get two good ideas from her: The first was bouncing on the stability ball. When we started sitting on the bouncing ball with Sixten in our arms, he calmed down. It seemed like he could finally feel himself and was able to relax enough to sleep. Today, it is unbelievable how many hours, meals, and nights we spent on those bouncing balls.

The second thing the reflexologist said was to consult a craniosacral therapist, since she could probably calm Sixten down even more by helping him feel his own body. That was a good experience, where Sixten could relax lying down, but it never changed the sleeping pattern or the eating disorder.

During all these sessions with therapists of all sorts, which were costly for economic reasons and in terms of time, our experiences were also tracked by the local municipality and our assigned nurse, which we felt was a good thing, so that others could benefit from the lessons we learned.

As the months went by, we were also tracked by the regional hospital to monitor Sixten and us as parents. Our personal feeling was that our own doctor and the hospital never really wanted to listen. They always had the notion that their base of knowledge was large enough, and Sixten just didn't fit in. Sixten was just a troubled boy, and we had to accept him as he was—which was a major frustration to our family. It is not normal to not be able to sleep, and it is not normal to reject things like "normal" food, oatmeal, porridge, bread, water, and the like.

One day, the physiotherapist with the local municipality came up with an idea that she learned about recently. She wanted to test Sixten for "tactile shyness," as SPD is called in Denmark, where we live. Before the actual test was implemented, we suddenly had that term to look up on the Internet, and there—right there—we could read about Sixten and all the other children with SPD. We were *not* alone!

The test results indicated that Sixten had a high level of "tactile shyness" regarding his surroundings and his body, and a very low level of sensitivity for his mouth and what was going in or out. We discovered, together with the physiotherapist, that the exact same regional hospital that had rejected us several times before employed a leading occupational

 Sensational Journeys

therapist who specialized in SPD and food disorders! This was a relief but also a major frustration to us—why hadn't the doctors within the same hospital suggested that we meet with the therapist long before? Why hadn't they listened or at least talked with their colleagues about what to do? The kicker was that one of the doctors' offices was located right across the hall from the occupational therapist.

Meeting the occupational therapist when Sixten was 12 months old was a major step in getting to know our own son. We learned that we never had really done anything wrong—we just had to do more of the same and work intensively with Sixten's disorder. As our therapist said to us, "We (doctors and therapists) might know the most, but parents know best!"

We learned that having a daughter before Sixten had helped us recognize Sixten's behaviors as being atypical, so we didn't expect him to "act like a normal baby should," as many others do with children who have SPD. But we also learned that resources are very limited on this subject in Denmark and in Europe, and for that reason, we started up a Facebook page with valuable links—some in Danish and a lot in English—together with our occupational therapist and another family. (As it turns out, there is another family who lives close by, and their wonderful little daughter has SPD and is just 6 months older than Sixten.)

During the past 8 months, Sixten has had 11 middle-ear infections with a severe fever (104°+) and loads of days spent at home with Mom or Dad. One of our own theories—which clinical studies have shown—is that when you get little to no sleep, your immune system is compromised quite considerably—meaning you are more receptive to getting infections.

Our social life went down the drain when Sixten came into our lives. We couldn't see other people, as Sixten had strong reactions for several nights after a visit, a dinner with friends, or even seeing our closest family members.

To sum Sixten's problems up:

- He is overresponsive to his surroundings—he can't calm down and rest if there happens too much going on around him.
- He has a low sensory level around his mouth and possibly his intestines and his bottom—he has a fear of things going into and out of his mouth, etc.
- Because of his eating sensitivities, he will not accept things into his

mouth and will only eat three different things.

- Because of his sleeping issues, he can't fall asleep and wakes up three to six times per hour.

- Socially, he is not accepted by peers, family, or our community—people do not understand him.

- He has multiple infections that seem to result from a compromised immune system.

Today, Sixten is a happy and fun boy, with loads of humor and talents. We call him "The Little Wizard," as he is always in a good mood in the morning, despite the tough nights with many impulses he cannot handle. That is the magic touch he brings to our family. Pernille, my wife, is not working right now, as the sleepless nights are too tough when you also have a normal job, and we are now considering our options as a family. Sixten still deals with all of his problems, but we are now even more focused, and once every month there might be just one night where we can all get 3 hours of sleep.

The proud father and mother of two wonderful children, Freya and Sixten (one with SPD and the other showing signs of SPD), **Christian Vindinge Rasmussen** *is chief-consultant in the Danish Ministry of Science, and* **Pernille Isabell Kray Rasmussen** *is a nurse for a medical practitioner.*

Early Intervention Matters

by Allison Fields

I always knew my son Cameron was different, even when he was still in the womb. At every ultrasound appointment, we were assured that our little boy was healthy, even though he insisted on staying in the breech position. He was born at 39 weeks via cesarean section, with no known health problems. Still, I would watch him sleep and think to myself, "Something is off." Over the next year, that nagging feeling continued, even though Cameron appeared completely healthy and normal to everyone but myself, despite a few minor gastrointestinal complications and issues with feeding. It was not until his 12-month checkup that I began to get validation for my concerns after I mentioned that Cameron had stopped talking and seemed to be going backward in his maturity. We were then referred to our state's early-intervention program for an evaluation. I had never even heard of early intervention in that capacity before that day. Now I can't imagine our life without it.

Cameron underwent therapy for developmental and speech delays. It was not until he was 17 months old that SPD and Cameron's name were used in the same sentence. The only thing I knew about SPD is that children that had it hated tags in their clothes and disliked loud noises and crowded places. I had no idea there was more to it than that! Cameron had always been a rough-and-tumble boy, preferring to crash his body into the couch or bang toys together over quiet, sedentary play. We all learned quickly to not give anything to Cameron that we were not okay with getting broken. He loved to rip thick board books apart and could turn the toy room upside-down in a matter of seconds. He even ripped a heater out of the wall.

Despite all of his rough play and his love for all things loud, he hated having his face touched, especially his mouth. When Cameron's speech-language pathologist witnessed his rough style of play but then could not get him to let her touch his mouth, it was then that she suggested he might have some sensory-processing issues going on and that we would likely benefit from a visit with an occupational therapist. I was highly confused, since my little boy loved loud noises and was never bothered by tags in his clothes.

The occupational therapist quickly identified SPD in Cameron and explained sensory avoidance versus sensory-seeking. Cameron, for the most part, is a sensory seeker. Suddenly, it all made sense. I now understood why he would repeatedly throw his body into the couch, rip wallpaper off the wall, and seem to actually enjoy loud noises that would startle and annoy most people. He craves deep hugs and will burrow his body into anyone holding him in an attempt to get more input. He enjoys spinning around and around in swings, not once bothered by dizziness. Not only did I have a new understanding of Cameron's behaviors, but I also learned that he has a bit of sensory avoidance in some areas, especially when it comes to sensations affecting his mouth. Knowing this helped not only me, but also his speech-language pathologist in understanding how to treat Cameron's issues with regard to feeding.

All of Cameron's special needs are invisible to the untrained eye. They're so invisible that he could easily fall through the cracks, especially at this young age. It would have been easy to say, "He's just being a boy," "Boys are always late bloomers," or "He'll grow out of it." But I didn't. I recognized that something was just not right with my son, even though I could not physically see it. I pushed for answers and treatment until I felt confident that we were doing the right things. Learning about Cameron's SPD allowed me to better understand some behaviors we were concerned about with my 3-year-old daughter, as well. After an evaluation with an occupational therapist, we now know that she too has SPD.

Since becoming a parent of a child with "invisible" special needs, I have become passionate about early intervention. Too often, I hear parents dismiss their concerns about their child's development or behaviors because of the child's young age. I now speak up and tell parents about our state's early-intervention program and how important it is for their child's future if that child does indeed have atypical needs. My children are proof that seeking early treatment does help. In a matter of weeks, my daughter, who once would not let me groom her because the sensations were too painful, is now asking me to braid her hair and clip her nails. Clothing that was once painful is now happily worn without throwing a fit. While not all children respond so quickly to therapy, it does go to show that it works. Cameron, though progressing wonderfully, will likely be in therapy for a long time, as he has many hurdles to overcome. However, getting him into therapy from such a young age gives him a huge advantage. It is our hope that with early intervention for both of our children, they will have a brighter future than they would have had without it. By the time they get to school age, we will have had several years to help them manage their SPD and other needs, even when they are not in our care.

Allison Fields *resides in eastern Tennessee with her husband and two children. She is passionate about raising awareness for SPD and speech disorders and the importance of early intervention.*

I Am Not Making This Up!

by Amy Temple Reiswig

It was 11 PM, and I was sitting at the computer in the spare room, writing. My son Daniel was screaming in my husband's arms in our bedroom. He had been screaming for about 45 minutes, with no end in sight. He had screamed for 3 hours straight in my arms earlier that day, and for shorter periods at other times, whenever I would put him down to use the bathroom or make some food for myself. Our days had been going like this for almost 3 months now, and we were all exhausted. I had no idea how long the screaming would last this time, before we could all finally go to sleep, and I was grateful that my husband Jaymz was home to take a turn.

So many thoughts ran through my head as I sat there writing: I thought about our pediatrician's advice (and that of several other people) to implement "cry-it-out" sleep training for Daniel. *But that just didn't feel like the right thing to do for him.* He already cried so much! I didn't want him to fall asleep alone and cry every night, too.

I thought about the suggestion that I (as Daniel's primary caregiver) was stressing him out with my anxiety about his crying, thus perpetuating the crying, and that we should hire a nanny to give me a break. But *any* parent would find their child's incessant screaming distressing, when it happened for such a large portion of the day, every day, without knowing what was wrong and not being able to fix it.

I thought about the way Daniel acted so differently from all the other babies I interacted with: He only napped for 20 minutes at a time, he didn't like to be around lots of people, he never wanted to be put down, and he screamed *so much,* but only at home, and only if Jaymz and I were the only people in the house. *I knew there was something wrong with my baby. I was not making this up.*

All of a sudden, the screaming stopped, and I snapped back into the present moment. I was puzzled at the sudden cessation, since Daniel usually wore himself out gradually over a period of hours, eventually "crashing" and falling asleep. This sounded different from that. I waited for the crying to start up again, but it didn't. Jaymz opened the door and walked into the room where I was, wearing Daniel on his chest in one of our baby carriers. Daniel was smiling and cooing, as happy as could be. I noticed that his footed pajamas were unsnapped at the feet and dangling around his ankles. I looked up at Jaymz with a questioning look on my face and said, "What happened?!" Jaymz replied, "I took his pajamas off of his feet, and he stopped crying. Now he's totally happy again…it's like nothing ever happened."

It was an eye-opening moment, to say the least. Jaymz and I just stood there, staring at each other for a few seconds, knowing that things were about to change. We realized that night that our suspicions that Daniel was dealing with sensory-processing issues were probably right.

Two-and-a-half months before that night, Daniel was about 4 months old. He had been fairly "colicky" for the first 3 months, with a consistent fussy period in the evenings that lasted from 1 to 4 hours. He required constant holding, walking, and bouncing during those hours, but the crying was intermittent, and it never occurred outside those evening hours. Other than the evening, Daniel would only cry if he needed something: to nurse, to have his diaper changed, or to take a nap. We had talked to our pediatrician about it, and he gave Daniel a clean bill of health and told us to wait it out. When those first 3 months were over, we saw a bit of a shift. Daniel didn't cry as much in the evenings, so we thought we were out of the woods.

A few weeks passed, and there was another shift: Daniel began crying more during the day. It started out slowly, with him crying for an hour here and there, maybe three or four times per day. Over the next few weeks, the crying progressed to lasting several hours in a row (often 2 or 3 hours, but sometimes up to 4) and several times per day (on the worst days, Daniel cried for 5-6 hours total). The crying changed, too. It went from being fussy, whiny crying, to all-out hysterical screaming. He cried real tears, his face got red and hot, his hands and feet got very cold (from flailing his extremities and also from the blood being diverted to his head), and he often screamed and cried until he started hyperventilating and hiccuping. The crying sessions almost always ended a crash—he would fall asleep from sheer emotional and physical exhaustion. It wasn't the kind of restful sleep that happens when you're tired at the end of a long day…Daniel would literally pass out from crying.

Jaymz and I had no idea what was wrong with our son. Daniel seemed fine sometimes, and other times, he just screamed and screamed. Daniel acted differently at home than he did when we were out somewhere or in a group, interacting with other families. When we were out or in a large group of people, he was very quiet and withdrawn, and he usually fell asleep. Jaymz and I thought this was strange, because he didn't sleep much during the day at home (only taking 20–30-minute naps). When I brought him home after going on an outing, he cried and cried, as if he needed to decompress from holding it all in while we were out.

His tendency to stay quiet and sleepy in public was especially difficult, because the meltdowns happened when no one else was witnessing them besides my husband and me. There were times when someone would come up to us when we were out together and comment on how well behaved (read: quiet and obedient) our kid was. We would look at each other and say, "This is real. He does scream all day at home. We are not making this up."

There was one exception: I had enrolled him in a baby music class (mostly to get myself out of the house on a regular basis), and every time we went there, he had a meltdown. I would stand in the corner of the class with my crying baby, looking at the other babies who were having the time of their lives and wonder, "What is going on here? Why is Daniel not like these children? What am I doing wrong?"

We took him to the pediatrician, who still couldn't find a physiological cause for Daniel's crying. The doctor suggested that perhaps Daniel and I were feeding off of each other's stress, and the more anxious I got about him crying, the more he cried. He advised that we hire a nanny to take care of Daniel for at least 3 hours two or more times per week to give me a break.

I walked away from that appointment feeling totally defeated. I know the doctor was trying to be helpful, and I certainly did need help during the day. But we couldn't afford to hire someone to care for Daniel, much less someone who we'd feel comfortable with taking care of him while he cried for 3 hours straight. Furthermore, I couldn't ignore the fact that my kid was crying for *hours on end.* This was not normal. There was something wrong.

He sent us home with a prescription for a reflux medication, just to see if it would help Daniel cry less. We agreed to try giving him the medication, because at that point we would've tried anything. Jaymz and I were pretty sure that reflux wasn't the problem, as the crying didn't seem to be at all related to when Daniel had last eaten. Still, we tried the reflux medication (and then a second, more expensive one), to no avail.

This whole time, I had been attending a weekly new-parent support group. I had been going back week after week, telling the parents and facilitators there about Daniel's worsening crying. I am so grateful to that group for providing me with a safe space to share everything that was going on. I am grateful to myself for continuing to go back every week, even when it felt like it would be too hard to get out of the house. It was so important for me to be around other mothers and experience other babies during that time. With Daniel being my only child, I think it would've been easy to assume that this is how all babies act or that I was doing something to make him this way. But being around other babies (in the support group and at music class) and seeing how very different Daniel was from those other kids really helped to validate what we were going through.

One day at the support group, someone mentioned sensory issues as a potential cause for Daniel's troubles. I had been hearing a lot of anecdotal things from other mothers, like, "I have a friend whose kid was like that, and he's still really sensitive, but it gets better." The mention of a possible cause for my son's distress was exciting for me. I decided to talk to Jaymz about it and read more.

I did a couple of Internet searches, but I couldn't spend much time on researching this idea because Daniel required so much of my constant energy and attention. He couldn't be put down during the day. I had this "sensory" idea in the back of my mind, but I didn't really know what my next step should be. We took him back to the pediatrician, and I mentioned that I thought Daniel had sensory troubles. The doctor acknowledged that it might be the cause of the crying, but maybe not, and told us that sensory therapies often aren't covered by insurance, so we should explore other avenues first. He advised that we hire someone to help us "sleep-train" him so we could all start getting more sleep. He also suggested that we try to do all the things that make him feel better and minimize the crying as much as possible to try to flood his brain with happy chemicals and see if we could "reset" whatever was going on with him.

I was pretty sure we were already doing our best to make him feel better, and he was still crying a lot. I decided to look into it further on my own. A few nights later, Jaymz walked into the room with Daniel's pajamas dangling off of his feet, and we knew something was definitely up.

That night, we decided to compile a list of things that we had figured out would exacerbate or alleviate the crying, so we could show it to whomever we found to help us.

Things That Usually Make It Worse	Things That Sometimes Make It Better
• Lying him down horizontally • Putting him down • Coming home after being around large groups of people or any unfamiliar people • High-pitched sounds, like laughing, sneezing, water running, or a chair scraping against the floor • Lots of stimulation, like baby music class • Being alone	• Wearing him upright, tightly against my chest in a baby carrier; tight swaddling • Holding him tightly against my chest while jumping up and down; bouncing vigorously on a stability ball • Rhythmic, hard thumping on his back with a flat hand • Petting very soft things/rubbing soft things on his skin • Loud, continuous sounds like a coffee grinder, food processor, or vacuum cleaner • Taking his clothes off • Being in the bathroom • Going outside

The next day, I went to meet with our marriage counselor. We had been going to counseling regularly during that time, on account of how difficult things had been at home. I talked to our therapist about what was going on with Daniel and about our suspicions that his crying was related to sensory-processing difficulties. I relayed to her the events of the previous night, and she agreed with our assessment of the problem. She offered to contact an occupational therapist colleague of hers for us, to see if she had any experience with the diagnosis and treatment of sensory issues in very young children. I took her up on her offer.

Within a couple of days, the occupational therapist offered to evaluate Daniel. She told us up front that she wouldn't charge us for the visit, because while she specializes in children, she had never treated a child so young and she wasn't sure she would be able to help us.

I still remember that day very vividly—Jaymz and I were exhausted. I cried during the appointment, and so did Daniel. She was able to reproduce situations that would make him cry—something that we had never been able to do. She told us it was obvious to her that he was having a lot of trouble regulating his nervous system. She also told us that we were doing an amazing job of regulating it for him and that she could teach us how to help Daniel learn to regulate himself. I was so relieved! We finally had an answer to what was wrong with our baby. We were not making it up, it was not something we were *doing to* him, and it wasn't going to go away on its own without some help.

That day, she taught us how to do brushing and joint compressions. We were instructed to do them at least eight times per day. We left feeling hopeful that things were about to change. We brushed him diligently every day. Exactly a week after we began the brushing, Daniel took two naps that lasted 2 hours each. I didn't know what to do with myself! He woke up happy and didn't cry for any extended periods that day.

Things continued that way: We were all getting more sleep and feeling much happier. Daniel wasn't spending hours upon hours every day crying. When we went back for a second visit with the therapist, we reported the success of the brushing protocol. She then asked us to add a couple more things, in addition to the brushing: swinging Daniel in a sheet or blanket once a day and playing music with a high-pass/low-pass filter while Daniel did tummy time several times per day. These therapies further improved his ability to self-regulate.

We've continued to see the occupational therapist, and the therapies have changed over the past few months on the basis of Daniel's needs. We're still working on decreasing his sensory defensiveness. In particular, we are still trying to help him regulate his vestibular system. We've had harder days and easier days, but it's never gotten back to the way it was for those months when Daniel was crying all the time.

I will always be grateful to all the people in our lives who helped and encouraged us along this path of discovering new things about how Daniel's brain works. If it wasn't for their knowledge and trust in our parental intuition, I don't know how we would be coping today.

Amy Temple Reiswig is a mom, wife, nurse, doula, and blogger. You can read about her adventures at anktangle.com.

Why Can't It Just Be Easy?

by Stacy Woodruff

Our story started in September about 5½ years ago. I had been friends with Brad for about 5 years at that point—but just friends (mostly because of the 21-year age difference and our very different places in life). He was turning 43, and I had just turned 22. But, we started hanging out a lot right around his birthday, and things grew from there. It got to be serious pretty fast, but we kind of tried to pretend it wasn't, mostly because of one big thing: kids. I wanted them, and he didn't. I have always wanted to be a mom, and although I didn't have any kids yet, they were part of the package. He already had a teenage son from a previous marriage, and he didn't want to start over. We even split up over it for a few days, but he came around to my way of thinking, which was a big leap on his part, considering I always said I wanted four kids—I wanted to have two and adopt two.

After about 2½ years together, we got married. For about 2 years, we had not been preventing pregnancy in any way, so a couple of months later we started going to a reproductive endocrinologist, otherwise known as the fertility doctor. I received a diagnosis of polycystic ovarian syndrome, or PCOS, and Brad had a low sperm count, likely due to his diabetes. I was always very open about all the treatments we were going through, and so was he. People would ask me why I was in such a hurry to have kids—I was young—I had plenty of time. I always told them that I didn't want Brad to be raising babies when he was 80—after all, he was no spring chicken!

We went through months of fertility treatments, from basic treatments with oral pills to intrauterine insemination coupled with injectible fertility drugs. It was exhausting—physically, financially, and emotionally. When I finally did get pregnant, I was so scared I was going to have a miscarriage. The numbers from all the blood work were really low, and we didn't see a heartbeat until fairly late in the game. I finally got to see a heartbeat via ultra-sound on Christmas Eve. I just cried and cried. Even after seeing a heartbeat, I still wouldn't fully believe that I was going to wind up with a real, live baby at the end of it all. I refused to buy anything for the baby or talk about names until well after 23 weeks, which is the earliest a baby can survive outside the womb with all the assistance available today. But, scared as I was, we did make it to the end, with a fairly uneventful pregnancy. The labor and delivery went smoothly, and we were rewarded with a gorgeous, 8-lb baby boy.

Travis has always been a pretty easy kid. At first he wanted to be held nonstop, but we managed to wean him off of that and get him to where he could be put down for more than a few minutes at a time. Looking back, I can see the sensory issues that were there even as an infant. He hated the swing and the bouncer with a passion. He had to be swaddled very tightly to sleep at all, and if the swaddling came undone, he woke up. He didn't seem to have a cutoff switch that told him when he was full, and he drank from his bottle until he vomited, and then cried for more. People looked at us like we were crazy when we limited his feedings—everybody said babies know when they're full, but he didn't. He slept through the night pretty early and has always been mellow, independent, and not very cuddly. He freaked out over noises, like birds singing or noisy people. He was a little bit behind on some of his milestones, but not so much that I was concerned about it. He has always been the kind of kid who doesn't try anything until he is sure he can do it, so I figured he would get to things when he was ready.

When he was 10 months old, we got our first set of foster kids—two sisters, aged 9 months and 21 months. Now, I know you're not supposed to compare kids, but his new Little Sis was a month younger than Travis and way more advanced, in pretty much all areas. For a while, we all blamed it on the differences between boys and girls. But then we started to notice more and more differences between the two.

We had the girls for 5 months, and while we had them, we were going through more fertility treatments to try for another baby. Talk about awkward—dragging three kids under the age of 2 to the fertility clinic for appointments! I considered wearing a sign that said, "Yes, I really am infertile!" We got some strange looks during those months, but we did manage to get pregnant. I was so excited when I saw that ultrasound, with two little beating hearts. Yep, twins! We knew there was a large possibility of that happening, so we were somewhat prepared for the news. In those first months of pregnancy, I was so sick and exhausted. We eventually had to have the girls moved to another foster placement because of my health and because even at 2 years old, Travis's Big Sis already had more issues than we were capable of dealing with. It was an excruciating decision, but it was best for everybody involved, including the girls. Looking back, I can see more clearly that moving the girls was the right thing to do, on so many levels. It has allowed me to focus on Travis's needs, whereas before, he was just fading into the background because he was so much less demanding than the girls.

Being primarily a sensory avoider, he is content to sit and watch Baby Einstein and Signing Time all day if he is allowed to. At one point, I read an article that a friend had posted on her Web site about SPD. It totally described Travis. I started noticing the sensory-related behaviors more and more and finally had to call early-childhood intervention to have him evaluated at about 15 months old. The only reason I even knew about early intervention was because I worked in a classroom with medically fragile teenagers for a few years. While doing that, I was around kids with many different diagnoses, but many of them were on the autism spectrum. More so than most people, I knew what services were available and how to get them. I also learned how valuable early intervention is and what a difference it can make. I called, and we set Travis up with occupational therapy twice a month, speech therapy twice a month, and sessions with the developmental coordinator twice a month. It is not really enough, but it's all that I can handle right now.

When Travis was 16 months old, I had to go back to work full time so that I would have health insurance that actually covered maternity care. We put him in daycare—he hates it, I hate it, and his dad hates it. But, it's just for a few more months, until the twins are born and I can stay at home.

At the daycare he attends, the class size is too big and he just doesn't get enough one-on-one attention. He has regressed since he started daycare, and the therapists are trying to work with his teachers, but they are just too busy to have much time for anything beyond meeting his basic needs. So now, we are torn between moving him to a daycare where the class sizes are smaller, but he would have to adjust to new teachers; or, just sticking it out for another 10 weeks until the babies are born. He does not adjust well to new people, but I also know that 10 weeks is a long time in the life of a kid who is only 20 months old.

We are still fairly new to this world of special-needs parenting and still don't know where the path is going to take us. The developmental doctors have mentioned that Travis may have autism, but it's too early to be sure. They are also saying he has a motor-planning problem, which is not at all surprising to me. Some days I find myself asking, "Why can't it just be easy?" We worked so hard just to even get him here that it seems like he (we) should get a pass on things like this. But I guess that's not how it's going to be. I'm just hoping that the two babies I am carrying now will have an easier time of it than their brother. But I'm not going to hold my breath for that, either. It will be what it will be, right?

Stacy Woodruff lives in central Texas with her husband, Brad, and son, Travis. Travis is not quite 2 and has SPD and some developmental and speech delays. Stacy is expecting twins, a boy and a girl, and is looking forward to holding her babies but not the imminent sleep deprivation. She is hoping to be able to find a balance between being a wife, the mother of twins, and the mother of and advocate for a special-needs child.

Chapter 10

It Will Get Better

by Hartley Steiner

Before I ever got a diagnosis of any sort for my oldest son Gabriel, I think everyone I knew had told me some version of the line, "It will get better." I knew they all meant well, but I wasn't dealing with your run-of-the-mill toddler tantrums with Gabe. Not even close. My son had *meltdowns*. Big, long, scary, excruciatingly loud meltdowns. Gabe would cry for hours on end for no apparent reason and crashed into walls for fun; this wasn't typical development in my book, and I couldn't understand why people were so quick to dismiss it with any of the old standbys ("He's just a boy" or "He'll grow out of it" or the noncommittal, "It will get better"). How could people think that it would just *get better*? I wanted to believe them, *I really wanted to*, but I had lived with the "out-of-sync" behavior for years, with no sign of it letting up, so I wasn't convinced that my son would just magically "get better" one day.

When Gabriel's first diagnosis of SPD came in at age 4, I was so relieved to finally know what was going on that I steamed forward—full speed—through occupational therapy and implementing a sensory diet at home and school, without so much as taking a breath. If that was what my son needed, then that was what I would do for him. After all, this is what would finally make things "get better," right?

But you know what? It wasn't easy, and it didn't just "get better" as quickly as I had hoped. I was tired of being told by family, friends, and therapists that things would "get better." Did these people really understand what I went through every single day? Did they understand how upset my son was over the smallest things? How hard school was for him? How hard having playdates was? How difficult it appeared for him to enjoy the simplest pleasures of being a child? If things were really going to get better, could they *please* hurry?

Then one day, about a year after Gabriel's diagnosis, I was just exhausted—the kind of exhausted that only a special-needs mom can relate to. This particular day was not really all that different from the hundreds before it; Gabriel, at almost 5 years old, was having the umpteenth meltdown of the day over some perceived infraction on the part of his 2-year-old brother, who sat statue still, watching him yell and throw things while I held my 3-month-old tightly to my chest, shushing and pacing with him because he hates loud noises. That was my breaking point. I needed things to "get better," and I needed them to do so *immediately*.

I remembered meeting a fellow SPD mom at the occupational therapist's office the week before and decided I needed to talk to someone who understood my life in a very real way—someone who could provide testimony that the elusive "It gets better" truly exists.

I rifled through my purse in the garage to find her name and phone number, which was scribbled on the back of a deposit slip. She said I could call her anytime. What did I have to lose? I dialed her number and was beyond relieved when she answered the phone. We ended up talking for over an hour—OK, I did most of the talking and all of the crying, but it felt great. At the end of the conversation, she quieted her voice, and in a tone so genuine and true, calmly said, "Keep doing what you are doing—it gets better." And I actually believed her.

I believed that if she had survived this journey of SPD that somehow, some way, I would, too. That my life wouldn't always be chaos and meltdowns, that somewhere in my future there would be a family meal that we all *sat* through (not to mention ate), that there would be fun family vacations and maybe even a day I didn't have to plan down to the minute. I was optimistic.

As shocking as it is, she turned out to be right. Today, Gabriel is 10 years old. He self-regulates and self-advocates at school, he asks for a "tight squeeze" when he needs it, he willingly takes the trash out for heavy work, and he often volunteers to take "quiet time" when he is overwhelmed—both at home and at school. He has an arsenal of chew toys and fidget toys to keep him focused and calm him when needed. And perhaps most impressive, Gabriel has generalized those skills and can *choose* to do virtually anything he wants—like wear special clothing for special occasions, even wearing cleats for football and a tie for holidays. He can tolerate gel in his hair for "crazy hair day" and wear makeup on his face for Halloween. He can attend a "jump party" without covering his ears and even takes his heavy blanket with him to the movie theater, "just in case" he needs it. Trust me when I say that this is *leaps and bounds* from where we were *just a few short years ago.*

So today, as many of you are reading this, and are probably living that same sense of crisis, between diagnosis and "It gets better," I want to assure you that your dedication to your child's daily sensory needs, to his or her continued therapy appointments, and to the millions of things you do every day to help teach your child to live in this often-overwhelming sensory world of ours will pay off—*in spades.*

Or, to put it simply: *It will get better.*

In Closing

Although the starting point may be different, with trouble conceiving, or with the birth of a second child, or in a far off country somewhere across the ocean, each of the families in this book have come to the same point: a diagnosis of Sensory Processing Disorder. Those three little letters—S-P-D—tie us all together along this journey and show us just how similar we are, no matter how different we may appear.

If you have ever felt alone, like no one knows what your family goes through, or if you've felt scared because you are the only one you know who is raising a child with SPD—think again. You are not alone—and as a matter of fact, you are in great company. Remember those SPD support group meetings I talked about? The ones where we laughed more than we cried? Consider yourself a part of them—you are now on this journey with thousands of other parents, just like you.

To ensure that I leave you laughing—and happy to be on this journey with me—here is a lighthearted look at parenting a sensational child.

And don't forget to take care of yourself!

You Know You're Raising a Child with SPD When...

1. You judge every playground by the number of swings or the amount of spinning equipment it has.

2. You hear the restaurant crew begin to clap and you immediately cover your child's ears to avoid the "Happy Birthday" song.

3. You have memorized where all of the automatic flushing toilets are in your whole town.

4. You have a trampoline in your main living area (probably not far from the TV or the kitchen).

5. You have objects that are OK for "chewing" but are not edible.

6. Your discussions with your doctor require a better understanding of acronyms than you need for doing your own taxes.

7. You wonder if you can write off a swing in your playroom as a "medical expense."

8. You haven't been on vacation...pretty much ever.

9. You consider reading your support-group forum an "afternoon out with friends."

10. You have turned down more invites for parties than you attended during *your entire college career.*

11. You spend the same amount of time convincing others that your child is "not" OK as you do that he "is" OK.

12. You own a pair of earphones that were so expensive, your spouse can't believe you let your child use them.

13. You carry gum, bubbles, straws, and earplugs in your purse, but no lipstick, powder, or mirror.

14. You have given up the idea that your child will sit through an entire meal (let alone eat what you are eating).

15. You are constantly asking yourself, "Is that a behavioral issue, or is it sensory?"

16. You have at least seven different strategies to get your child's hair cut. (So what if he is 5 and has only had two haircuts in his entire life?)

17. If challenged to remove the words "inappropriate," "overstimulated," or "input" from your vocabulary, you wouldn't last 10 minutes.

18. You know the meaning of "heavy work."

19. You can name all eight senses and wish you would've learned them in school!

20. You do not own a single article of clothing that has its original tags in it.

21. For your family, "OT" doesn't stand for "overtime."

22. You are bombarded every day with, "What is that sound?" even though you can't hear a thing.

23. Your child can operate a shaving cream container before the age of 4.

24. Your child can hear the humming of the lights but cannot hear you call his name. Even after yelling it five times.

25. You have looked into buying noise-canceling headphones—only the headphones aren't for you.

26. You are surprised that *everyone* doesn't know who Carol Kranowitz is.

27. You hoard bubble wrap for those days when you can't think of anything else to keep your kid busy.

28. You have *encouraged* your child to hide under the table in a restaurant.

29. You know how to perform at least six different "animal walks" and have likely done them all in public.

30. The insurance company knows you by name, but you are not sure if that is good.

31. You own ice-cream–flavored toothpaste, but your child still doesn't like brushing his or her teeth.

32. You celebrate the little things, like a perfectly written word.

33. You own a collection of ancient twisty straws with applesauce caked inside them.

34. You know what a "no-thank-you bite" is.

35. You do your grocery shopping after the kids to go sleep.

36. Your child refuses to wear a coat—even though it is snowing outside—and you are OK with it.

37. When you tell your child it is time to "brush," you aren't talking about his teeth.

38. You talk about "engines" all day long but know nothing about cars.

39. You are tired of explaining that your child does not have "behavioral issues," but rather sensory issues that affect his behavior.

40. You follow The SPD Foundation's updates on the *Diagnostic and Statistical Manual* with greater interest than current affairs, movie releases, or fashion trends.

41. You spent more time planning, preparing for, and researching your child's 504/IEP meeting than you did your own wedding.

42. You aren't on Facebook to connect with lost high-school friends, as you originally intended.

43. You know that a sensory diet has nothing to do with eating and is probably the most important "diet" you'll ever do.

44. You used to browse the newest bags at *Coach.com,* but now you spend more time "dreaming" over the latest from *FunandFunction.com.*

45. You are no longer surprised when your child greets someone by crashing into them at full force.

46. You hear other women talk about the next "Twilight" movie, but you are just hoping for a sequel to "Autistic-Like: Graham's Story."

47. You beam with pride when your child asks to be squeezed or chooses to swing without being told.

48. You remember the day you found support.

49. You pass the contact information for your newfound support on to everyone you can think of.

50. You wouldn't trade being the mom of your kid for any other "typical" kid in the world.

About the Author

Hartley Steiner lives in the Seattle area with her husband and three sons. She is the award-winning author of the SPD children's book, *This Is Gabriel Making Sense of School*, the founder of the SPD Blogger Network *(www.spdbloggernetwork. com)*, and a contributing writer for the SPD Foundation's blog, *S.I. Focus* magazine, and *Autism Spectrum Quarterly*, among dozens of other online Web sites and blogs. You can find her chronicling the never-ending chaos that is her life on her own blog, Hartley's Life With 3 Boys *(www.hartleysboys.com)*, and on Twitter as @ParentingSPD. When she isn't writing or dealing with a meltdown, she enjoys spending time in the company of other adults—preferably with good food and even better wine.

Resources

The SPD Foundation—*www.spdfoundation.net*

The SPD Foundation is a world leader in research, education, and advocacy for Sensory Processing Disorder, a neurological condition that disrupts the daily lives of many children and adults. Originally called the KID Foundation, The SPD Foundation has been providing hope and help to individuals and families living with SPD.

SPD Blogger Network—*www.spdbloggernetwork.com*

The SPD Blogger Network is a group blog designed for those who write—or want to write—about raising a child with SPD. It is a place to share stories—*all* of our stories. Please join us in our sensational chaos, sensational joys, and sensational lives.

Sensory Planet—*www.sensoryplanet.com*

Sensory Planet's goal is to bring a positive, purposeful, and valuable social network community to those whose lives are affected by SPD. By building a network that brings all resources together, we will greatly strengthen understanding on an individual level, as well as a community level.

Soft Clothing—*www.softclothing.net*

Many children are extra-sensitive to the texture and feel of clothing. Soft Clothing is the first line designed with the needs of all children in mind. Flat seaming and seamless construction are used for extra comfort, as well as the softest combed cotton and specially developed soft sensory blends, wide collars, encased elastic waistbands, printed labels (tagless), custom fits, and much more.

Fun and Function—*www.funandfunction.com*

Launched by pediatric occupational therapist Aviva Weiss and her husband, Haskel, Fun and Function has been lauded for "normalizing" the experience of being different and helping children achieve their fullest potential. Weiss was inspired to start her own company when she discovered that one of her children had SPD. She was frustrated by the lack of kid-friendly products, inconsistent quality, and high pricing, and set out to change all that.

Additional Resources

Paula Aquilla, Ellen Yack, & Shirley Sutton
*Building Bridges through Sensory Integration,
2nd edition*
www.sensoryworld.com

Britt Collins & Jackie Olson
*Sensory Parenting: From Newborns to Toddlers—
Everything Is Easier When
Your Child's Senses Are Happy!*
www.sensoryworld.com

Marla Roth-Fisch
*Sensitive Sam: Sam's sensory adventure has a
happy ending*
www.sensoryworld.com

Dr. Temple Grandin
The Way I See It and *Thinking in Pictures*
www.fhautism.com

Carol Gray
The New Social Story Book
www.fhautism.com

Jennie Harding
Ellie Bean, the Drama Queen
www.sensoryworld.com

David Jereb & Kathy Koehler Jereb
MoveAbout Activity Cards: Quick and Easy Sensory Activities to Help Children Refocus, Calm Down or Regain Energy
www.sensoryworld.com

Joan Krzyzanowski, Patricia Angermeier, & Kristina Keller Moir
Learning in Motion: 101+ Fun Classroom Activities
www.sensoryworld.com

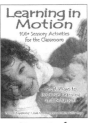

Jane Koomar, Stacey Szklut, Carol Kranowitz, et al
Answers to Questions Teachers Ask about Sensory Integration
www.sensoryworld.com

Aubrey Lande & Bob Wiz
Songames™ for Sensory Processing (CD)
www.sensoryworld.com

Rebecca Moyes
Building Sensory Friendly Classrooms to Support Children with Challenging Behaviors
www.sensoryworld.com

Laurie Renke, Jake Renke, & Max Renke
I Like Birthdays…It's the Parties I'm Not Sure About!
www.sensoryworld.com

Dr. John Taylor
Learn to Have Fun with Your Senses!
The Sensory Avoider's Survival Guide
www.sensoryworld.com

Kelly Tilley
Active Imagination Activity Book:
50 Sensorimotor Activities to Improve
Focus, Attention, Strength, & Coordination
www.sensoryworld.com

Carol Kranowitz
The Out-of-Sync Child, 2nd ed; *The Out-of-Sync Child Has Fun*,
2nd ed; Getting Kids in Sync (DVD featuring the children of St.
Columba's Nursery School); *Growing an In-Sync Child*; Sensory
Issues in Learning & Behavior (DVD); *The Goodenoughs Get in Sync*;
Preschool Sensory Scan for Educators (Preschool SENSE) Manual and
Forms Packet ~ www.sensoryworld.com